POWER QUERY BEYOND THE USER INTERFACE
Solving Advanced Data Cleaning Problems using M

by
Chandeep Chhabra

Holy Macro! Books
PO Box 541731
Merritt Island, FL 32953

Power Query Beyond the User Interface
Solving Advanced Data Cleaning Problems using M

First Publication: April 2025

Author: Chandeep Chhabra

Copy Editor: Kitty Wilson

Tech Editors: Geert Delmulle

Indexer: Cheryl Lenser

Compositor: Bronkella Publishing

Cover Design: Chris Dorning

Published by: Holy Macro! Books, PO Box 541731, Merritt Island FL 32954

Distributed by Independent Publishers Group, Chicago, IL

ISBN 978-1-61547-081-5 (print) 978-1-61547-167-6 (digital)

Library of Congress Control Number: 2024951813

Version: 20250108

Contents at a Glance

Foreword

One of the most flattering things for any teacher is for one of their students to become a teacher in their own right and to start teaching you things. The book you are reading is an example of that.

When we wrote *M Is for (Data) Monkey*, Miguel and I set a goal to teach how to use Power Query to solve common business problems. As you might have guessed from the original title, our first thought was to explore the M language more thoroughly, but it became apparent to us as we began writing that there was just so much that could be done via the user interface. In what was one of the first books in the Power Query space, we decided that our priority was to focus on teaching people to use Power Query to get the job done. While we did cover M, we filled our book with examples where reaching past the user interface really wasn't necessary. When we released *Master Your Data*, we rewrote and expanded our M code section, but we stopped short of including extensive examples of solving practical business problems that could not be solved via the user interface. Our intention at that point was really to say "Hey, if you *do* want to dive into this language, here are the basics to get you into the journey."

Little did I know that in 2016, Chandeep would encounter Power Query for the first time, pick up our book to start his journey, and eventually write a book to pick up where we left off. And honestly, I could not be happier about this!

One of the greatest things about Power Query is that it gives you the ability to visualize the output of your actions. Every action you take gets recorded, and you can preview the results in the output window—at least until you can't. And at that point, you need to be able to figure out your goal, determine the syntax needed to achieve it, and visualize the results without being able to actually see the intermediate values. I honestly think that is one of the most difficult jumps to make when programming, whether with VBA, DAX, SQL, or M. Can you visualize the virtual tables or lists that are being used to generate your output? How do you validate that your vision is correct?

One of the most important things that Chandeep does here is illustrate these intermediate steps during his problem-solving journey. Getting to the end results is important, but understanding *how* you got there is critical to being able to develop your own solutions in the future, and Chandeep's explanations will help you do exactly that. From the foundational concepts of tables, lists, and records and how to move between them, to advanced concepts like `List.Generate`, Chandeep does a great job of explaining the concepts in a layered way, using business-focused examples. He's even included practice sets and examples for you to hone your skills.

That's enough from me, though. It's now time for Chandeep to show truly that M is for (us) data monkey(s). 😊

Ken Puls, FCPA, FCMA, MVP

Co-author of M Is for (Data) Monkey and Master Your Data with Power Query in Excel and Power BI

https://excelguru.ca, https://skillwave.training

Dedication

Dedicated to the three most important women in my life: Daya, Manjeet, and Sonika.

Acknowledgments

A big THANK YOU to:

Ashutosh Zawar for everything that I've learned from him. **Ken Puls** for helping me write this book from the very start. **Darin Spence** for consistently throwing nasty data cleaning problems at me. **Geert Delmulle** for proving his valuable feedback. (This book would have been a mess without him. If you still find it a mess, I am to be blamed for that. 😄) **Bill Jelen** for being so generous and allowing me to extend the deadline. I bet he initially thought that I wouldn't complete this at all. My friend and business partner, **Sourabh Kushwaha**, for proofreading this book multiple times. The incredible copy editor, **Kitty Wilson**, for putting up with my shenanigans and patiently fixing my bad English.

And all the genius Power Query minds that I have learned a lot from, including **Imke Feldmann, Ben Gribaudo, Rick De Groot, Mellissa De Korte, Victor Wang, Brian Julius, Bhavya Gupta, Owen Price, Mike Girvin, Chris Webb, Aditya Darak, Marcel Beug, Daniil Maslyuk**, and even people behind aliases like **mma173**.

Introduction

I participated in World Excel Champ (a worldwide competition to find the nerdiest Excel jockey) back in 2016. I could create fancy charts and cube-driven pivot tables, and I could even break the spreadsheet with array formulas. I thought I'd do well in the contest. The first two rounds were indeed charts and formulas, and I did okay. Round 3 was Power Query questions, and I kid you not, that is when I opened the Power Query window for the first time in my life.

I was zapped, staring at whole new window of tools and functionality opened on top of Excel. I couldn't do a thing, and I lost! But that got me thinking: If Power Query is being tested at a global competition, it might be a thing in the future.

For the next few months, I laid my hands on all the Power Query materials I could get on the web, including the book *M Is for (Data) Monkey* by Ken Puls and Miguel Escobar. There's a good chance that you've also read that book, or maybe its successor, *Master Your Data*.

Each time I learned something new in Power Query, I kicked myself for not having learned Power Query earlier. Turning pages, I'd say to myself, "This is so awesome. Why didn't I learn this sooner?" But until that time, I had been the user interface guy. I just knew the clicks to solve most problems.

Fast forward to early 2018, when I met up with my close friend Ashutosh, who runs a data analytics company in Mumbai. The awesomeness of Power Query was bound to dominate our conversation. In the midst of the chatter with lemonade and wada-pav (Indian burger), he mentioned that his team was grappling with Power Query's limitations. I couldn't believe his words.

I stopped drinking the lemonade and said, "Grappling with Power Query! Really? It's the most awesome automation tool ever built in Excel. Maybe your team doesn't know how to use it." I tried to quash his point without even listening to his problem.

Ashutosh is a smartass. He didn't mind that I wasn't drinking the lemonade anymore and turned his laptop to show me a peculiar case. Let me summarize the case to the best of my memory.

One of his clients had shared with him CSV files for sales data, but each file had slightly different column headers, and there was no real pattern to the changes. He asked, "How would you dynamically combine data from all these CSV files, given that the column headers aren't always the same, and there's no pattern to them?"

The problem was indeed hard to solve (at least with the Power Query user interface), and I felt the same way I'd felt when I'd faced Power Query for the first time in 2016. There was work to be done beyond the UI.

I scraped the Internet again and found a whole new world behind Power Query's user interface and that was the M language. I guess that was a reason Ken titled his book ***M Is for (Data) Monkey***. 😁

In the next few months, I took my Power Query skills to a whole new level. Although M isn't the most friendly-looking code, once you learn how it works and what it can do, every bit of its ugliness is worth it.

In this book, I've put together solutions to many of the problems that business users like Ashutosh struggle with every single day—problems that are clearly beyond the scope of Power Query's UI capabilities. This book will turn you into an advanced data monkey. (I really wanted to be able to say that.) 😁

Who This Book Is For

I have made a few assumptions about you as the reader of this book:

- You already know the "clicks" of Power Query, either in Excel or Power BI.
- You already know how to create basic queries that can combine data, remove columns, filter and unpivot rows, and the like.

- You have come across a few data cleaning problems that have made you scratch your head and wonder, "How am I going to do that?"
- Most importantly, you could relate to Ashutosh's plight in the Introduction. (Don't tell me you skipped that! 😳)

If you were mostly nodding through this list: Congratulations! You are my ideal reader! Enjoy the book!

How to Use This Book

I've written this book in a structured way, leveling up the complexity one page at a time. It's ideal for you to read the book in its written order. Fundamental building blocks like lists, records, tables, and navigation are discussed in the first few chapters. More complex topics like iterations, custom functions, and patterns and recipes are then built on top of these fundamentals in later chapters.

I did start with a story, but this isn't a story book. To truly master M, you need to practice. I've got two suggestions for you:

- After you read a concept or an example, close the book and practice it on your own. This will help you recall the concepts and apply the learning to your own data.
- Spend some time with the exercises that appear at the end of most chapters. Do your best to solve those questions before looking at the solutions.

I've provided companion files for you to practice, tweak, and tinker with. You can download them from https://tinyurl.com/pq-book or by scanning the QR code below.

Chapter 0: Warming Up

As a basic to intermediate Power Query user, you're already sold on how awesome Power Query is, so I won't be a pesky over-the-top salesman. Instead, let's start by warming up with some Power Query basics you already know.

> **Note:** Before you go any further in this book, be sure to download the companion files for the book from https://tinyurl.com/pq-book. For this chapter, open the file Intro.xlsx (which you'll find in the Warmup folder). As you work through this chapter, you'll be able to walk through the examples by using the queries provided in this file.

Power Query's User Interface

Refer to the query Data.

I am sure you've clicked enough UI buttons in Power Query to clean your data, and this sample query will look familiar:

Figure 0-1 *A sample query created using the Power Query user interface.*

Maybe you've even peeked into the Advanced Editor (in the View tab) and seen a scary mashup of all possible special characters like the one shown below:

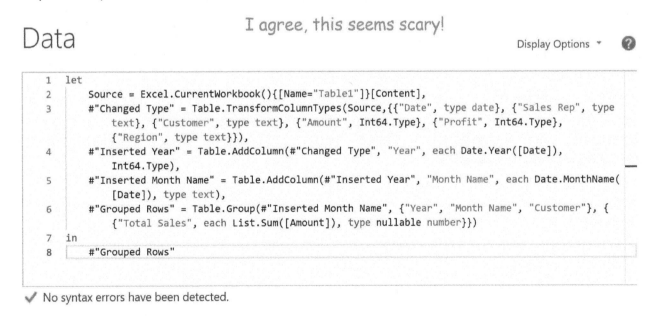

```
1  let
2      Source = Excel.CurrentWorkbook(){[Name="Table1"]}[Content],
3      #"Changed Type" = Table.TransformColumnTypes(Source,{{"Date", type date}, {"Sales Rep", type
           text}, {"Customer", type text}, {"Amount", Int64.Type}, {"Profit", Int64.Type},
           {"Region", type text}}),
4      #"Inserted Year" = Table.AddColumn(#"Changed Type", "Year", each Date.Year([Date]),
           Int64.Type),
5      #"Inserted Month Name" = Table.AddColumn(#"Inserted Year", "Month Name", each Date.MonthName(
           [Date]), type text),
6      #"Grouped Rows" = Table.Group(#"Inserted Month Name", {"Year", "Month Name", "Customer"}, {
           {"Total Sales", each List.Sum([Amount]), type nullable number}})
7  in
8      #"Grouped Rows"
```

✔ No syntax errors have been detected.

Figure 0-2 *The Advanced Editor in Power Query.*

The first time I opened the Advanced Editor in Power Query, I said it out loud: "Damn! look at all these worms floating around. What a mess!"

Don't let the Advanced Editor scare you into giving up on the idea of learning M. Microsoft has built an almost perfect user interface on top of the M language, so the average Joe never has to be bothered by how ugly and complex M looks.

Now that we share a common notion of M's poor first impressions, let me show you, page by page, why the M language is awesome and what we can do with it.

What Is M, and Why Do We Need It?

Refer to the query Example.

M, short for Mashup, is the language behind Power Query. The good news is that M gets generated for you automatically as you do your data cleaning clicks in the Power Query UI; therefore, you never have to write a bit of it.

In the query shown here, if you remove a column by selecting the column and pressing Delete, Power Query automatically creates the new step Removed Columns, along with the M code to do that.

Figure 0-3 *A sample query to delete a column.*

Power Query offers hundreds of other data cleaning options that are accessible with a click or two, and it feels magical.

But (there is always a but, which is why entire books are written) after the excitement of Power Query settles and you get more accustomed to working with it, you are likely to run into problems beyond the scope of those clicks in the user interface.

"Really?" you might ask. "Do you have any examples of such problems?" Oh, yes! This book is all about solving such problems. Here are a couple examples to pique your interest.

Example 1: Combining Data from Multiple Excel Files with Inconsistent Headers

Say that you need to combine data from three Excel files, but the column names in the files are inconsistent, as shown here. Although you could solve this problem by using the UI, it would be a mess. (Recall that my friend Ashutosh faced a similar issue.)

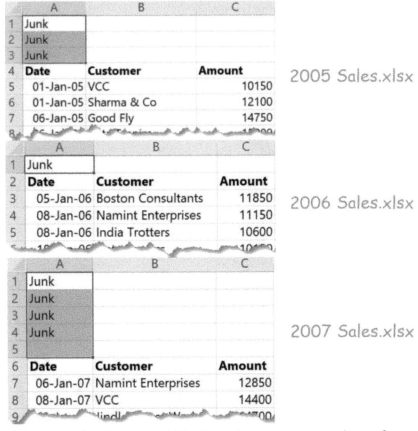

Figure 0-4 *Data from three Excel files with inconsistent column names.*

Example 2: Combining Data from Multiple Excel Files That Contain Junk Rows

Now say that the column names are the same across the three files, but the files have unequal numbers of rows at the top that contain the text "Junk."

Figure 0-5 *The three Excel files have inconsistent numbers of rows that say "Junk."*

These quirky problems make the queries unscalable (and possibly even unsolvable), especially when created solely with the UI. This is where your journey begins to move beyond the user interface to learning the M language.

My aim in this book is to help you boost the awesomeness of Power Query by teaching you how to solve hard problems using the M language. More importantly, I want to teach you how to think by teaching you concepts behind the M language so that you can apply them to your own diverse problems with confidence.

Where Is M in Power Query?

When you're working with Power Query in Excel or Power BI Desktop, you can find M in three places in the Power Query window: in the formula bar, in the Advanced Editor, and in the Custom Column box.

In the Formula Bar

You already know that Power Query creates steps for you. You can see the M code for each step in the formula bar.

	Date	A^B_C Sales Rep	A^B_C Customer	1²₃ Amount
1	01-01-2005	Jaspreet	VCC	10150
2	01-01-2005	Charley	Sharma & Co	12100
3	06-01-2005	Jaspreet	Good Fly	14750
4	06-01-2005	Ramesh	Data Tronics	15000
5	09-01-2005	Ramesh	VCC	13550
6	11-01-2005	Abhay	MNTL	12400
7	12-01-2005	Anshika	Shyam & Sharma Co	14300
8	14-01-2005	Charley	Boston Consultants	10700
9	14-01-2005	Varsha	MNTL	10850
10	26-01-2005	Jaspreet	White Associates	13150
11	29-01-2005	Bruce	VCC	12350

Formula bar: `= Table.RemoveColumns(#"Changed Type",{"Region", "Profit"})`

Query Settings — PROPERTIES — Name: Example — All Properties — APPLIED STEPS: Source, Changed Type, ✕ Removed Columns

Figure 0-6 *The formula displayed for the Removed Columns step.*

If, for some reason, you cannot see the formula bar in your Excel or Power BI Power Query window, you need to activate it by clicking the View tab and selecting Formula Bar. (Throughout the book we use the notation View → Formula Bar as a shortcut for this type of selection.)

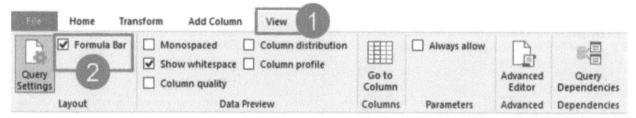

Figure 0-7 *The formula bar can be activated from the View tab in Excel or Power BI Desktop.*

In the Advanced Editor

The next place you can see the M code for a query is in the Advanced Editor (View → Advanced Editor).

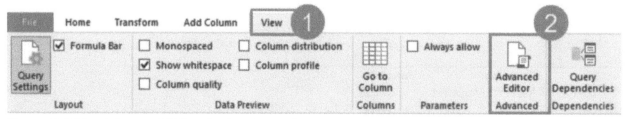

Figure 0-8 *The Advanced Editor in the View tab.*

Whereas the formula bar shows the code for the active step, the Advanced Editor shows the code for the entire query—all the steps at once, as shown here:

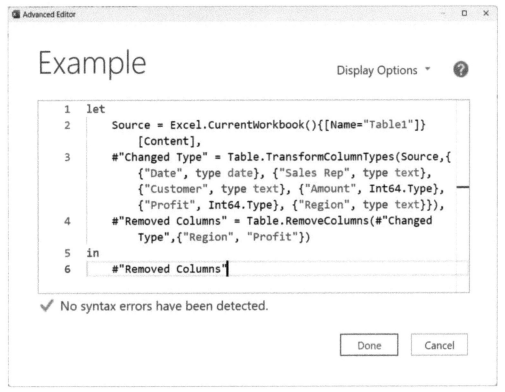

Figure 0-9 *M code in the Advanced Editor.*

In the Custom Column Box

An often-overlooked place where you can write M code is the Custom Column box (Add Column → Custom Column).

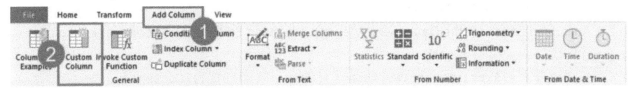

Figure 0-10 *Selecting Custom Column in the Add Column tab.*

The Custom Column box, shown below, is made exclusively for writing formulas that apply to each row of the table. (You'll learn more about this later in the book.)

×

Custom Column

Add a column that is computed from the other columns.

New column name

Amount Plus 10

Custom column formula ⓘ

```
= [Amount] + 10
```

Available columns

Date
Sales Rep
Customer
Amount

<< Insert

Learn about Power Query formulas

✓ No syntax errors have been detected.   OK   Cancel

Figure 0-11 *A sample formula in the Custom Column box.*

M Syntax: A Few Basics

Refer to the query Data.

Let's use a sample query to discuss a few general principles that will help you read and understand the M language.

The let and in Keywords

In the Advanced Editor for the Data query (View → Advanced Editor), the M code looks like this:

```
1  let
2      Source = Excel.CurrentWorkbook(){[Name="Table1"]}[Content],
3      #"Changed Type" = Table.TransformColumnTypes(Source,{{"Date", type date
4      #"Inserted Year" = Table.AddColumn(#"Changed Type", "Year", each Date.Y
5      #"Inserted Month Name" = Table.AddColumn(#"Inserted Year", "Month Name
6      #"Grouped Rows" = Table.Group(#"Inserted Month Name", {"Year", "Month
7  in
8      #"Grouped Rows"
```

Figure 0-12 *The query is in between the* let *and* in *keywords.*

Note that:

- Almost all queries start with the let and in keywords. There are a few exceptions, but we'll ignore them for now.
- In between the (lowercase) let and in keywords are the steps Power Query created based on clicks in the user interface.
- After the in keyword, Power Query by default places the last step (in this case, #"Grouped Rows") as the result to be displayed.

Comma After Each Step

In this figure, notice that M includes a comma at the end of each step except for the last one:

```
1   let
2       Source = Excel.CurrentWorkbook(){[Name="Table1"]}[Content],
3
4       #"Changed Type" = Table.TransformColumnTypes(Source,{{"Date", type date}, {"Sales Rep", type text}
            , {"Customer", type text}, {"Amount", Int64.Type}, {"Profit", Int64.Type}, {"Region", type
            text}}),
5
6       #"Inserted Year" = Table.AddColumn(#"Changed Type", "Year", each Date.Year([Date]), Int64.Type),
7
8       #"Inserted Month Name" = Table.AddColumn(#"Inserted Year", "Month Name", each Date.MonthName(
            [Date]), type text),
9
10      #"Grouped Rows" = Table.Group(#"Inserted Month Name", {"Year", "Month Name", "Customer"}, {
            {"Total Sales", each List.Sum([Amount]), type nullable number}})
11  in
12      #"Grouped Rows"
```

Figure 0-13 *Each step except the last one ends with a comma.*

Note that:

- Power Query places a comma at the end of each step except for the last one in order to separate the steps.
- The last step before the `in` keyword does not end with a comma.
- The output step (after the `in` keyword; in this case, `#"Grouped Rows"`) also doesn't end with a comma.

Step Referencing

Steps in Power Query use very special notation, with each step referenced in the next step:

```
1   let
2       Source = Excel.CurrentWorkbook(){[Name="Table1"]}[Content],
3       #"Changed Type" = Table.TransformColumnTypes(Source,{{"Date", type date,
4       #"Inserted Year" = Table.AddColumn(#"Changed Type", "Year", each Date.Y
5       #"Inserted Month Name" = Table.AddColumn(#"Inserted Year", "Month Name
6       #"Grouped Rows" = Table.Group(#"Inserted Month Name", {"Year", "Month N
7   in
8       #"Grouped Rows"
```

Figure 0-14 *Each step is referenced in the next step.*

Note that:

- Steps are like variables, and each step holds an intermediate result of the M formula used.
- Each step is referenced in the next step to further build the query.
- Notice in lines 3 to 6 that each step name starts with a pound sign (#) and is wrapped in double quotes, like this: `#"Changed Type"`. This syntax is mandatory if a step name has a special character or a space in it.
- Notice in line 2 that the `Source` step is written without any pound sign (#) or double quotes (" ") because it doesn't include any spaces or special characters.

> **Tip:** To avoid having to use the pound sign and double quotes notation (for example, `#"Grouped Rows"`) when writing and referencing steps, I like to simply use CamelCase (for example, `GroupedRows`). This makes the query look cleaner and more readable.

Example 1: Writing a Simple M Query

> Refer to the query Query1.

Now that we have established a few ground rules, let's write a simple query from scratch in the Advanced Editor:

1. Create a blank query (Home → New Source → Other Sources → Blank Query).Open the Advanced Editor (View → Advanced Editor). You now see the `let` and `in` keywords and an empty Source step.

2. Replace all that code with the code shown here and then click Done.

```
1   let
2       step1 = 100,
3       step2 = 5,
4       step3 = step1 * step2
5   in
6       step3
```

✔ No syntax errors have been detected.

Done   Cancel

Figure 0-15 *Creating a simple three-step query in the Advanced Editor.*

Let's quicky recap the syntax used in this example:

- We started off with the (lowercase) `let` keyword.
- We then declared three steps and their values, ending each step except for the last one with a comma.
- We closed the steps with the (lowercase) `in` keyword.
- After the `in` keyword, we called out the last step (in this case, `step3`).

At this point, if we were to open the Power Query user interface, the query would look like this:

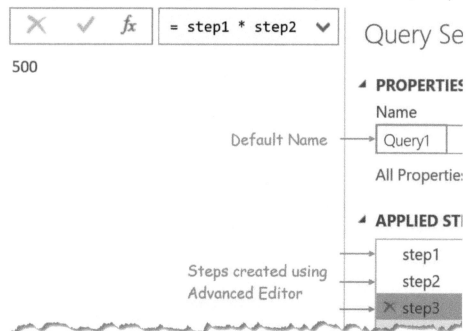

Figure 0-16 *The Power Query UI shows the three steps created using the Advanced Editor.*

If you want to create another step in this query, you can do so by using the formula bar, like this:

1. Click the fx button next to the formula bar. Power Query creates a new step with the default name Custom1. By default, this step refers to the previous step (in this case, `step3`).

2. Change the formula for the Custom1 step to `step3 + 100`. The query now shows the result 600.

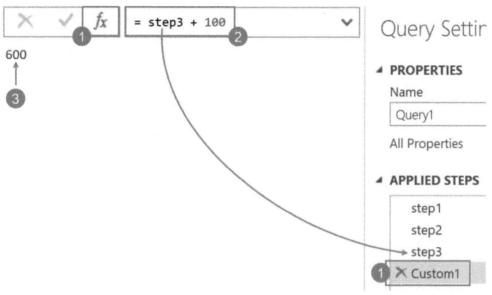

Figure 0-17 *Creating a new step by using the formula bar.*

> **Note:** Here are a few important things to keep in mind when creating custom steps:
> - When you create a custom step using the formula bar, it's a good idea to rename it using CamelCase.
> - To rename a step, right-click the name of the step and select Rename. Alternatively, you can select the step and press the F2 key. Then give the step a new name, using CamelCase.
>
> Two steps cannot have the same name.

Writing M in the Advanced Editor Versus the Formula Bar

There are a few differences between writing M in the Advanced Editor and in the formula bar:

- The formula bar allows you to write the M code for the active step and not for the entire query.
- When writing M code in the formula bar, you don't have to worry about declaring the step name. Each new step created is by default named Custom1, Custom2, and so on, and you can easily rename these steps whenever you want.
- The formula bar is slightly easier to work with than the Advanced Editor because you don't have to worry about adding a comma at the end of each step. Power Query adds it for you. 😎

In this book, we'll use both the formula bar and the Advanced Editor (whichever is easiest in the moment to get the job done).

Example 2: Writing Another Simple M Query

Refer to the query SalesData.

Let's create another (slightly more meaningful) query, similar to what you'd create by using the Power Query UI but now using the Advanced Editor:

1. Create a blank query (Home → New Source → Other Sources → Blank Query).
2. Rename the query SalesData.
3. Open the Advanced Editor (View → Advanced Editor). You should see the `let` and `in` keywords along with an empty `Source` step.
4. Change the `Source` step to look as shown here and then click Done:

```
1   let
2   |      Source = Excel.CurrentWorkbook(){[Name = "Dataset"]}[Content]
3   in
4   |      Source
```

Figure 0-18 *The Source step connects to a table in the current Excel file.*

Note: Because Source is the only step declared between the let and in keywords, it doesn't need a comma at the end.

The Power Query UI gives you a preview of the data from the Dataset table in the current Excel file. At the moment, you do not need to understand the code shown in this example. The goal right now is to just become familiar with the syntax.

Year	Customer	Column1	Sales
2022	Ae	null	10150
2022	Bee	null	12100
2022	Cee	null	14750
2022	Dee	null	15000
2022	Ee	null	13550
2023	Ae	null	12400
2023	Bee	null	14300
2023	Cee	null	10700
2023	Dee	null	10850
2023	Ee	null	13150

Formula bar: `= Excel.CurrentWorkbook(){[Name = "Dataset"]}[Content]`

Query Settings — PROPERTIES — Name: SalesData — All Properties — APPLIED STEPS: Source

Figure 0-19 *The Source step pulls data from the Dataset table in the current file.*

If you examine the table shown above, you'll notice an unwanted and empty column called Column1. It might be very tempting to use the user interface to select and delete the column, but here we'll do it by using the formula bar instead:

1. To create a new step, click the fx button next to the formula bar. Power Query creates a step named Custom1.

2. Right-click the new Custom1 step and rename it RemovedCols.

3. In the formula bar, write the following code (where Source refers to the table in the previous step):

```
= Table.RemoveColumns(Source, "Column1")
```

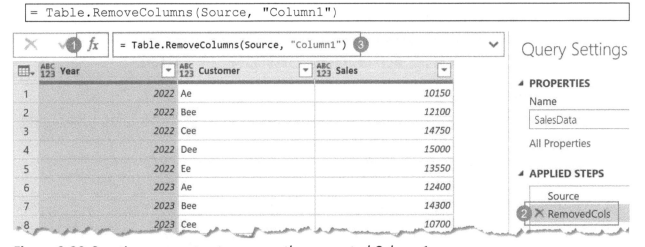

Formula bar: `= Table.RemoveColumns(Source, "Column1")`

Year	Customer	Sales
2022	Ae	10150
2022	Bee	12100
2022	Cee	14750
2022	Dee	15000
2022	Ee	13550
2023	Ae	12400
2023	Bee	14300
2023	Cee	10700

Query Settings — PROPERTIES — Name: SalesData — All Properties — APPLIED STEPS: Source, RemovedCols

Figure 0-20 *Creating a new step to remove the unwanted Column1.*

For the last step of the query, we can ease up a bit and use the UI to set the data types for all columns. Press Ctrl+A to select all columns and then select Transform → Detect Data Type. At this point, the query should look like this, with a new step, Changed Type, added:

In PQ User Interface

In Advanced Editor

```
1   let
2       Source = Excel.CurrentWorkbook(){[Name = "Dataset"]}[Content],
3       RemovedCols = Table.RemoveColumns(Source, "Column1"),
4       #"Changed Type" = Table.TransformColumnTypes(RemovedCols,{{"Year", Int64.Type},
            {"Customer", type text}, {"Sales", Int64.Type}})
5   in
6       #"Changed Type"
```

Figure 0-21 *Our new query with three steps.*

Creating this tiny query from scratch might feel like too much at this point. Don't worry: By the end of this book, you will be creating much more complex queries, so hang in there.

Feed Power Query What It Eats

I was sitting at the breakfast table in London on the morning of February 7, 2024. It was drizzling, and I had butterflies in my stomach. I was scheduled to present on the stage at the Global Excel Summit that afternoon, and I didn't know how to start my talk. I was trying to think of an opener that would be catchier than "Good afternoon, everyone!"

As I started to eat my veggies and omelet—the same breakfast I've eaten every day for the past five years—I began to feel better. The first bite in, I murmured to myself, "Feed Chandeep what he eats every day. He likes it." It's astonishing how our brains make connections. The next moment, I was thinking about Power Query and how much my mindless murmur resonated with the M language. When I presented that afternoon, this was my first slide, and the audience loved it:

This has been the most eye-opening concept in my personal journey in learning M. Unfortunately, I didn't have cool lingo for it yet, but now I do. I will be stressing the importance of feeding Power Query what it eats multiple times throughout the book, and this section presents a primer to get you started. I hope you'll love it as much as I did, speaking about it in London.

Refer to the query PromoteHeaders.

Notice the Promoted Headers step:

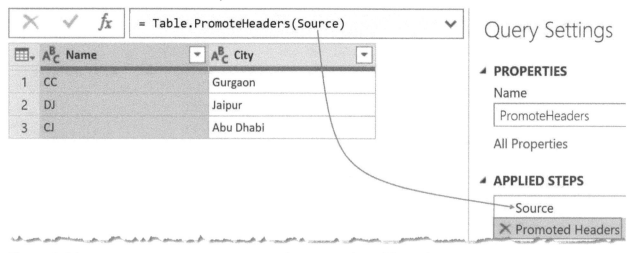

Figure 0-22 *Table.PromoteHeaders is referring to the table in the previous step.*

The Promoted Headers step uses the `Table.PromoteHeaders` function, which has the following syntax:

```
= Table.PromoteHeaders(
    table as table,                       // 1
    optional options as nullable record   // 2
) as table                                // 3
```

Note: In the above code, I've included the numbers 1, 2, and 3 after // (double forward slash) as reference points to the explanation below. Anything after // is a comment and is not executed in Power Query.

Note that:

1. The first argument is asking for a table as input. If you provide anything other than a table, you will get an error. As I said, feed Power Query what it eats!

2. The second argument is optional, and you can leave it out for now.

3. The output of this function will be a table (notice `as table` at the end).

Now consider another formula:

```
= Table.RowCount(
    table as table)    // 1
    as number          // 2
```

Note that:

1. This formula is asking for a table as input.

2. The output of the function will be a single number that shows the row count value.

You must carefully observe such subtleties in M functions and feed Power Query the correct type of input. If you don't, your formula won't work.

As you grow stronger in your understanding of M, you'll find this concept incredibly useful for understanding the types of arguments needed to make your formulas work.

Remember: "Feed Power Query what it eats!"

Order of Evaluation

Refer to the query Query Evaluation.

When you're busy clicking buttons in the Power Query UI, the steps are automatically created in a coherent order, one after the other, but (there is always a but) that is not how those steps are evaluated. To see what I mean, look at these three query steps:

	ABC 123 Customer	1.2 Total Sales
1	Sharma & Co	74750
2	VCC	64300
3	White Associates	62450
4	India Trotters	121650
5	Data Tronics	89750
6	Boston Consultants	49550
7	Jindle Power Works	112300
8	Shyam & Sharma Co	85800
9	Good Fly	101200

▲ PROPERTIES

Name

Query Evaluation

All Properties

▲ APPLIED STEPS

① Source
② Filtered Rows
③ Grouped Rows

Figure 0-23 *A query with three steps.*

You might think it works like this:

1. The query evaluation starts from the Source step (i.e., the data is brought in).
2. The table is filtered.
3. The data is summarized (i.e., grouped).

Although this is a logical way to think about it, the query is not actually evaluated from the top down. Rather, Power Query evaluates the query from the bottom up. To see how it works, let's take a look at the same query in the Advanced Editor (View → Advanced Editor). Here's how it looks:

```
1   let
2     ③ Source = Excel.CurrentWorkbook(){[Name="Table1"]}[Content],
3     ② #"Filtered Rows" = Table.SelectRows(Source, each ([Region] = "East")),
4     ① #"Grouped Rows" = Table.Group(#"Filtered Rows", {"Customer"}, {{"Total
          Sales", each List.Sum([Amount]), type nullable number}})
5   in
6       #"Grouped Rows"
                          └── Evaluation Starts
                              here and goes up top.
```

✔ No syntax errors have been detected.

Done   Cancel

Figure 0-24 *The Advanced Editor window, showing three query steps.*

Here is how the evaluation takes place:

1. Because the final output is Grouped Rows, the query begins by evaluating the last step. You don't need to understand the code, but it is helpful to know that the Grouped Rows step is

summarizing the data by customer. When I say "data" in this case, I mean the table in the previous step (i.e., `#"Filtered Rows"`).

2. Before the data is passed on to the Grouped Rows step, it is filtered (`[Region] = "East"`).

3. In this case, we're connected to the current Excel file in the Source step. However, we can assume that if the Source step connects to a SQL database, it will request only the filtered data (`[Region] = "East"`) and then pass it on to Grouped Rows step.

Bottom-up evaluation makes the query lazy and efficient as it works selectively on limited data. Furthermore, even if we were to jumble the steps, the query wouldn't break, and it would still evaluate from the bottom up, as shown here:

```
 3  //       # Filtered Rows  = Table.SelectRows(Source, each ([Region] = "East")),
 4  //       #"Grouped Rows" = Table.Group(#"Filtered Rows", {"Customer"}, {{"Total Sales",
        each List.Sum([Amount]), type nullable number}})
 5  // in
 6  //       #"Grouped Rows"
 7
 8  let
 9    ❷#"Filtered Rows" = Table.SelectRows(Source, each ([Region] = "East")),
10    ❶#"Grouped Rows" = Table.Group(#"Filtered Rows", {"Customer"}, {{"Total Sales",
             each List.Sum([Amount]), type nullable number}}),
11    ❸ Source = Excel.CurrentWorkbook(){[Name="Table1"]}[Content]
12  in
13       #"Grouped Rows"
```

Figure 0-25 *The steps are jumbled, but the query still works.*

> **Note:** To retain the original steps, I duplicated them and commented them out (by selecting lines 1–6 and using the shortcut Ctrl+/).

However, because this query is now not in the logical order used in the user interface, the UI stops displaying the steps:

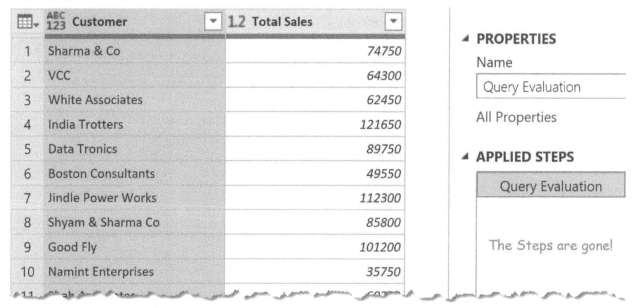

🔢	ABC 123 Customer	1.2 Total Sales
1	Sharma & Co	74750
2	VCC	64300
3	White Associates	62450
4	India Trotters	121650
5	Data Tronics	89750
6	Boston Consultants	49550
7	Jindle Power Works	112300
8	Shyam & Sharma Co	85800
9	Good Fly	101200
10	Namint Enterprises	35750

PROPERTIES

Name

Query Evaluation

All Properties

APPLIED STEPS

Query Evaluation

The Steps are gone!

Figure 0-26 *If you jumble the steps in the Advanced Editor, Power Query removes the steps in the UI.*

In the examples up to this point, you've seen steps in a logical order in the Power Query UI. But once you understand that queries are evaluated as you reference the steps in different Power Query functions, you can do a lot more in fewer steps (even if the steps are not in a coherent order). I know, it can be hard to imagine its utility now, but as your understanding grows throughout the course of this book, your mind will begin to make serendipitous connections. 😊

Chapter 1: Working with Lists

After warming up, there is no better place to start your M workout than with a list. Lists can make your queries a lot more robust and adaptive to changes in your data. In this chapter, we'll talk about what lists are, explore their nuances and behavior, and use them to solve a few practical problems.

> **Note:** For this chapter, we'll be using the file Lists.xlsx (which you'll find in the Lists folder). As you work through this chapter, you'll be able to walk through the examples by using the queries provided in this file.

What Is a List?

Refer to the query ListExample.

In the query ListExample, I've hard-coded a list that contains a few numbers and letters.

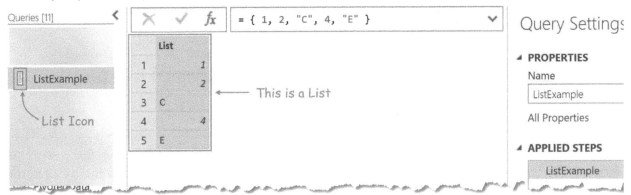

Figure 1-1 *This is how a list looks in Power Query.*

Here are a few things to keep in mind about lists:

- In the Power Query UI, a list appears as a single column, and the list icon appears next to the query's name. Note that a table with one column is not a list. (You'll learn more about tables later in this book.)
- A list can store any value (a number, text, a date, or even a structured value like a table or another list).
- A list is typed in curly brackets ({ }), and the list items are separated by commas—for example, ={1, 2, "Apple"}. In this example, because Apple is a text value, it is wrapped in double quotes.
- A list doesn't have a header. To help you understand that something is a list, Power Query adds the default header label List (which you can't change).
- A list uses zero-based sequencing, which means the position of the first value in a list is 0. For example, in Figure 1-1, the letter E is in position 4 and not 5 (even though it appears in position 5 in the UI).

How to Create a List

Refer to the query My First List.

Let's start off by creating a hard-coded list:

1. In Power Query, create a blank query (Home → New Source → Other Sources → Blank Query).
2. Name this query My First List.
3. Write the following code in the formula bar:

```
= {"Hello", "How", "are", "you?"}
```

This is what you get:

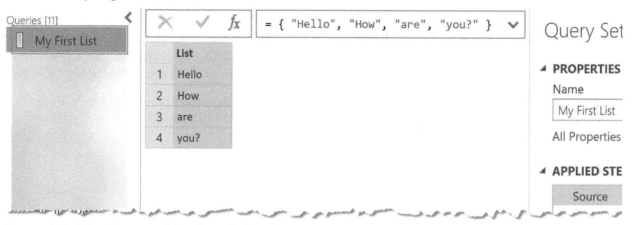

Figure 1-2 *A list is created inside curly brackets.*

Refer to the query Interesting List.

Now let's look at a slightly more interesting example of creating a list:

1.   Create another blank query (Home → New Source → Other Sources → Blank Query).

2.   Name the new query Interesting List.

3.   Write the following code in the formula bar:

```
={"Chandeep",100,{"Sleeping","Running","Creating lists"}}
```

Here we have created a nested list (a list inside a list) by using curly brackets within the outer curly brackets.

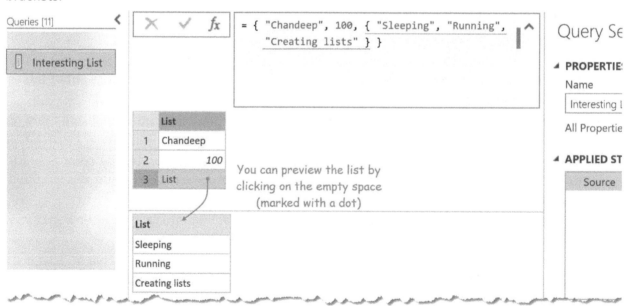

Figure 1-3 *An example of a nested list.*

At this point, creating a nested list might seem useless, but there are several advanced problems you can solve by using the nested list structure (as discussed later in this chapter).

How to Extract a List from a Table

Refer to the query ExtractList.

A lot of Power Query functions require you to work with lists. You've already seen that you can create a static list by hard-coding list values in curly brackets. Sometimes, though, you need to use dynamic lists. Let's start with a simple example of creating a dynamic list by extracting a column of a table as a list.

Consider this table:

	ABC 123 Category		ABC 123 Product		ABC 123 Sales	
1	Mid		A		100	
2	Mid		B		50	
3	Top		C		70	
4	Top		D		350	
5	Top		E		710	

Figure 1-4 *A table with three columns.*

From this table, say that we'd like to extract the Sales column as a list. We can do so in two simple steps:

1. Create a new step by clicking the fx button next to the formula bar. Power Query creates a new step that automatically refers to the previous step, Source.

2. Add the column name Sales in square brackets (so you have = `Source[Sales]` in the formula bar) and press Enter. The Sales column is extracted as a list.

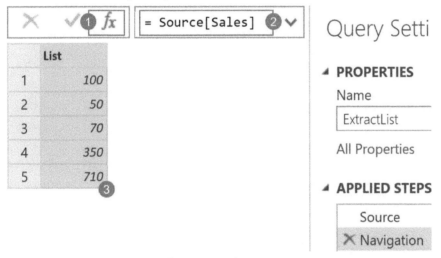

Figure 1-5 *Extracting a column as a list.*

Let's pause to reflect on what just happened:

• Notice that Source is the name of the previous step, which refers to the three-column table in Figure 1-4.

• By referencing the column name in square brackets ([ ]) after the table reference, we extract that column as a list.

> **Note:** You don't need to wrap the column name in quotation marks, even if it contains spaces:
>
> `= table[column name] // returns the column as a list.`
>
> However, you do need the pound sign and quotes if the column name contains special characters, such as an exclamation point. In that case, the M code looks like this:
>
> `= table[#"column name!"]`

Not surprisingly, you can create the same list by right-clicking on the Sales column and choosing Drill Down. So, we've done nothing remarkable here, but allow me a few more paragraphs before I start to blow your mind. 😉

How Lists Behave

Refer to the query ListBehavior.

A common behavior of a list is to expand to create rows. To see this in action, let's take a slightly more practical use case. Take a look at this three-column table:

	Category	Product	Sales
1	Mid	A	100
2	Mid	B	50
3	Top	C	70
4	Top	D	350
5	Top	E	710

PROPERTIES
Name
ListBehavior
All Properties

APPLIED STEPS
Source

Figure 1-6 *A table with three columns.*

Say that you'd like to add a column to this table and duplicate each row for the years 2019 and 2020. The result should look like this:

	Category	Product	Sales	Year
1	Mid	A	100	2019
2	Mid	A	100	2020
3	Mid	B	50	2019
4	Mid	B	50	2020
5	Top	C	70	2019
6	Top	C	70	2020
7	Top	D	350	2019
8	Top	D	350	2020
9	Top	E	710	2019
10	Top	E	710	2020

Figure 1-7 *The expected output with 10 rows: 5 for 2019 and 5 for 2020.*

To create a list with two values for each row of the table, we follow these steps:

1. Create a custom column (Add Column → Custom Column).
2. Name the new column Year.
3. In the Custom Column Formula box, create the list ={2019, 2020} and click OK.

New column name

Year

Custom column formula ⓘ

= {2019, 2020} ⟶ Created a List within Curly Brackets

Figure 1-8 *Using curly brackets to create a list.*

We've now created a list with two values for each row of the table.

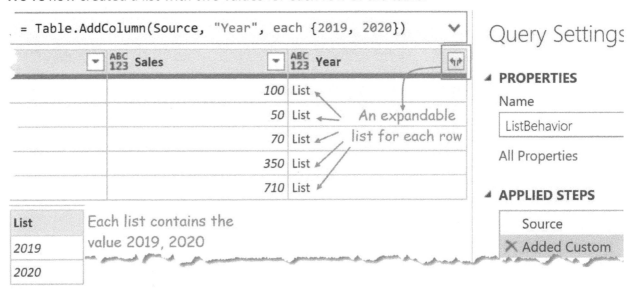

Figure 1-9 *An expandable list with two values for each row in the Year column.*

Notice the little expand button on the Year column. If you click the expand button and select Expand to New Rows, you end up with values for both years in the table, as shown here. Sweet!

Figure 1-10 *When you expand the Year column, the table includes a row for each year.*

To summarize, when you create a list in each row of a table, the list can be expanded to create more rows (or columns). This is incredibly useful when you want to dynamically expand a table's rows (or columns).

Example 1: Expanding Dynamic Columns

Refer to the query Dynamic Expansion.

Let's level up to a trickier problem. Say that we are working with three tables in the Lists.xlsx file (on the sheet named Sales Data), as shown here, and we want to append them into a single table.

Table Name:
| Year05 |

Sales Rep	Customer	Amount
Jaspreet	VCC	10150
Charley	Sharma & Co	12100
Jaspreet	Good Fly	14750
Ramesh	Data Tronics	15000
Ramesh	VCC	13550
Abhay	MNTL	12400
Anshika	Shyam & Sharma Co	14300
Charley	Boston Consultants	10700
Varsha	MNTL	10850
Jaspreet	White Associates	13150
Bruce	VCC	12350

Table Name:
| Year06 |

Sales Rep	Customer	Amount
Bruce	Boston Consultants	11850
Varsha	Namint Enterprises	11150
Swati	India Trotters	10600
Bruce	Data Tronics	10150
Jaspreet	White Associates	11750

Table Name:
| Year07 |

Sales Rep	Customer	Amount
James	Shyam & Sharma Co	12150
Bruce	Data Tronics	10350
Charley	Jindle Power Works	13650
Veronica	Boston Consultants	12350
Jaspreet	Data Tronics	14150
Abhay	Good Fly	12000
Veronica	White Associates	12050
Bruce	India Trotters	10150
Abhay	Sharma & Co	11700

Figure 1-11 *Three tables with the same columns.*

Let's fire up Power Query and gather the three tables by following these steps:

1. In the Power Query window, create a blank query (Home → New Source → Other Sources → Blank Query).
2. Rename the new query Dynamic Expansion.
3. In the formula bar, write the function `= Excel.CurrentWorkbook()` to retrieve all the tables in the current Excel file.

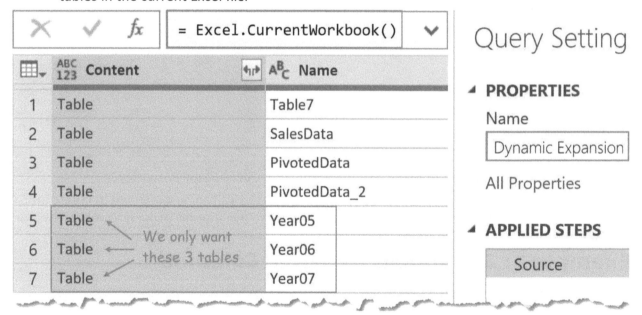

Figure 1-12 `Excel.CurrentWorkbook()` *returns all tables and named ranges in the current Excel file.*

To append only the Year tables, we can conveniently apply a filter on the Name column to keep the values that start with the string `"Year"`.

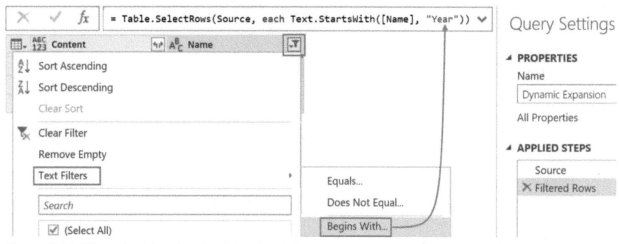

Figure 1-13 *Filtered tables that begin with Year.*

At this stage, I am pretty sure you're familiar with this view, which has nested tables waiting to be expanded:

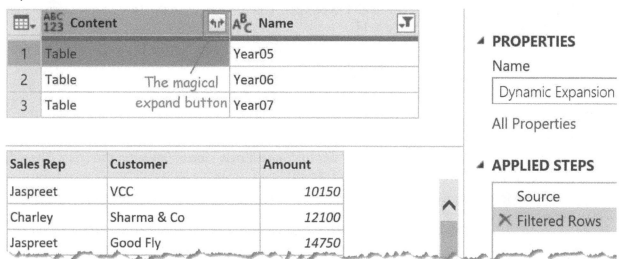

Figure 1-14 *The Content column has three tables that can be expanded.*

Here's the challenge: When we expand these tables, the column names get hard-coded, which means any new columns added to the source data will not dynamically expand. Bad!

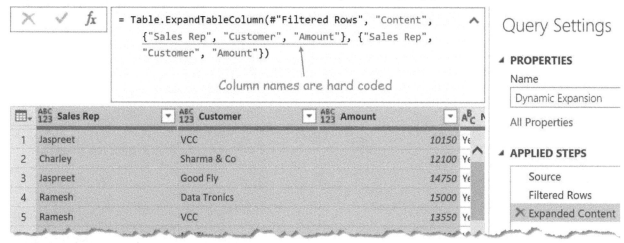

Figure 1-15 *Upon expansion, the column names are hard-coded into the formula.*

But what if we want to automatically show any new columns that are added? Before we look at how to do that, we need to take a step back and understand the function used in the Expanded Content step:

```
= Table.ExpandTableColumn(
    #"Filtered Rows",                        // 1
    "Content",                               // 2
    {"Sales Rep", "Customer", "Amount"},     // 3
    {"Sales Rep", "Customer", "Amount"}      // 4
)
```

Note that:

1. The first input is a reference to the table in the previous step (i.e., #"Filtered Rows").

2. The second input is the hard-coded name of the column to be expanded (i.e., "Content"; refer to Figure 1-14).

3. The next input is a list of columns to be expanded. Notice the curly braces: {"Sales Rep", "Customer", "Amount"}.

4. The last input is a list to rename the columns that are expanded, and it is optional.

A Logical Way to Think About the Solution

Here is a two-step process that will get us the result we want:

1. Start by creating a dynamic list of all the possible column names in the three tables (from the Content column; refer to Figure 1-14).

2. Once we have the list of columns, replace the hard-coded list (in Figure 1-15) with our dynamic list, and it should work.

Let's give this a shot.

Step 1: Creating a List of Columns

Here is how we can create a dynamic list of column names:

1. Click the fx button next to the formula bar to create a new step in between the steps Filtered Rows and Expanded Content.

2. Write the following M code in the formula bar to get a list of column names from the three tables:

```
=Table.ColumnNames(
    Table.Combine(#"Filtered Rows"[Content])
)
```

3. Right-click the new step and rename it ColList.

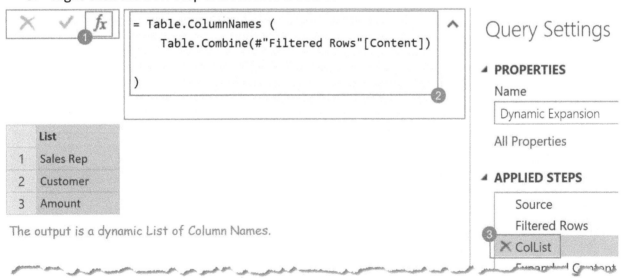

The output is a dynamic List of Column Names.

Figure 1-16 *Creating a new step that returns a dynamic list with column names from the three tables.*

Let's dissect the formula from the inside out:

- #"Filtered Rows" is the name of the table in the previous step (refer to Figure 1-14).

- In the event that we reference the column name ([Content]) after the table name, we'll get a list that contains three tables like the one shown here:

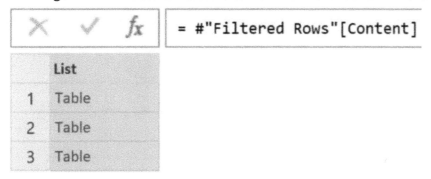

Figure 1-17 *This is how the list looks if we extract the Content column from the previous step (Filtered Rows).*

- The Table.Combine function accepts a list that contains the tables that are to be appended). Sure enough, we have that, so it is legit to write the full formula as Table.Combine(#"Filtered Rows"[Content]). However, this function is literally going to append the data from all three tables (regardless of the column names), and we don't want that to happen yet.

- Therefore, we have the final wrapper Table.ColumnNames, which accepts a table as input and extracts the column names as a list that is not hard-coded. (In comparison, see the formula with the hard-coded list in Figure 1-15.)

Step 2: Plugging the List Back into the Expanded Content Step

Now if we go to the Expanded Content step, we get an error because we added a step in between, and Expanded Content no longer refers to the correct table.

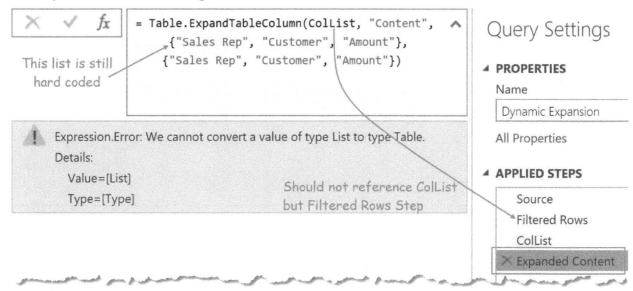

Figure 1-18 *The Expanded Content step returns an error.*

Let's fix this. Here is the revised M code for the Expanded Content step:

```
=Table.ExpandTableColumn(
    #"Filtered Rows",
    "Content",
    ColList
)
```

And here's how it differs from the original code:

- The first input is now #"Filtered Rows" (the table on which expansion will happen).
- The "Content" column name remains the same because it was hard-coded.
- The list to be expanded now refers to the ColList step that we've created.
- We don't want any renaming to be done, so we've removed the optional renaming list.

Figure 1-19 *The* Table.ExpandTableColumn *function now references the dynamic list of columns.*

Now, if any new columns are added in the base tables, the query is robust enough to expand them automatically.

> **Gotcha!** 😕 Because we omitted the last input (renaming the list) from the Table.ExpandTableColumn function, the function might return an error if any of the expanded columns have the same name as the existing columns. An easy solution for this is to make sure the existing table columns are renamed before the Expanded Content step.

Recap: Feed Power Query What It Eats

It'll be worthwhile to see what it looks like to feed Power Query what it eats (my cool lingo from the previous chapter). Take a close look at the input and output values of the functions used in creating the ColList and Expanded Content steps:

```
ColList =
  Table.ColumnNames(
    Table.Combine(#"Filtered Rows"[Content])
  )                             // 1 Creating Col List

#"Expanded Content" =
  Table.ExpandTableColumn(
    #"Filtered Rows",
    "Content",
    ColList
  )                             // 2 Expanded Content
```

Note that:

1. The Table.Combine function can only work if we input a list containing tables. The output it returns is a single table. Table.ColumnNames can only work if the input is a table. The output it returns is a list of column names.

2. Table.ExpandTableColumn can only work if the third argument is a list. The output it returns is appended tables with expanded columns.

Note that the output value of each function matches the input value of the wrapper function. Here is a table to help you see this vividly:

Function	Input	Output
#"Filtered Rows"[Content]		list
Table.Combine	list	table
Table.ColumnNames	table	list
Table.ExpandTableColumn(#"Filtered Rows", "Content", ColList)	3rd input is a list	table

Figure 1-20 *The output values of the functions match the input values of the wrapper functions.*

I said this earlier, but I'd like to say it again: Pay attention to the input and output values as you learn different M functions. A mismatch between what a formula is asking for and what you are feeding in the formula will at the very least return an error and will definitely lead to frustration. 😣

Example 2: Expanding Dynamic Columns, Part 2

Refer to the query Dynamic Expansion Part 2.

In the previous example, our intermediate query looked like this right before we expanded the Content column:

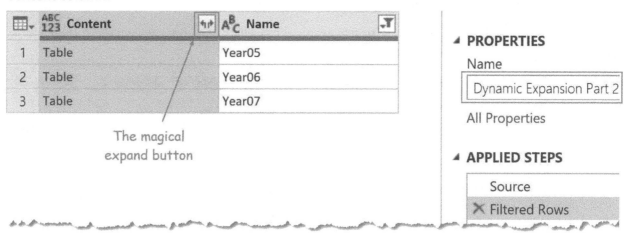

The magical
expand button

Figure 1-21 *Expanding the nested tables hard-codes the names of the columns.*

To make the expanded columns dynamic, we created a dynamic list of column names and then plugged that list into the `Table.ExpandTableColumn` function. **Very important:** This allowed us to retain the existing Name column along with the expanded columns (refer to Figure 1-19).

But what if we're only interested in expanding the columns from the tables in the Content column and don't want to retain any of the existing columns?

We can do that—and it is way easier. Here's how:

1. Create a new step by clicking the fx button.
2. Write the following code in the formula bar:

```
= Table.Combine (#"Filtered Rows"[Content])
```

This combines all the tables in the Content column. Neat! Right-click the new step and rename it `CombinedAllTables`.

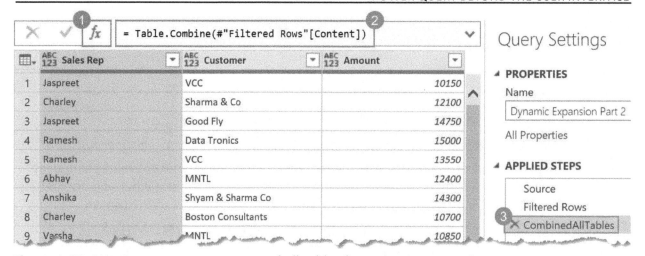

Figure 1-22 *Creating a new step to append all tables from the Content column.*

Example 3: Dynamically Unpivoting Other Columns

Refer to the query PivotedData.

Now let's consider an interesting unpivoting example where lists can come very handy. Take a look at this data:

Product	Color	31-Jan-22	28-Feb-22	31-Mar-22	30-Apr-22	31-May-22	30-Jun-22
A	Red	180	156	113	179	142	126
B	Red	110	117	166	140	185	157
C	White	149	199	184	139	172	183
D	Blue	180	120	137	157	193	138
E	Blue	153	180	121	142	101	132
F	Black	112	157	155	148	113	165

Figure 1-23 *Cross-tabulated (pivoted) data shows sales for product and color, by month.*

The data is obviously pivoted (or cross-tabulated) with month-ending dates in columns and product and color in rows.

A typical unpivoting technique in Power Query would be to select both the Product and Color columns, right-click, and select Unpivot Other Columns. And boom! You'd be done!

However, if you do that, you get output like this, where the Product and Color columns are hard-coded as a list:

	Product	Color	Attribute	Value
	= Table.UnpivotOtherColumns(Source, {"Product", "Color"}, "Attribute", "Value")			
1	A	Red	31-Jan-22	180
2	A	Red	28-Feb-22	156
3	A	Red	31-Mar-22	113
4	A	Red	30-Apr-22	179
5	A	Red	31-May-22	142
6	A	Red	30-Jun-22	126
7	B	Red	31-Jan-22	110
8	B	Red	28-Feb-22	117

Query Settings

▲ PROPERTIES

Name

PivotedData

All Properties

▲ APPLIED STEPS

Source

✕ Unpivoted Other Columns

Figure 1-24 *The Unpivoted Other Columns step hard-codes the Product and Color columns in the formula.*

What if we add a Category column as the third column in the source data?

Product	Color	Category	31-Jan-22	28-Feb-22	31-Mar-22	30-Apr-22	31-May-22	30-Jun-22
A	Red	Top	180	156	113	179	142	126
B	Red	Top	110	117	166	140	185	157
C	White	Top	149	199	184	139	172	183
D	Blue	Mid	180	120	137	157	193	138
E	Blue	Mid	153	180	121	142	101	132
F	Black	Low	112	157	155	148	113	165

Figure 1-25 *A new Category column is added.*

Now if we refresh the query with the new column added, the Category column is also unpivoted because only the Product and Color columns were hard-coded in the formula.

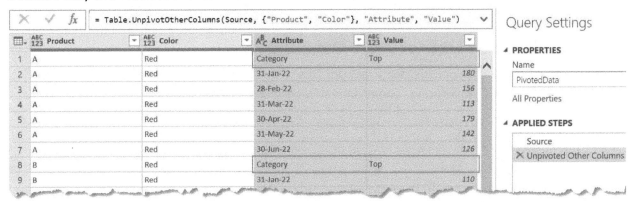

Figure 1-26 *The Category column was also unpivoted since it was not included in* `Table.UnpivotOtherColumns`*.*

How do we fix this in such a way that the Product and Color columns aren't hard-coded but are formed using a dynamic list? Let's think this through. We could do it like this:

1. Extract all column names as a list.

2. Filter the list for only non-date values (because only dates are supposed to be unpivoted).

3. Plug the filtered list into the `Table.UnpivotOtherColumns` function instead of hard-coding the column names.

This should work. Let's give it a shot.

Step 1: Extract All Columns as a List

Let's start by creating a list of all column names:

1. Create a new step in between Source and Unpivoted Other Columns.

2. Write the following code in the formula bar to extract all the column names as a list:

```
= Table.ColumnNames(Source)
```

3. Rename the new step ColNames. (Renaming custom steps and using CamelCase for clarity is a good hygiene practice.)

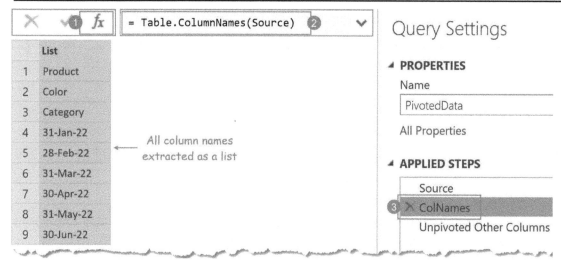

Figure 1-27 *Extracting all columns from the Source step as a list.*

Step 2: Filter the List for Non-Date Values

To filter the list, we can use another list function, `List.Select`, which checks each item of the list against a condition. In this case, our condition can be loosely written like this:

```
= List.Select(
    Column Name List,
    each value  <> a date
)
```

Let's wrap the existing M code in the following `List.Select` function:

```
= List.Select(
    Table.ColumnNames(Source),
    each ( try Date.From(_) ) [HasError]
)
```

	List
1	Product
2	Color
3	Category

Figure 1-28 `List.Select` *returns a list of values that are not dates.*

Momentarily refer to the query ListMagic.

Okay, I might have stretched your gray cells a bit too much here. There is a lot going on in these two lines. Let me explain:

- `Table.ColumnNames(Source)` gets us the list of all column names (refer to Figure 1-27).
- For each value in the list, we use the `try` keyword (which is synonymous with Excel's `IFERROR` function) to convert each value into a date:

```
each (try Date.From(_))
```

If we write the same code slightly differently, the results are more visual:

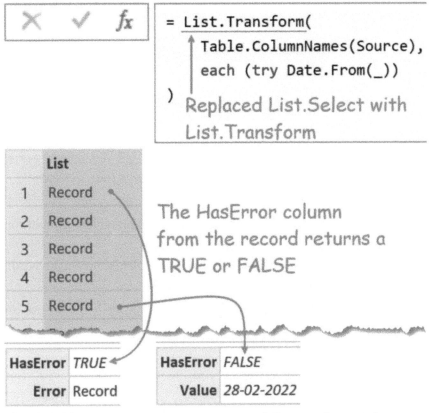

```
✗  ✓  ƒx      = List.Transform(
                  Table.ColumnNames(Source),
                  each (try Date.From(_))
              )
```
Replaced List.Select with List.Transform

List

	List
1	Record
2	Record
3	Record
4	Record
5	Record

The HasError column from the record returns a TRUE or FALSE

HasError	TRUE
Error	Record

HasError	FALSE
Value	28-02-2022

Figure 1-29 *Using* `List.Transform` *and the* `try` *keyword returns a record.*

- The output of `List.Transform` will not be a filtered list but a list where each value is tried using the `Date.From` function to transform it into a date.

- The `try` keyword returns a record for each row with a field HasError that has TRUE or FALSE as output. We get TRUE as the output if an error occurred (i.e., if the value was not converted to a date) and otherwise FALSE.

- Now the Product and Color columns and the newly added Category column contain text values, and our formula will return an error because it cannot convert them into dates.

- The error value is (by default) stored in a HasError field as TRUE or FALSE. So, we simply extract TRUE or FALSE from the HasError field.

> **Note:** When we replace `List.Transform` with `List.Select`, it evaluates each value of list against a TRUE/FALSE condition. All values where the condition returns TRUE are retained, and the rest are removed.
>
> Another important thing that could easily be overlooked is that `try Date.From(_)` returns a record, and in order to refer to the HasError field from the record, we have to surround `try Date.From(_)` with parentheses, like this: `(try Date.From(_)) [Has Error]`.

It's okay if your eyes glazed over just now. You'll get a more detailed understanding of working with `each _` (underscore), records, and `try...otherwise` in the next few chapters.

Step 3: Plug the Filtered List into Table.UnpivotOtherColumns

Refer to the query PivotedData.

In our PivotedData query, if we go to the Unpivoted Other Columns step, Power Query shows an error. This is expected because we added a step before it, causing it to point to the ColNames step rather than to the correct table (via the Source step). Let's fix that.

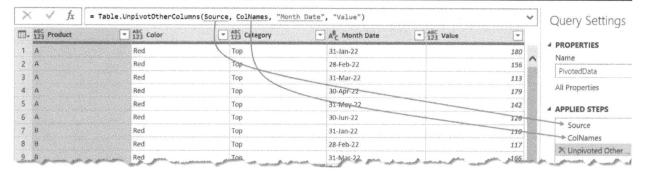

Figure 1-30 *The hard-coded list has been replaced with a dynamic list of columns (i.e., ColNames).*

In the function `Table.UnpivotOtherColumns`:

- Change the first input to `Source` (because the Source table is the table on which unpivoting will happen).
- Ensure that the list of columns refers to the dynamic list (step) we've created (i.e., `ColNames`).
- To omit an additional step, rename the Attribute column Month Date.

Now, if any new (non-date) columns are added to our base table, they'll automatically be left out of unpivoting. How awesome is that?! 😎

Lists of Lists (a.k.a. Nested Lists)

Refer to the query Creating List of Lists.

We can use nested lists—that is, lists of lists, where one or more lists are wrapped in another list—to solve more advanced problems. Before we jump to a practical example of nested lists, let's warm up a bit by creating a nested list. Take a look at this M code:

```
= {                          // Outer List
    {1,2},                   // Nested List 1
    {"A","B"},               // Nested List 2
    {"C",4}                  // Nested List 3
}
```

This code creates three nested lists within a list.

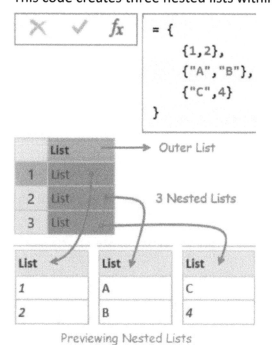

Previewing Nested Lists

Figure 1-31 *Three nested lists within a list. Each list is surrounded by curly brackets.*

Notice a few things:

- The outer list is wrapped in curly brackets (as you'd expect).
- The inner lists are separated with commas and also wrapped in curly brackets.
- All items of the inner lists are also separated by commas.

And that's about it. We've created a nested list. Now let's use this list of lists in a practical setting.

Example 4: Removing Errors from Multiple Columns (Using a List of Lists)

Refer to the query Replacing Errors.

Consider this table in the Source step, which contains errors. In this case, the source data from Excel had a few #N/A errors, and Power Query also marked each of those cells with "Error."

	Invoice	Date	Product	Sales	Units
1	INV-7	03-01-2023 00:00:00	D		350	29
2	INV-2	Error	D		350	27
3	INV-6	04-01-2023 00:00:00	E		710	6
4	INV-6	05-01-2023 00:00:00	A	Error		13
5	INV-3	05-01-2023 00:00:00	C		70	22
6	INV-9	06-01-2023 00:00:00	A		100	9
7	INV-3	06-01-2023 00:00:00	B		50	21
8	INV-6	07-01-2023 00:00:00	E		710	29
9	INV-5	08-01-2023 00:00:00	C		70	7
10	INV-5	10-01-2023 00:00:00	B		50	28

⚠ DataFormat.Error: Invalid cell value '#N/A'.

Figure 1-32 *A table with errors in the Date and Sales columns.*

Say that we'd like to replace each error with a null value. Sure enough, we could do that in the user interface, but what if we want the replacement to be dynamic, so that errors are replaced in all columns even if columns are added (or removed)?

To solve this problem, we can take hints from the UI and see what M code gets generated if we replace errors in the Date and Sales columns with null values:

1. Select the Date and Sales columns.
2. Select Transform → Replace Values drop-down → Replace Errors.
3. In the box that appears, enter `null` (all lowercase because Power Query is case-sensitive).

The errors are replaced with null values, giving us code like this:

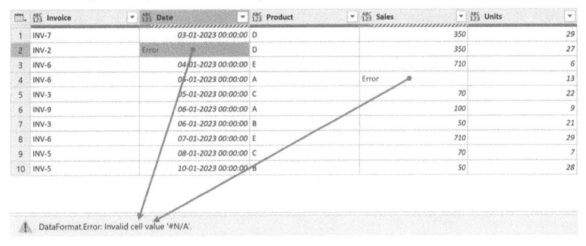

Figure 1-33 *The `Table.ReplaceErrorValues` function uses a nested list to replace errors in each column.*

Notice a few interesting things:

- `Table.ReplaceErrorValues` needs a table to work with (i.e., the Source step) in the first argument.
- In the second argument, the function accepts a nested list. Each inner list has two parts: the column name (as a text value) and the replacement value (`null`).
- To make this formula dynamic, we need to produce a nested list, and each inner list must have two values: the column name (as a text value) and `null`.
- Also, the dynamic nested list should contain all columns from the Source step.

Let's get to work.

Step 1: Creating a List

Let's start by generating column names as a list (not as a nested list—yet):

1. Create a new step in between the Source and Replaced Errors steps.

2. Write this M code in the formula bar to get the list of column names:

```
= Table.ColumnNames (Source)
```

3. Rename the new step AllColsList.

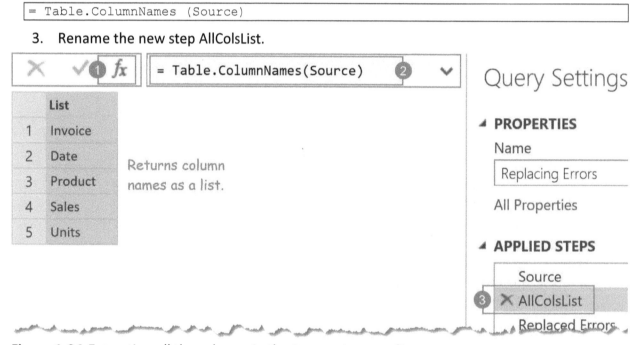

Figure 1-34 *Extracting all the columns in the Source step as a list.*

Step 2: Converting a List into a List of Lists

So far, we've been able to produce a list of columns (refer to Figure 1-34), but we need a nested list structure to make this work. Let's revise our M code further, as shown here:

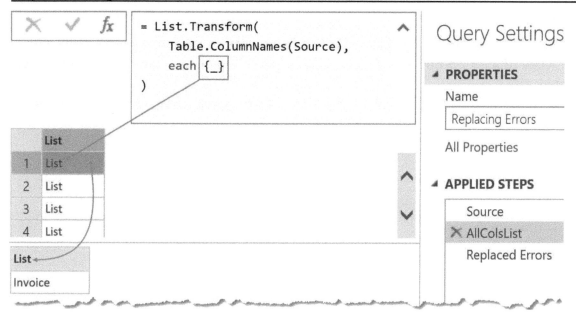

Figure 1-35 *Using* `List.Transform` *to create a list of lists.*

What just happened?

- We started by wrapping the existing formula in the `List.Transform` function.
- The first argument is a list to be transformed (that's our column names list—`Table.ColumnNames(Source)`).
- The second argument is the transformation. In this case, we'd like to nest each value into a list.
- The underscore (_) represents each value, and the curly brackets are used to nest each value in a list.

The only problem: We need to have two values in each list: a column name and null. We already have the column name. Now let's get the null.

Step 3: Adding Null Values to the Nested Lists

Here is a slight modification to the code to add null values to the nested lists:

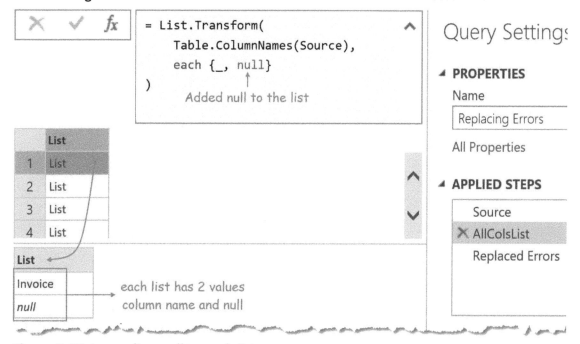

Figure 1-36 *Appending null to each list.*

Note the following:

- Along with the underscore, we append (using a comma) a second value in the list (`null`).
- A preview of each list now shows two values—the column name and `null`—just like we wanted. 😊

Step 4: Plugging the List of Lists into Table.ReplaceErrorValues

Once again, the Replaced Errors step must have errored out because we added a step in between, so let's fix that.

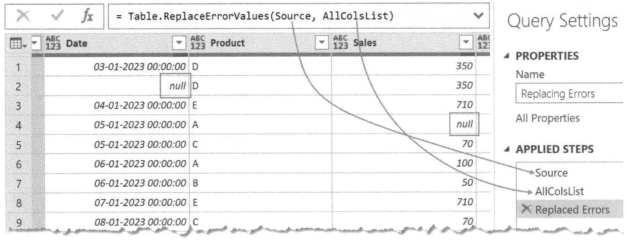

Figure 1-37 *Replacing the hard-coded list with the dynamic list of lists.*

In the third step, Replaced Errors:

- The first argument refers to `Source` (i.e., the table).
- The second input is the dynamic nested list we created as a new step (i.e., `AllColsList`).

Now if any error shows up in any column of the source table, it'll automatically be replaced by a null value.

Exercises

Here are a few exercises to test your understanding. Ready?

> **Note:** Open the Excel file List Exercises - Unsolved in the Lists folder and then use the Power Query Editor to work through these exercises.

Exercise 1: Create a List

Create a list of lowercase letters from a to j. The output should look like this:

	List
1	a
2	b
3	c
4	d
5	e
6	f
7	g
8	h
9	i
10	j

Figure 1-38 *Expected output.*

Exercise 2: Extract and Sum a Column as a List

From the three-column table shown here, extract the Amount column as a list and sum it. The output should be a single value: the sum of the Amount column.

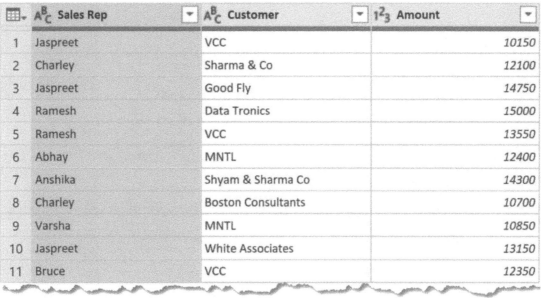

	A^B_C Sales Rep	A^B_C Customer	1^2_3 Amount
1	Jaspreet	VCC	10150
2	Charley	Sharma & Co	12100
3	Jaspreet	Good Fly	14750
4	Ramesh	Data Tronics	15000
5	Ramesh	VCC	13550
6	Abhay	MNTL	12400
7	Anshika	Shyam & Sharma Co	14300
8	Charley	Boston Consultants	10700
9	Varsha	MNTL	10850
10	Jaspreet	White Associates	13150
11	Bruce	VCC	12350

139300

Figure 1-39 *A table with three columns with the expected output below (i.e., the sum of the Amount column).*

Exercise 3: Dynamically Remove Junk Columns

Here is a table with a few columns. Notice that the last two columns have the ~ suffix at the end of the column name (and are junk).

Your task is to remove all the columns that have the ~ symbol at the end of the column name. Make sure that your solution is dynamic and the column names are not hard-coded.

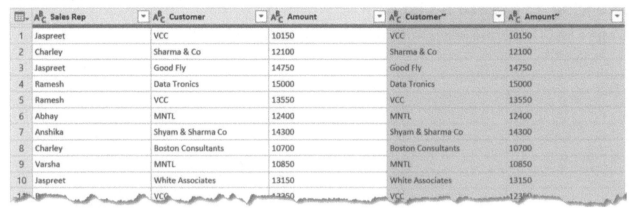

Figure 1-40 *A table with junk columns (with a ~ suffix on the column names).*

Exercise 4: Dynamically Rename Columns

The table below has the suffix 1 with each column name. Your task is to dynamically rename all the columns by removing the 1. The solution should not have any hard-coded column names.

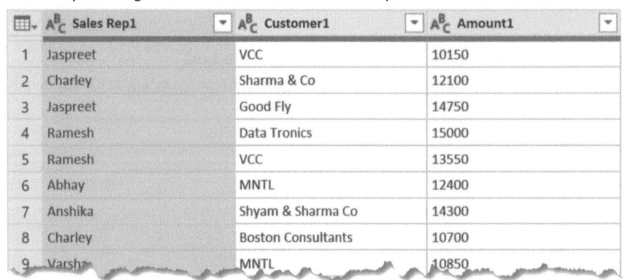

Figure 1-41 *Column names suffixed with the junk value 1.*

> **Note:** When you're done with these exercises, you can compare your answers against the ones I provide in the Solutions chapter at the end of this book or refer to the Excel file List Exercises - Solved or do both. 😊

Chapter 2: Working with Records

"Do you have a record of that?"

"My record in the system went missing!"

These sentences conjure images of rows or line items in a dataset. This is also the most intuitive way to understand records in Power Query. In simple terms, a record in Power Query is a single row of a table. That's it!

In this chapter, we'll see how to create, extract, and understand the behavior of records. You'll also be able to apply what you learn by solving a few practical problems.

> **Note:** For this chapter, we'll be using the file Records.xlsx (which you'll find in the Records folder). As you work through this chapter, you'll be able to walk through the examples by using the queries provided in this file.

Visualizing a Record

Refer to the query RandomData.

Consider this three-column table. Each row in this table is—you've guessed it—a record.

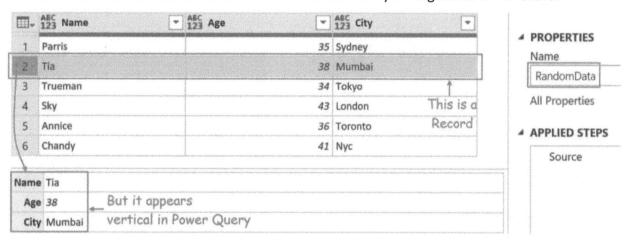

Figure 2-1 *A record in Power Query.*

Keep in mind a few things about records:

- Records are rows of a table, so 1 record = 1 row.
- Each record has two parts: the field (column) name and the field's value. For example, the record highlighted above consists of three unique field names (Name, Age, and City) and their respective field values (Tia, 38, and Mumbai).
- The field values can be primitive values (e.g., text, numbers, dates) or structured values (e.g., tables, lists, records, data types).
- Just like tables, records cannot have duplicate field or column names.

Creating a Record

Refer to the query ARecord.

Just like lists, records can be created manually. To create a record, we need to specify one or more field names and their respective field values in square brackets ([ ]).

Let's create a record in a blank query:

1. Create a blank query (Home → New Source → Other Sources → Blank Query).
2. Name the query ARecord.

3. Write the following M code in the formula bar:

```
= [
    Full Name = "Maria Jones",
    Age = 38,
    #"Phone No." = "9999-999-9"
]
```

Figure 2-2 *Creating a record with hard-coded values.*

Notice a few things:

*   Each field/value pair except for the last one is followed by a comma.
*   Even though the field name Full Name includes a space, there is no need to write it in quotes (or using any other special method).
*   A field name that includes any special character (such as the dot in the field name Phone No.) needs to be prefixed with a pound symbol and wrapped in double quotes, like this: #"Phone No".

Extracting a Record

Refer to the query Extracting Record.

You won't always create records from scratch. In many cases, you will need to extract records from tables. A record (i.e., a row) can be extracted from a table using this simple syntax:

```
= TableReference {rownumber}
// Since records are rows of a table,
// writing the row number after the table reference
// in curly brackets extracts the record.
```

In the table below, we'd like to extract the fourth record as a new step. (By now I'm sure you know how to create a new step: Click the fx button next to the formula bar.)

In the formula bar for a new step (named ExtractingRecord), we can refer to the table and row number like this:

```
= #"Changed Type"{3}
```

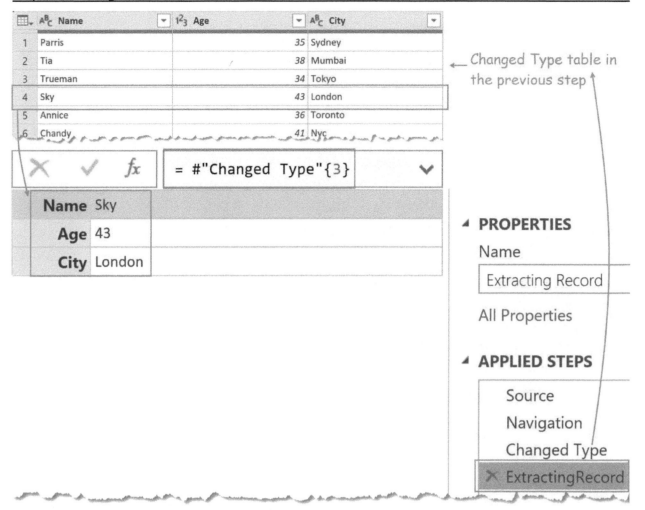

Figure 2-3 *Extracting a record in a new step.*

Notice a few interesting things in our code above:

- #"Changed Type" is the table from the previous step, and it refers to the third row in curly brackets.
- Since the indexing in Power Query starts with 0, writing #"Changed Type"{3} will extract the fourth record and not the third.

Creating and extracting records are insignificant tasks that don't mean much themselves. Let's now do something significant, yet simple, using records.

How Do Records Behave?

> **Note:** A record can have multiple fields (i.e., columns), and it expands to add columns when used as a column in a table.

Refer to the query ExpandingRecords.

Let's start with an interesting example using this tiny table:

Dealer	Start Date	USD Sales	Units
Boston Consultants	11-Apr-83	17500	1000
Data Tronics	08-Jun-85	7700	700
Good Fly	18-Apr-87	8200	2000
White Associates	13-Nov-83	60000	500
India Trotters	05-Jun-82	12000	1000
VCC	11-Oct-86	14000	3500
MNTL	12-May-85	22000	500
Good Fly	31-Dec-84	15000	1500

Figure 2-4 *A table with four columns.*

In this table, we'd like to add the following three calculated columns using Power Query:

- `Price = [USD Sales] / [Units]`
- `Years = (Today's Date - [Start Date]) / 365`
- `Cost = [USD Sales] * 35%`

The output should look like this:

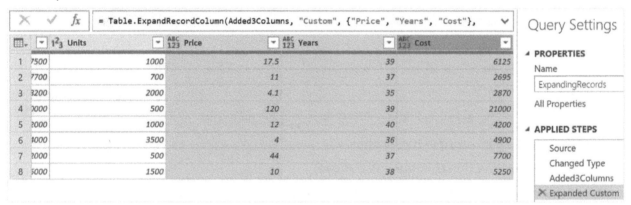

Figure 2-5 *The expected output, with Price, Years, and Cost columns added.*

This is a straightforward problem. All you do is create a custom column and pin down its formula, and you're good to go. However, you'll have to add three custom column steps if you want to add three columns.

To make this leaner, we can use the magic of records:

1. Add a custom column (Add Column → Custom Column).
2. In the Custom Column box, create a record with three columns (Price, Years, and Cost) by using the following formula:

Custom Column

Add a column that is computed from the other columns.

New column name

```
Custom
```

Custom column formula ⓘ

```
= [
    Price = [USD Sales] / [Units],
    Years =
        Number.RoundDown(
            Duration.Days(
                DateTime.LocalNow() - [Start Date]
            ) /365
        ),
    Cost = [USD Sales] * 0.35
]
```

Figure 2-6 *Using records to create a custom column formula.*

Let me enlighten you on the M code above:

- The entire formula is in square brackets, which means it's a record.
- The first column, Price, is straightforward: `Price = [USD Sales] / [Units]`.
- The second column, Years, uses a mix of date functions to calculate the years and then rounds down to a whole number. (Note that today's date will be different when you're reading this book, and so the output will differ.)
- The third column, Cost, is also straightforward: `Cost = [USD Sales] * 0.35`.

This results in a record with three fields in each row of the table:

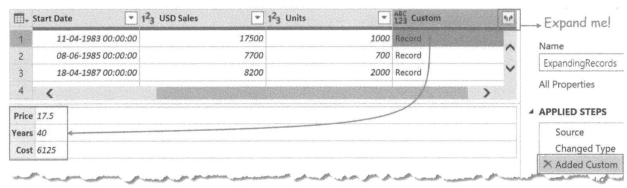

Figure 2-7 *The custom column shows a record for each row that can be expanded.*

The only thing left to do is to expand the custom column:

Figure 2-8 *When the custom column from* **Figure 2-7** *is expanded, three columns are added.*

We've created three columns in just two steps. We could create five or even more columns using these same two steps. We can add as many columns as we want with even more complex logic and expand them in a single go. This is bananas! 🍌

Long story short: Records expand to create columns when used in a column of a table.

Example 1: Summing Columns of a Table

Refer to the query Summing Columns.

Let's do more with records. In this table, we'd like to add a Total column that sums the values for all four months:

Add this column to the table →

ABC 123 Name	ABC 123 Jan	ABC 123 Feb	ABC 123 Mar	ABC 123 Apr	ABC 123 Total	
1 Chandeep	13	18	18	13	62	
2 Mike	17	14	17	12	60	
3 Tommy	20	12	20	17	69	
4 Rehet	19	14	15	10	58	

Figure 2-9 *A table with four months' worth of data, where a Total column is to be added.*

One way of solving this using the UI would be to add a new column and reference the four columns individually, like this: =[Jan]+[Feb]+[Mar]+[Apr]. However, this would be a manual method, and any new columns added wouldn't be included in the total.

We could arguably do some unpivoting, grouping, and re-pivoting to add a Total column, but that's too much effort for such a tiny total column. Instead, let's go with this extremely simple option that uses records:

1. Create a custom column (Add Column → Custom Column).
2. Name the new custom column Total.
3. Write the following code in the Custom Column Formula box:

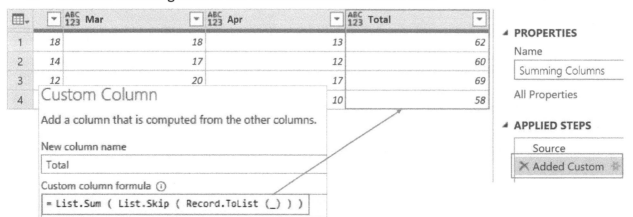

Figure 2-10 *Using records to add a Total column.*

Let's explore this code, from the inside out:

- The _ (underscore) here is used to extract the record for each row of the table. I promise to teach you more about underscores in upcoming chapters, but for now, this picture is worth a thousand words:

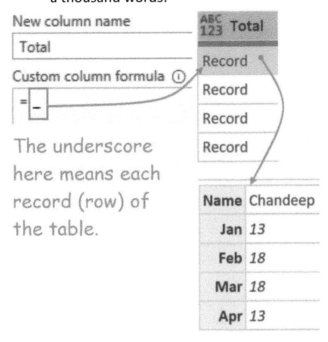

Figure 2-11 *The _ (underscore) returns a record for each row of the table.*

- Because we cannot sum a record, we need to transform the record into a list, and we do that by using `Record.ToList (_)`. Here is another pretty picture for you:

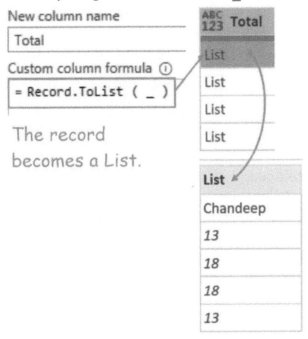

Figure 2-12 *The record is transformed into a list.*

- Another problem is that the list has five values (the name and the four numeric values for each month). Because we cannot sum a text value, we skip the first value by using `List.Skip*`, which returns only the numbers.
- Finally, `List.Sum` produces the sum of all the numbers in the list.

And we get our Total column in one little step:

		ABC 123 Mar		ABC 123 Apr		ABC 123 Total	
1		18		18		13	62
2		14		17		12	60
3		12		20		17	69
4		14		15		10	58

Figure 2-13 *Total column added.*

Pretty nifty, right? 😎

> **Tip:** *`List.Skip` by default skips the first value in the list. However, we can customize the number of items to be skipped by using a number or a condition. Here are two examples:
>
> ```
> = List.Skip(list, 2)
> // will skip the first two items in the list
>
>
> = List.Skip(list_of_numbers, each _ < 5)
> // will stop skipping when the condition becomes false
> // (i.e., it hits the first number >= 5)
> ```
>
> We can also make our code slightly more robust by adding a condition in `List.Skip`, where the list items are skipped until the first value is a number. This will provide for more columns that can be added at the start of the table (e.g., a Category column, which ideally should not be included in the list to sum). The code looks like this:
>
> ```
> = List.Skip (Record.ToList (_), not (each _ is number))
> // the not reverses the logic and skips
> // the non-number values from the start of the list
> ```
>
> You'll learn more about the `is` keyword later in this book. 😉

Example 2: Extracting an Intermediate Step from a Query

> Refer to the query ExtractingAStep.

Quite often, you'll find yourself stuck in a position where you'd like to extract an intermediate step from a query into a new query. Yup, you've read this right: A step in between is to be extracted! This isn't technically possible because when you reference a query, you always see the result of the last step and not an intermediate step. Well, guess what. We've got records, and this could be the most insane (and probably useful) application of records.

We're facing the same problem discussed in Example 1, where we used the query named Summing Columns, but this time we're solving it by using the user interface because we want to have a bunch of steps to work with.

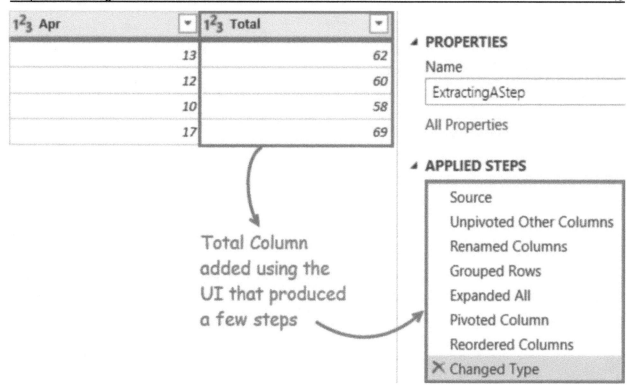

Figure 2-14 *Using the UI to add the Total column (which generates a few steps).*

We are not interested in going through the steps to solve the problem in this case. Instead, we are interested in extracting an intermediate step—any one of them.

Step 1: Transforming the Query into Records

To pull off the extraction of an intermediate step, we need to convert our query into a record. You'll understand when you see it.

Here's how we transform our query into a record:

1. Select the View tab.
2. Click Advanced Editor.
3. Comment out the `let` (at the start) and the closing `in` statement (at the end), along with the last step (i.e., `#Change Type`) by prefixing each with a double forward slash (`//`).
4. Wrap the query in square brackets. If we've done everything correctly, we'll see a green checkmark and the text "No syntax errors have been detected," as shown below.
5. Click Done.

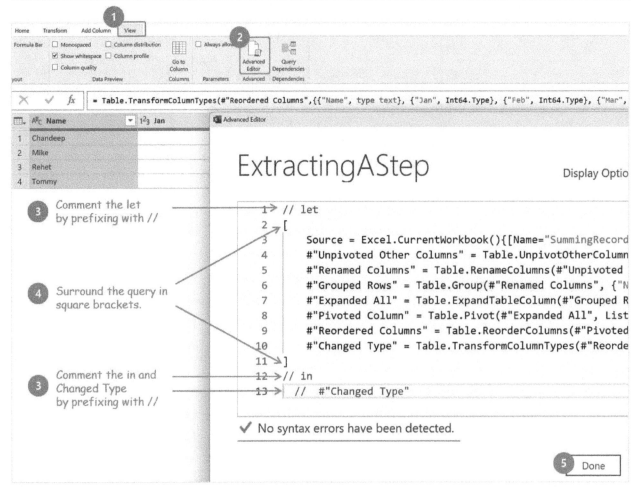

Figure 2-15 *Converting the entire query into a record.*

Here is how the query looks now:

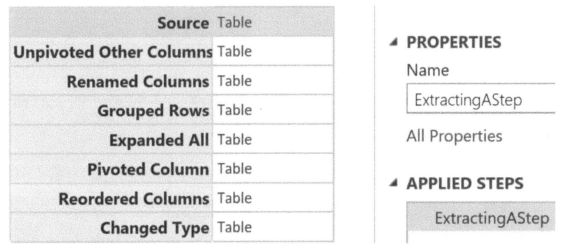

Figure 2-16 *The query has been converted into a record. The steps have become fields (shown vertically), and each field value contains a table as the output of the step.*

What just happened? Here is a quick refresher on records:

- Now the query sits between square brackets, and hence it is a record.
- A record has two parts: the field name and the field value. Each step name is now a field, and the formula used is rendering a table as the field value.

Step 2: Extracting the Intermediate Step in a New Query

If you aren't jumping in excitement, you've haven't realized what we've just done. Maybe you need to see what happens next to feel the appropriate euphoria.

To reference an intermediary step we can:

1. Create a new query blank query (Home → New Source → Other Sources → Blank Query).

2. Reference it back to the ExtractingAStep query that contains all the records (i.e., the steps) in the formula bar.

3. Click on the table from the Grouped Rows step. Voila! That step's table gets loaded.

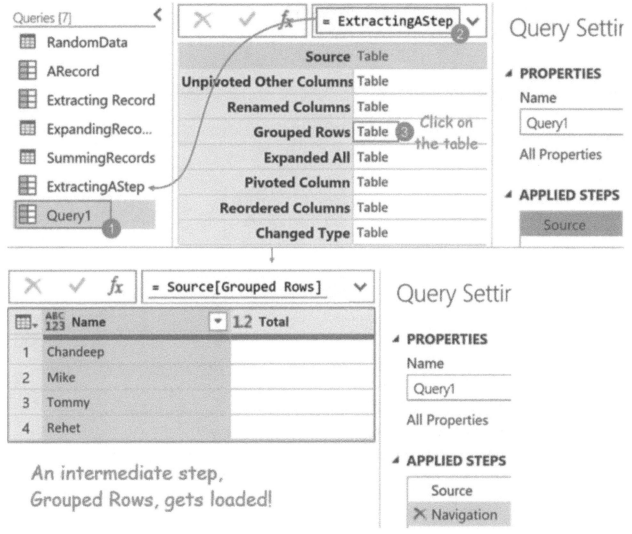

Figure 2-17 *In a new query, we reference an intermediate step of another query.*

When I first discovered this, my mind was blown. I hope you are feeling a similar emotion. Keep in mind a couple of nuances:

- Once you convert your initial query into a record, it becomes useless as it cannot be loaded into Excel or Power BI. You'll always have to reference a step that you want to extract as a new query. To avoid this, you can duplicate the initial query and convert the duplicated query into a record.

- This technique can be helpful for extracting interim steps for more complex queries.

Exercises

Here are a few exercises to test your understanding. Ready?

> **Note:** Open the Excel file Record Exercises - Unsolved in the Records folder and then use the Power Query Editor to work through these exercises.

Exercise 1: Create a Record

In a new query, create a record with two columns:

- Name—populated with first names
- Cities Lived—populated with list of City A, City B, City C, etc.

The output should look like this:

Name	Chandeep
Cities Lived	List

List
Dubai
Mumbai
Bangalore
Gurgaon
Pune

Figure 2-18 *Expected output as a record with two fields.*

Exercise 2: Extract a Record from a Table

From this table with three columns, extract the third row as a record.

	1²₃ Employee ID	AᴮC Name	AᴮC Department
1	101	Alice	Finance
2	102	Bob	Marketing
3 ←	103	Charlie	IT
4	104	David	HR
5	105	Eve	Operations

Employee ID	103
Name	Charlie
Department	IT

Figure 2-19 *A table with three columns and the expected output below (the third row, extracted as a record).*

Exercise 3: Add Custom Columns Using a Record

This table contains some sales data.

	Date	ABC Product	123 Quantity	123 Selling Price
1	31-01-2023	Product A	3	150
2	28-02-2023	Product B	2	200
3	31-03-2023	Product C	5	250
4	30-04-2023	Product A	4	180
5	31-05-2023	Product B	2	160
6	30-06-2023	Product C	3	225
7	31-07-2023	Product A	1	90
8	31-08-2023	Product B	4	320
9	30-09-2023	Product C	2	140
10	31-10-2023	Product B	5	300
11	30-11-2023	Product C	4	210

Figure 2-20 *Sales data.*

Add four custom columns to the table above, using the following logic:

Column Name	Calculation Logic
Year	To be extracted from the Date column
Month	Month name, to be extracted from the Date column
Sales	Quantity x Selling price
Commission	Sales x 10%

Hint: For each row, you should create all the columns in a record and then expand it. Refer to the ExpandingRecords query in the section "How Do Records Behave?" earlier in this chapter.

Note: When you're done with these exercises, you can compare your answers against the ones I provide in the Solutions chapter at the end of this book or refer to the Excel file Records Exercises - Solved or do both. 😊

Chapter 3: Working with Tables

Tables are so ubiquitous in the world of data that most people never take time to think about what makes a table a table. Technically this entire book is about tables because almost everything that you end up working with or producing as output in Power Query is a table.

In this chapter, I'll talk about some nuances of working with tables, how they are formed, and a few nifty tricks with tables beyond the Power Query user interface.

> **Note:** For this chapter, we'll be using the file Tables.xlsx (which you'll find in the Tables folder). As you work through this chapter, you'll be able to walk through the examples by using the queries provided in this file.

What Are Tables?

Refer to the query A Table.

A table in Power Query is always identified with a table icon.

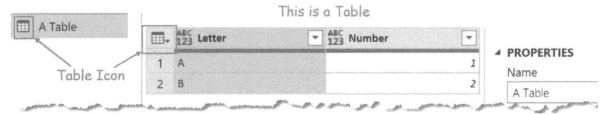

Figure 3-1 *A table in Power Query.*

An interesting thing about tables in Power Query is that they can hold primitive values (e.g., numbers, text, dates) as well as structured values (e.g., tables, lists, records).

Refer to the query Complex Table.

Here is a table where one of the columns contains a list.

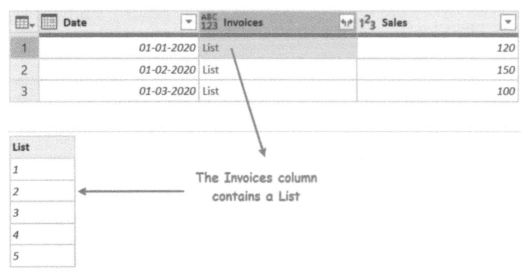

Figure 3-2 *A table can contain a mix of structured and primitive values.*

How to Create a Table

There are a few ways in which you can create a table in Power Query:

- The most obvious way is to import data as a table from any data source (e.g., Excel, CSV file, SQL).

- Another way to create a table is to paste in the data using the Enter Data option (on the Home tab). This works well for smaller datasets, but it would be impossible to copy and paste millions of rows in this way.
- The third way to create a table—and the method we'll explicitly talk about here—is by using the `#table` function. This is still a manual method, but it can be very useful in scenarios where you are building a solution that needs a hard-coded table.

Here is the basic syntax of the `#table` function:

```
#table (
    Columns as any,    // 1
    Rows as any        // 2
)
```

Note that:

1. The first argument should be a list of column names or a single number. If the input is a number—let's say 2—the column names of the table that is created will default to Column1 and Column2.
2. Since there could be multiple rows in a table, all rows must be wrapped in a list, with each row's value also being a list.

Refer to the query A Table.

Here is how a query is created using the `#table` function:

```
1    #table (
2        {"Letter", "Number"},  ←— column headers
3        {
4            {"A", 1},  ←— 1st row
5            {"B", 2}   ←— 2nd row
6        }
7    )
```

ABC 123 Letter	ABC 123 Number
1 A	1
2 B	2

Figure 3-3 *Using the `#table` operator to create a table.*

Note that:

- The column names are a list.
- All rows are wrapped in a list, and each row is also a list.

Creating a Table with Explicit Data Types

Refer to the query Table With Data Types.

Here is a variation of using the `#table` function where you can also declare columns and their data types by modifying the code:

```
1   #table (
2       type table
3       [ Letter = text, Number = number ],
4       {
5           {"A", 1},
6           {"B", 2}
7       }
8   )
```

- declaring type table.
- Column names and their data types as a record.

	A^BC Letter		1.2 Number	
1	A			1
2	B			2

Figure 3-4 *Using explicit data types to create a table using* `#table`.

Note that:

- The `#table` function starts with the `type table` keyword.
- The column name and data types are declared as fields in a record, in square brackets (`[ ]`).

Gotcha! 😊 The rows that don't match the data type of the column will error out once the data is loaded.

Creating a Complex Table (with a Mix of Primitive and Structured Values)

Refer to the query Complex Table.

Creating a slightly more complex table is not very different from creating a simple one. However, in this case we will nest lists into a column of a table, and our output table will look like this:

	Date		Invoices		1.2 Sales	
1	01-01-2020	List				120
2	01-02-2020	List				150
3	01-03-2020	List				100

Figure 3-5 *A complex table with data types defined for each column.*

Here's how we create this slightly more complex table:

1. Create a blank query (Home → New Source → Other Sources → Blank Query).
2. Select Home → Advanced Editor.
3. Delete the existing code, paste in the following code, and click Done:

```
1    #table(
2        type table
3        [Date = date, Invoices = list, Sales = number],    Invoice column is a list.
4        {
5            {#date(2020,1,1), {1,2,3,4,5}, 120},               Each row of Invoice
6            {#date(2020,2,1), {6,7,8}, 150},                  column is typed as a list
7            {#date(2020,3,1), {9,10}, 100}                      (in curly brackets)
8        }
9    )
```

	Date		Invoices		1.2 Sales	
1	01-01-2020		List			120
2	01-02-2020		List			150
3	01-03-2020		List			100

List
1
2
3
4
5

Figure 3-6 *Creating a table with a mix of primitive and structured data types.*

Note that the Invoices column is defined as a list data type. This means that each row value of the Invoices column also needs to be a list—hence the curly brackets.

Cross-Join Example Using #table

Refer to the query SalesPeople.

Consider these tables. The one of the left contains information on salespeople and their vehicles, and the one on the right shows a weekly schedule.

Salesman	Vehicle
Wyatt	T13
Darleen	D15
Marty	H11
Wendy	A15
Ruth	U20
Charlotte	B20
Jonna	J19

Weekday	Route No
Mon	3
Tue	5
Wed	4
Thu	1
Fri	9

This table is static
and unlikely to change.

Figure 3-7 *Two tables with salesperson info and a weekly schedule.*

The task is to cross-join these tables so that each row in the SalesPeople query expands to five rows so that for each salesperson, we have a row for each weekday and the route number for that day. Here is the expected output:

	Salesman	Vehicle	Weekday	Route No
1	Wyatt	T13	Mon	3
2	Wyatt	T13	Tue	5
3	Wyatt	T13	Wed	4
4	Wyatt	T13	Thu	1
5	Wyatt	T13	Fri	9
6	Darleen	D15	Mon	3
7	Darleen	D15	Tue	5
8	Darleen	D15	Wed	4
9	Darleen	D15	Thu	1

The Expected Output

Figure 3-8 *The expected cross-joined table.*

Given the fact that the second table is unlikely to change, we can create that as a static table using the #table function rather than import it from a data source. One less data source is always good. 😄

Here's how we cross-join the two tables:

1. Add a new custom column (Add Column → Custom Column).

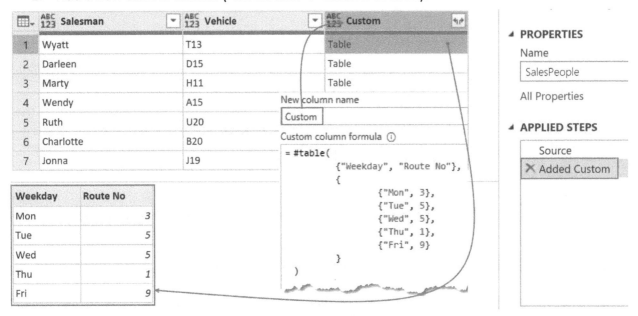

Figure 3-9 *The #table function creates a static table for each row.*

2. Write the following #table code in the formula bar:

```
#table(
  {"Weekday", "Route No"}, // list of columns
  {{"Mon", 3},{"Tue", 5},{"Wed", 5},{"Thu", 1},{"Fri", 9}}
  // each nested list above is a record/row of the table
)
```

3. Play the standard UI game of expanding the custom column. Voila! We have the cross-join ready.

Figure 3-10 *Cross-join of the two tables.*

What Can You Do with a Table (Beyond the UI)?

When you work with a table in Power Query, the ribbon provides a host of clickable transformation options, such as for transforming a column, merging a table, and adding a new column.

I am sure you have plenty of experience using those options, so let's explore what we can do with tables beyond the UI.

Example 1: Table Schemas

> Refer to the queries Table1 and Table2.

Let's say we're working with these two tables:

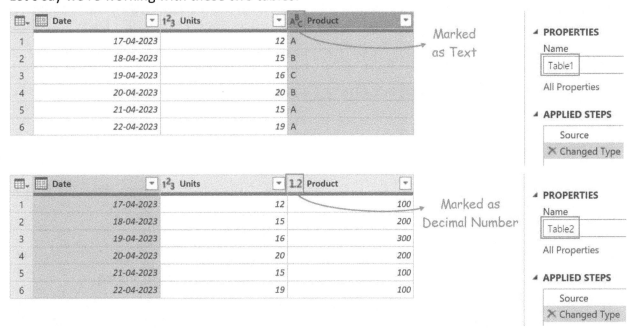

Figure 3-11 *Two tables with slightly different data and data types.*

> Refer to the query Schema.

We'd like to compare the schemas of the two tables. By *schema* I mean the column names, the column positions, data types, etc. To do this, we can use the `Table.Schema` function:

1.   Create a new blank query (Home → New Source → Other Sources → Blank Query).
2.   Name the query Schema.
3.   In the formula bar, write the following M code:

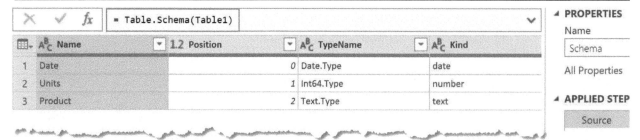

Figure 3-12 *Using the* `Table.Schema` *function.*

This function returns a table with its schema (the column names, positions, data types, and a few other column properties). Interesting! Now we can enhance the formula by simply comparing the schemas of the two tables:

```
= Table.Schema(Table1) = Table.Schema(Table2)
```

FALSE

Figure 3-13 *Since the schemas of the two tables don't match, the output is* `FALSE`.

Refer to the query Schema Name and Position.

Now let's say that instead of comparing all the schema info from the two tables, we'd like to compare only the column names and their positions. In this case, we can modify our code a bit:

```
= Table.Schema(Table1) [[Name], [Position]] =
  Table.Schema(Table2) [[Name], [Position]]
```

TRUE

Figure 3-14 *The output is* `TRUE` *because the column names and their positions match.*

You may be wondering why I used nested square brackets here (`[[Name], [Position]]`). This technique, called *using projections*, involves using nested square brackets to extract the columns from a table as a table. (You'll learn more about this later in the book.)

Alternatively, you could select only the Name and Position columns from both the tables. However, that would involve more M code and be a lot less {M}agical. 😄

Example 2: Table Profiling

Refer to the query TableProfile.

Another interesting function to store in your arsenal is `Table.Profile`. There is nothing complicated about its syntax, so I am going to jump straight to its use.

Say that we want to remove all blank columns from this table:

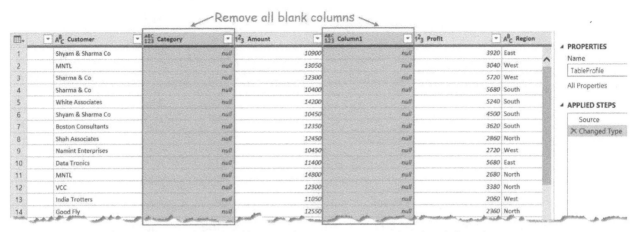

Figure 3-15 *A table with two blank columns that are supposed to be deleted.*

Although it would be very tempting to just select and delete the columns that show all null values, there are two catches:

- Power Query shows a preview of the first 1000 rows, but what if there are values beyond the first 1000 rows that are not blank? In that case, we wouldn't be able to delete the column by simply selecting it in the user interface and pressing Delete.

- What if the number of blank columns increases or decreases? In that case, any hard-coded column names would produce an incorrect result.

Here are the steps we need to take to solve this problem:

1. For each column, check whether all the rows are blank, which we can do by using the `Table.Profile` function.

2. Extract as a list the names of all columns that have blank rows.

3. Use that list in the `Table.RemoveColumns` function.

Step 1: Checking Whether All the Rows Are Blank

First, we need to create the new step TableProfile and use the `Table.Profile` function.

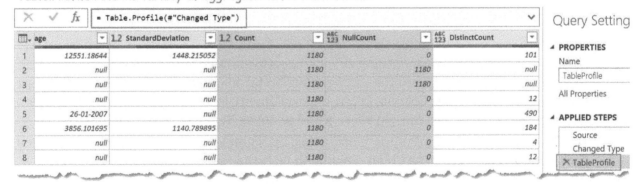

Figure 3-16 `Table.Profile` *returns aggregations like* `Min, Max, Count,` *and* `NullCount`*.*

`Table.Profile` references the previous step's table and returns a few interesting aggregations for all the columns. Take a closer look at the Count and NullCount columns.

age	StandardDeviation	Count	NullCount	Dist
1	12551.18644	1448.215052	1180	0	
2	null	null	1180	1180	
3	null	null	1180	1180	
4	null	null	1180	0	
5	26-01-2007	null	1180	0	
6	3856.101695	1140.789895	1180	0	
7	null	null	1180	0	
8	null	null	1180	0	

Figure 3-17 *The Count and NullCount columns have the same numbers of values.*

It is reasonable to say that if the Count column equals the NullCount column, then all the rows of that column are blank.

Step 2: Extracting a List of the Columns That Have Blank Rows

To extract a list of the columns that have blank rows, we need to create a new step and write the following M code:

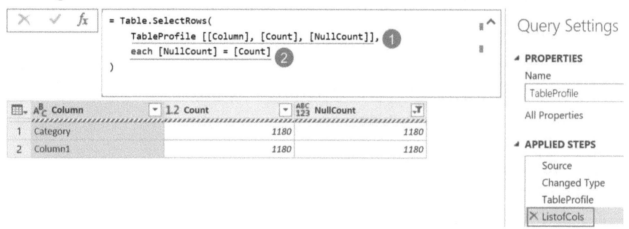

Figure 3-18 *Filtered table where* `[NullCount] = [Count]`.

Note that:

- For some weird reason, we cannot directly apply filters to the table returned by `Table.Profile`, so in this example, we've used the same projection technique used in Figure 3-14 to select the relevant columns (i.e., Column, Count, and NullCount). Instead of using the nested square brackets, we could do this by right-clicking and selecting Remove Other Columns.

- The wrapper `Table.SelectRows` function applies a simple condition to check whether the NullCount column equals the Count column to filter the relevant rows.

However, the output is a table and not a list of columns, so we've got to further modify our M code.

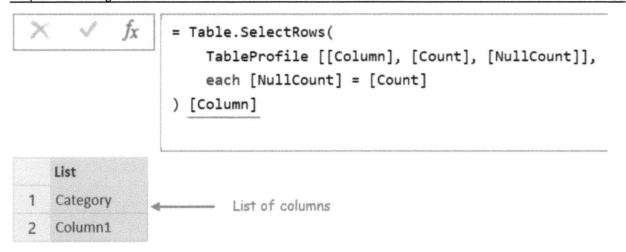

```
= Table.SelectRows(
    TableProfile [[Column], [Count], [NullCount]],
    each [NullCount] = [Count]
) [Column]
```

	List
1	Category
2	Column1

◄——— List of columns

Figure 3-19 *Extracted column names as a list.*

By adding `[Column]` at the end of the code, we can extract the column as a list. (Refer to Figure 1-5 in Chapter 1.)

Step 3: Using the List in the Table.RemoveColumns Function

We can create the new (and final) step NoBlankCols by using `Table.RemoveColumns` to remove the empty columns:

```
= Table.RemoveColumns(#"Changed Type", ListofCols)
```

	▼	A^B_C Sales Rep	▼	A^B_C Customer	▼	1²₃ Amount	▼	1²₃ Profit	▼
1	27-12-2005	Varsha		Shyam & Sharma Co		10900		3920	
2	20-04-2006	Veronica		MNTL		13050		3040	
3	24-05-2006	Ramesh		Sharma & Co		12300		5720	
4	19-11-2007	James		Sharma & Co		10400		5680	
5	25-06-2005	Rajat		White Associates		14200		5240	
6	14-09-2008	Varsha		Shyam & Sharma Co		10450		4500	
7	19-09-2005	Swati		Boston Consultants		12350		3620	
8	12-11-2008	Charley		Shah Associates		12450		2860	
9	02-06-2005	Mark		Namint Enterprises		10450		2720	
10	14-04-2007	Abhay		Data Tronics		11400		5680	
11	28-04-2006	Varsha		MNTL		14800		2680	

Query Settings

▲ PROPERTIES
Name
TableProfile
All Properties

▲ APPLIED STEPS
Source
Changed Type
TableProfile
ListofCols
✕ NoBlankCols

Figure 3-20 *The table, with empty columns removed.*

We input the table (i.e., Changed Type) and the dynamic list of columns (i.e., ListofCols) into the `Table.RemoveColumns` function, and it becomes a dynamic solution for removing blank columns.

In summary, you can use `Table.Profile` function to just see the aggregations of columns and even use those aggregations to make your queries more robust.

> **Tip:** If you're trying this on a very large table, it would be wise to make a sample of rows—let's say the first 5000 rows—to profile and then, if the first 5000 rows are blank, you'd remove the columns. In that case, your code would look like this:
> ```
> = Table.Profile (Table.FirstN (LargeTable, 5000))
> ```

Example 3: Appending Tables by Using &

Refer to the query Using&.

You can literally (and intuitively) use the `&` operator to append tables in Power Query. It works like this:

```
= Table1 & Table2
```

Consider this M code to append two tables:

Advanced Editor

```
1   let
2   Table1 =
3       #table(
4           {"ColA", "ColB"},        ──────▶  Table1 has 2 columns
5           {{"Car", 100}}
6       ),
7   Table2 =
8       #table(
9           {"ColA", "ColB", "ColC"},  ──▶  Table2 has 3 columns
10          {{"Plane", 1000, "Sonic"}}
11
12      )
13  in
14      Table1 & Table2  ──────▶  Using & to Combine 2 tables
```

Resulting Table

🞕▾	ABC 123 ColA	▾	ABC 123 ColB	▾	ABC 123 ColC	▾
1	Car		100		null	
2	Plane		1000	Sonic		

Figure 3-21 *Using the & operator to append two tables.*

Although this example shows that it's possible to combine two tables by using the & operator, it is not a very useful example. Let's look at a more practical example.

Refer to the query TableCombine.

Consider this data and the expected transformation:

Male Customers			Female Customers			
Date	Product	Units	Date	Product	Units	◀────── Pivoted Data
17-Apr-23	A	82	17-Apr-23	Z	76	
18-Apr-23	B	11	18-Apr-23	G	80	
19-Apr-23	C	82	19-Apr-23	H	71	
20-Apr-23	B	57	20-Apr-23	I	84	
21-Apr-23	A	12	21-Apr-23	G	75	
22-Apr-23	A	78	22-Apr-23	K	89	

Date	Product	Units	Customer Type	
17-04-2023	A	82	Male	◀────── Expected Output - Unpivoted Data
18-04-2023	B	11	Male	
19-04-2023	C	82	Male	
20-04-2023	B	57	Male	
21-04-2023	A	12	Male	
22-04-2023	A	78	Male	
17-04-2023	Z	76	Female	
18-04-2023	G	80	Female	
19-04-2023	H	71	Female	
20-04-2023	I	84	Female	
21-04-2023	G	75	Female	
22-04-2023	K	89	Female	

Figure 3-22 *Data and its expected output.*

If you were to solve this problem with your hands (yes, with your physical hands), you'd just take the block of columns for female customers and place it underneath the block for male customers and of course add a column for customer type. Done!

This is exactly what we'll do but in Power Query. Since this is largely a UI problem, let me summarize the steps very quickly:

1. Remove the first row, which contains junk (Home → Remove Rows → Remove Top Rows → 1).

2. Promote the headers (Home → Use First Row as Headers).

3. Keep only the columns for male customers (i.e., the first three columns) by selecting the Date, Product, and Units columns, right-clicking, and selecting Remove Other Columns.

4. Add a custom column for customer type (Add Column → Custom Column → Male → OK).

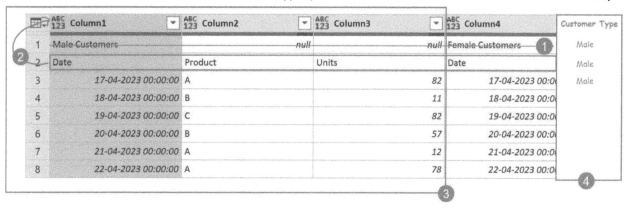

Figure 3-23 *UI transformations on the table.*

Here is how the query looks so far (with the steps renamed):

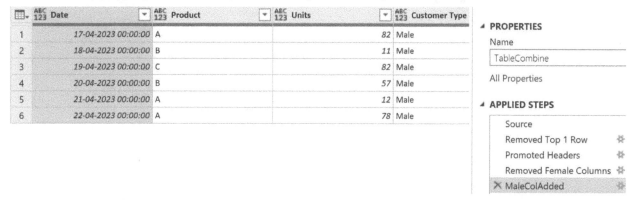

Figure 3-24 *Transformation steps for male customer columns.*

Next, we create a new step, reference the Promoted Headers step, and repeat the transformations done earlier but now for female customers, making sure to rename the columns Date, Product, and Units. Here are the next few steps and the query so far:

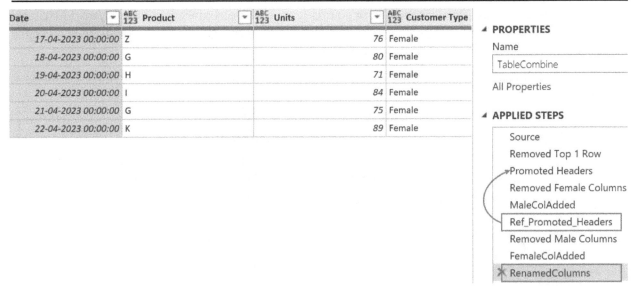

Figure 3-25 *Transformation steps for female customer columns.*

At this stage, the steps RenamedColumns and MaleColAdded have the same column headers, so we just append them by using the & operator:

```
= MaleColAdded & RenamedColumns
```

Then we add the customary Changed Type step at the end.

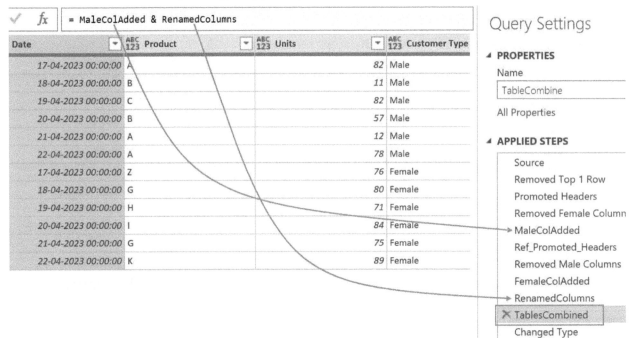

Figure 3-26 *Combining the two tables by using the & operator.*

Boom! We're done!

> **Gotcha!** 😕 In case you're half impressed, I'd agree that this solution has several limitations. What if the number of customer types increases (e.g., males, females, and kids), or what if the number of subheaders increases or decreases? Sure enough, this query would break.
>
> My goal in this example is just to demonstrate the use of the & operator to combine tables. Don't be disappointed! I have provided a more robust solution to this problem in a later chapter.

Chapter 4: Navigation

If you've read between the lines in Chapters 1, 2, and 3, you'll probably realize that we've already covered the concept of navigation implicitly, but I want to talk about it explicitly in this short chapter because I don't want this important concept to fizzle out.

> **Note:** For this chapter, we'll be using the file Navigation.xlsx (which you'll find in the Navigation folder). As you work through this chapter, you'll be able to walk through the examples by using the queries provided in this file.

Navigation...Meaning?

Refer to the query Navigation.

There isn't anything formally documented as "navigation" in Power Query, but to me it seems an appropriate word to use. Let me use an example to describe what it is.

Consider this table, where I'd like to navigate to the value Green in row 2, column 3:

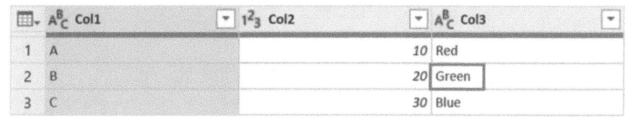

Figure 4-1 *A table with three columns.*

I can create a new step using code like this:

```
= #"Changed Type" {1} [Col3]
```

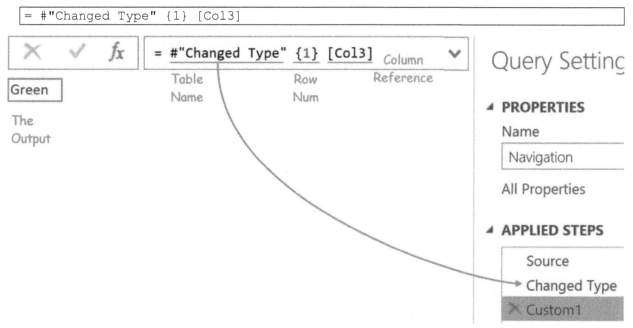

Figure 4-2 *Navigating to the value Green.*

This code has three parts:

- **Table name:** This is the previous step (i.e., `#"Changed Type"`).
- **Row number:** The row number in curly brackets after the table name (`{1}`) means we navigate to the second row or record. (Remember that the count starts with 0.)
- **Column reference:** The column reference `[Col3]` means we navigate to the value Green in that record.

This combination of `table {row} [col]` can be written in several ways, and each method will result in different output. The Power Query UI often calls this step Navigation.

> **Tip:** Keep in mind that a table reference can also be a formula that returns a table. So, this M code is legit:
>
> ```
> = Table.TransformColumns(
>     #"Changed Type",
>     {"Col1", Text.Lower}
>   ) {1} [Col3] // row number & column reference is used
>               // after the table expression
> ```
>
> `Table.TransformColumns` returns a table, and then a row number and column reference are used. As I said, we can write this in several ways, and each way results in different output:
>
> ```
> = Table[Column Reference] // Returns the column as a list
> = Table{Row Number} // Returns the row as a record
> = Record[Column Reference] // Returns the value
>                             // in the column
> = List{Row Number} // Returns the value
>                     // based on the position
> ```
>
> Depending on the output required, you can play around with the three parts: the `Table.TransformColumns` (or any other) formula that returns a table, the row number, and the column reference.

Lookup Operators

Refer to the query Navigation Tricks.

In the combination `table {row} [col]`, it can be tedious to hard-code the row number. Instead, we can use a lookup operator in Power Query. A lookup operator is a condition that can look for a record within a table. It is similar to the `MATCH` function in Excel.

Reconsider this earlier example:

⊞▾	A^B_C Col1	▾	1$^2_3$ Col2	▾	A^B_C Col3	▾
1	A			10	Red	
2	B			20	Green	
3	C			30	Blue	

Figure 4-3 *A table with three columns.*

Now say that we still want to navigate to Green, but we don't want to hard-code the row number (`{1}`). Instead, we want to write a condition to look for the value B in column 1 and then navigate to its corresponding value in column 3 (i.e., Green).

Here is how we can write a lookup operator to do this in a new step:

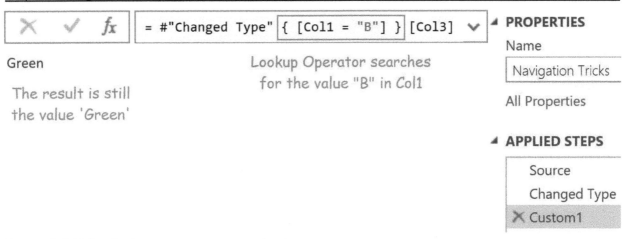

Green

The result is still
the value 'Green'

Lookup Operator searches
for the value "B" in Col1

PROPERTIES

Name

Navigation Tricks

All Properties

◢ **APPLIED STEPS**

Source

Changed Type

✕ Custom1

Figure 4-4 *Using lookup operators to navigate.*

The lookup operator in this example is wrapped in curly brackets and uses a record (in square brackets) to search for the value B in column 1. Here are a couple of things to keep in mind when using lookup operators:

- A lookup operator must return only one row (record) as output; otherwise, Power Query throws an error.

- You can use multiple lookup operators to navigate to a single record, like this:

```
TableReference {[Column 1 = "value", Column 2 = "value"]} [Column4]
```

- You can use a question mark to mitigate errors in the event that a record or the column is not found. Here are a few examples:

```
// this returns an error since there are only 3 columns
#"Changed Type" {[Col1 = "B"]} [Col4]

// writing a ? at the end of column reference
// returns a null instead
#"Changed Type" {[Col1 = "B"]} [Col4] ?

// ? can be written after the lookup operator too.
#"Changed Type" {[Col1 = "NewValue"]} ?

// ? can also be written both after
// the column and row reference
#"Changed Type" {[Col1 = "NewValue"]} ? [Col4] ?
```

Getting Data from the Current Excel File with a Lookup Operator

Refer to the query Navigation Tricks.

This chapter wouldn't be complete if we didn't go through the literal Navigation step in Power Query. Here is the Source step in the query Navigation Tricks:

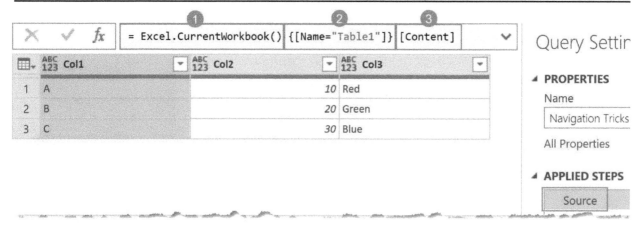

Figure 4-5 *Source step formula.*

The formula in the Source step has three parts:

```
= Excel.CurrentWorkbook()     // 1
  {[Name = "Table1"]}         // 2
  [Content]                   // 3
```

Note that:

1. `Excel.CurrentWorkbook()` returns a table containing all the tables and named ranges in the current Excel file. If this function were written alone, it would render a table like this:

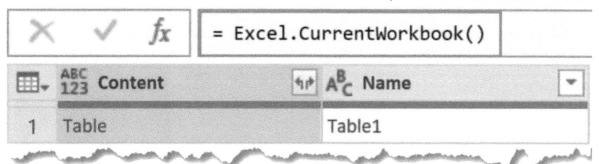

Figure 4-6 `Excel.CurrentWorkbook` *returns a table with Content and Name columns.*

2. `{[Name = "Table1"]}` is the lookup operator that navigates to Table1 in the Name column. If written together with the formula above, it would return a record like this:

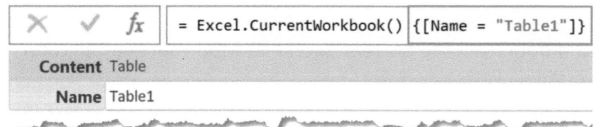

Figure 4-7 *A table and row reference (using a lookup operator) returns a record.*

3. `[Content]` extracts the value (i.e., the table) in the Content field (column) and returns the table Table1:

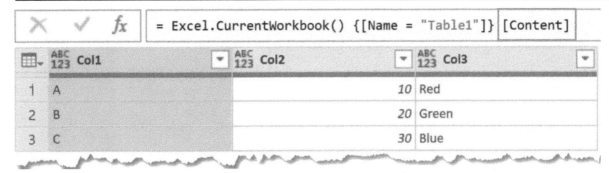

Figure 4-8 *Table1 is returned as output.*

But where is the Navigation step? Well, it is created by default when you click on Table in the Content column (refer to Figure 4-6).

Refer to the query NavigationStep.

Here you can see the default Navigation step:

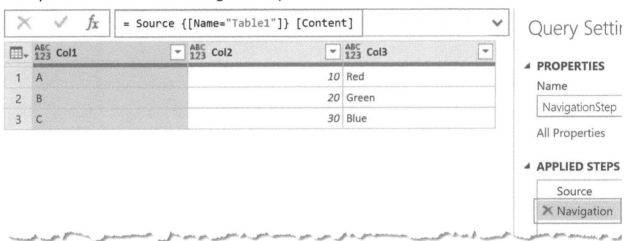

Figure 4-9 *The default Navigation step is created using the UI.*

This formula contains the same three parts we've seen before:

- **Source:** The table that is returned by the `Excel.CurrentWorkbook` function in the Source step
- `{[Name = "Table1"]}`: The lookup operator
- `[Content]`: The field/column reference

Exercises

Here are a few exercises to test your understanding. Ready?

Note: Open the Excel file Navigation Exercises - Unsolved in the Navigation folder and then use the Power Query Editor to work through these exercises.

Exercise 1: Navigate a List

Navigate to the third value in this list. The answer should be the value C.

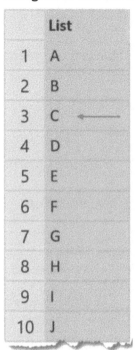

	List
1	A
2	B
3	C ←
4	D
5	E
6	F
7	G
8	H
9	I
10	J

Figure 4-10 *A list of letters in alphabetical order.*

Exercise 2: Navigate to a Record

In the table below, navigate to the first row/record.

	A^B_C Prod	1²₃ Units	A^B_C Color
→ 1	A	10	Red
2	B	12	Black
3	C	15	Black
4	D	11	Red
5	E	13	Blue
6	F	15	Red

Figure 4-11 *A table with three columns.*

This is the expected output:

Prod	A
Units	10
Color	Red

Figure 4-12 *Expected output.*

Exercise 3: Use a Lookup Operator

In the table below, use a lookup operator for the month February to navigate to the corresponding value in the Visitors 000 column. The expected output is the value 11.3.

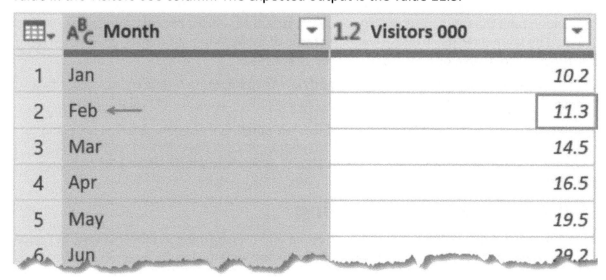

Figure 4-13 *In this table, navigate to the value for the month February.*

> **Note:** When you're done with these exercises, you can compare your answers against the ones I provide in the Solutions chapter at the end of this book or refer to the Excel file Navigation Exercises - Solved or do both. 😄

Chapter 5: Manipulating Between Lists, Records, and Tables

Once you understand the three most important object structures—lists, records, and tables—a step further would be learning to mash up between the three of them. When writing M, you'll often need to convert records to a table or a record to a list or vice versa.

The next few pages will help you better understand how to manipulate between lists, records, and tables. Once you have built that {M}uscle, we can get down to solving some real problems.

> **Note:** For this chapter, we'll be using the file Manipulating Between Lists Records and Tables.xlsx (which you'll find in the Manipulating Between Lists Records and Tables folder). As you work through this chapter, you'll be able to walk through the examples by using the queries provided in this file.

Nesting Versus Transforming

I am not even sure if there are official terms for nesting and transforming in Power Query, but once you understand these concepts, you'll be able to follow along with my intuitive naming conventions just fine. 😄

So, What Is Nesting?

> Refer to the query Nesting_VS_Transforming.

To get an idea of what nesting is, let's start with this table:

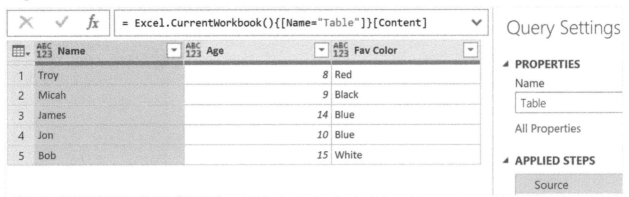

Figure 5-1 *A three-column table.*

To implement nesting in this table, we can add a new step and reference the Source step (i.e., the table above) in curly brackets. Here is what we get:

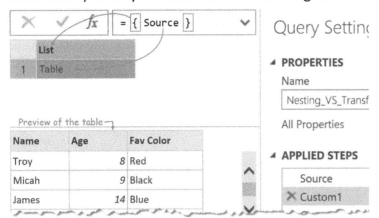

Figure 5-2 *Referencing the Source step (i.e., a table) in curly brackets causes the table to be nested in a list.*

Note that:

- The original table is now nested in a list because we referenced that table in the curly brackets, like this: `={Source}`.

- The nested value is still a table. It hasn't been transformed into a list (or anything else).

> **Note:** Let's take a time-out. Using curly brackets (`{ }`) around a table, record, or list doesn't transform the value; it only nests it. Moreover, nesting can be done in several ways. Here are a few examples (where the code is not valid syntax but just provides a representation of the logic):
>
> ```
> = [my table = table]   // Nesting the table in a record.
>                        // Records also have field names;
>                        // hence we wrote the field name as
>                        // my table.
> = {record}             // Nesting a record in a list.
> = {list}               // Nesting a list in a list.
> = {table}              // Nesting a table in a list.
> ```

What Is Transforming?

To understand transforming, let's take our example further by creating another step and writing the following code in the formula bar:

```
= Table.ToList(
    Source,
    each Text.Combine(
            List.Transform(_, each Text.From(_)), ", ")
)
```

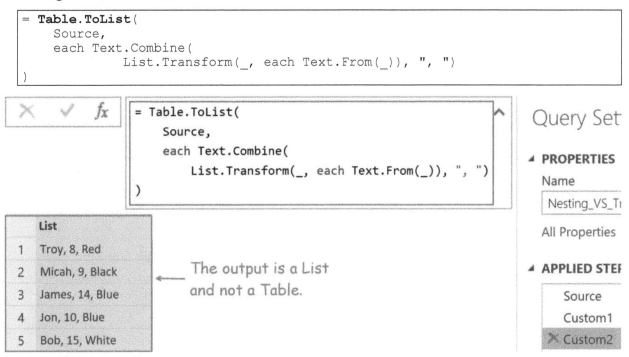

Figure 5-3 *The Source table is now transformed into a list.*

I don't want to get into the nitty-gritty of the M code at this point. For now, just note these two very important details:

- I used the `Table.ToList` function to transform the table into a list.

- The table from the Source step isn't a table anymore. It has been transformed into a list.

> **Note:** Let's take another time-out. There are many transformation functions that can transform one structured value (e.g., table, list, record) to another structured value. Here are a few examples (again not using valid syntax but showing how these functions behave):
>
> ```
> = Table.ToRecords  // transforms a table to records.
> = Record.ToList    // transforms a record to a list.
> = Record.FromList  // transforms a list to a record.
> ```

You might have felt a bit uninspired by this discussion of nesting and transformation theory. However, the subtleties of nesting and transformation will either make your M code happy and error free or stressed and error prone.

Let's spice up the learning with some practical examples.

Nesting Example: Creating a Table from Records

Refer to the query Nesting Example.

If you glance through the official M documentation at https://learn.microsoft.com/en-us/power-query-m, you'll notice that the Microsoft website doesn't provide data sources as downloadable Excel files, and quite often it shows the function `Table.FromRecords` being used to create tables on the fly, as shown here:

```
Table.Combine({
    Table.FromRecords({[CustomerID = 1, Name = "Bob", Phone = "123-4567"]}),
    Table.FromRecords({[CustomerID = 2, Name = "Jim", Phone = "987-6543"]}),
    Table.FromRecords({[CustomerID = 3, Name = "Paul", Phone = "543-7890"]})
})
```

```
Table.Distinct(
    Table.FromRecords({
        [a = "A", b = "a"],
        [a = "B", b = "b"],
        [a = "A", b = "a"]
    })
)
```

```
Table.Contains(
    Table.FromRecords({
        [CustomerID = 1, Name = "Bob", Phone = "123-4567"],
        [CustomerID = 2, Name = "Jim", Phone = "987-6543"],
        [CustomerID = 3, Name = "Paul", Phone = "543-7890"],
        [CustomerID = 4, Name = "Ringo", Phone = "232-1550"]
    }),
    [Name = "Bob"]
)
```

Figure 5-4 *A random snapshot from the official documentation on Power Query M.*

This function clearly demonstrates the nesting concept. Consider these records nested in a list:

```
{
   [Name = "Chandeep", Weight = 75, Country = "India"],
// record 1

   [Name = "Rehet", Weight = 21, Country = "India"]
// record 2
}
```

In the Power Query UI, it looks like this:

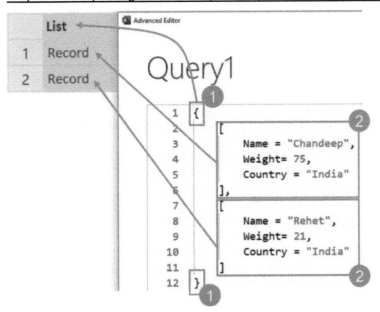

Figure 5-5 *Two records nested in a list.*

Note that:

- The starting and ending curly brackets create a container list.
- The nested square brackets are used to create two records nested in the list.

Now let's wrap this list containing two records in the `Table.FromRecords` function:

```
Table.FromRecords(
    {
       [Name = "Chandeep", Weight= 75, Country = "India"],
       [Name = "Rehet", Weight= 21, Country = "India"]
    }
)
```

This returns a table:

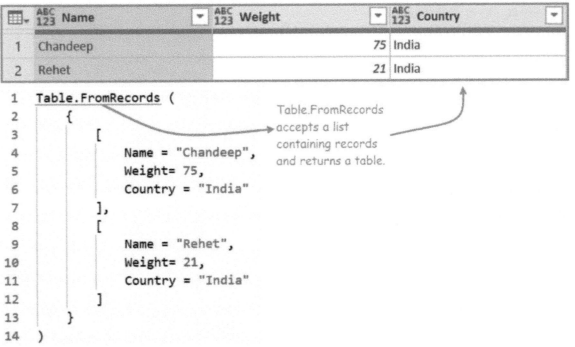

Figure 5-6 *A table is formed using the* `Table.FromRecords` *function.*

Notes:

- Even though the `Table.FromRecords` function feeds on records, it needs those records to be nested inside a list.
- The list is just a container. It doesn't transform the records into a list.

As you can see with this example, there are some instances in which you need a wrapper around a value. The key to identifying such instances is to look at the syntax of the function. For instance, here is what the official documentation says about `Table.FromRecords`:

```
= Table.FromRecords(
    records as list,  // it clearly says,
                      // input the records as a list.
    optional columns as any,
    optional missingField as nullable number
) as table
```

As another example, the `Table.Combine` function needs one or more tables as input, and those tables need to be wrapped in a list:

```
= Table.Combine(
    tables as list,  // tables need to be wrapped
                     // in a list. Refer to Figure 1-17.
    optional columns as any
) as table
```

Transformation Example: Removing Random Blank Values

Refer to the query RemovingNulls.

To explain the transformation of an object, I've got an interesting example for you. Consider this table, which is riddled with random null values:

123 ID	Date	123 Value	
1	1	null	100	Row 1
2	null	02-02-2022	null	
3	2	null	null	
4	null	null	300	Row 2
5	null	01-01-2021	null	
6	null	10-03-2022	null	
7	3	null	null	
8	null	null	400	Row 3

Figure 5-7 *A table with random null values.*

Here is how we'd like the clean table to appear:

123 ID	Date	123 Value
1	1	02-02-2022	100
2	2	01-01-2021	300
3	3	10-03-2022	400

Figure 5-8 *The expected output.*

The problem is, we can't apply a "remove nulls" filter because that would also remove legit values from other columns. So, what do we do? Here is way to approach the problem:

1. Transform each column into a list.
2. Remove nulls from each list.
3. Transform the lists back into a table.

Step 1: Transforming Each Column into a List

Refer to the query RemovingNulls.

Let's start by creating a new query step and using the `Table.ToColumns` function. This function will transform each column of the table (i.e., Source) into a nested list.

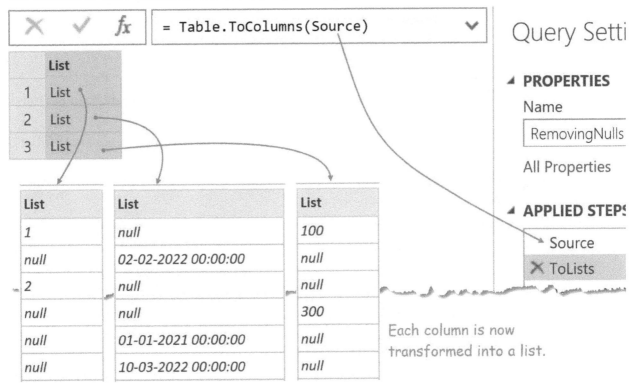

Figure 5-9 *Each column of the table is transformed into a list.*

Notes:

- The `Table.ToColumns` function transforms each column of a table into a list. The input argument is a table, and the output is a nested list (where each sublist is a column).
- If you preview a nested list, you will see the column values from the previous step's table.

Step 2: Removing Nulls from Each List

In a new step, we write the `List.Transform` function to remove the nulls from each list:

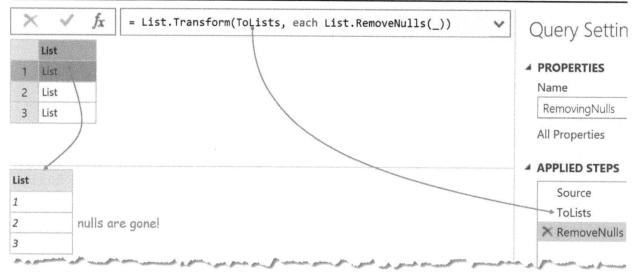

Figure 5-10 *Removing nulls from each list.*

If you preview a nested list, you see that the nulls are now gone. Let's take a moment to understand the code shown above:

- The first argument, `ToLists`, is a list to be transformed. The previous query step, ToLists, contains nested lists.

- The second argument, `List.RemoveNulls`, is a function that removes the `null` values from each sublist.

> **Note:** Don't miss the subtlety here: `List.RemoveNulls` only accepts the input as a list, and if we didn't have a nested list structure, our formula would return an error. Reminder: Feed Power Query what it eats! 😊
>
> You could use this alternative (and shorter) code to skip the `each` keyword:
>
> `= List.Transform(ToLists, List.RemoveNulls)`
>
> You'll learn more about this technique later in the book.

Step 3: Transforming Lists into a Table

I want you to look again at Figure 5-10. In step 2, we were working with three lists, which were technically three columns of our table. Now we need to put those three lists back into a table of three columns, as shown here:

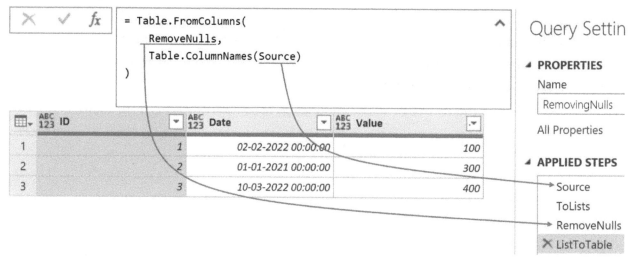

Figure 5-11 *Creating a table from lists.*

It is worth spending a few minutes on the `Table.FromColumns` function, which does the magic here:

- In the first argument, we feed the nested list from the RemoveNulls step, and each inner list will become a column of the table.
- Since a list doesn't have a column header (and a table does), the column names need to be drawn from the Source step.
  - If we don't include the second argument, `Table.ColumnNames(Source)`, we end up with generic column headers (e.g., Column 1, Column 2), but we'll still get a legit table as output.
  - However, if we do provide column names either using a function or by hard-coding them within a list (e.g., `{"ID", "Date", "Value"}`), we need to make sure the count of column names is equal to the count of nested lists. Otherwise, the formula will error out. Here is how the formula would look for hard-coded column names:

```
= Table.FromColumns(RemoveNulls, {"ID", "Date", "Value"})
```

> **Note:** The `Table.FromColumns` function is the inverse of the `Table.ToColumns` function: It converts the lists back into a table with an additional input parameter for adding column headers.

Combining the Three Steps into One

Refer to the query RemovingNullsSingleStep.

If you want to perform like a ninja, you can choose to do the transformation just shown all in a single step. Here is the pretty one-step M code for you:

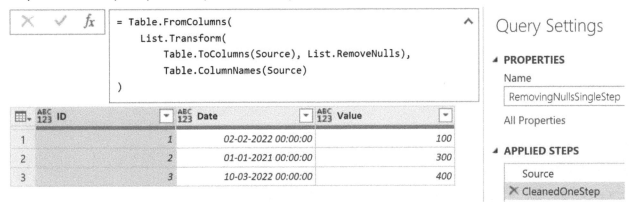

Figure 5-12 *The same transformation example, solved in a single step.*

> **Note:** Keep in mind that nesting and transforming values as standalone concepts do not help solve mighty problems, but they are building blocks for interconnecting values within functions that accept input in a certain way. In examples later in this book, both nesting and transforming will come in handy as we work with different functions.

Exercises

Here are a few exercises to test your understanding. Ready?

> **Note:** Open the Excel file Manipulation Exercises - Unsolved in the Manipulating Between Lists Records and Tables folder and then use the Power Query Editor to work through these exercises.

Exercise 1: Nest Lists in a Record

Consider this M code, which produces three lists as three different steps in a query:

```
let
    List1 = {1,2,3},
    List2 = {4,5,6},
    List3 = {7,8,9}
in
    List3
```

For this query, the UI view looks like this:

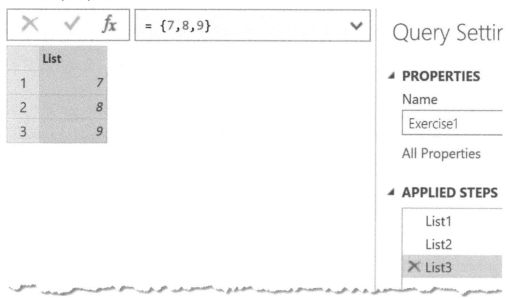

Figure 5-13 *Query view showing three lists in three steps.*

As the fourth step in this query, nest all three lists in a single record.

Exercise 2: Transform Records into a Table

Here is the M code for a query that produces three records as three steps:

```
let
    Record1 = [Name = "Bob", Age = 20],
    Record2 = [Name = "Mary", Age = 21],
    Record3 = [Name = "Tanya", Age = 19]
in
    Record3
```

In the UI view, it looks like this:

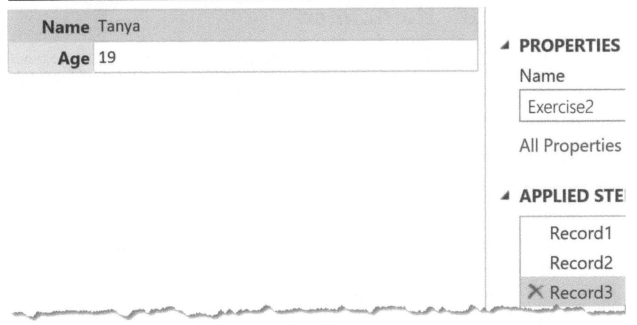

Figure 5-14 *Query view showing three records in three steps.*

As the fourth step in this query, transform the three records (i.e., steps) into a table.

> **Note:** When you're done with these exercises, you can compare your answers against the ones I provide in the Solutions chapter at the end of this book or refer to the Excel file Manipulation Exercises - Solved or do both. 😄

Chapter 6: If...then...else

The IF statement is fundamental to building any logical test, and every programming language has its own subtleties for writing IF statements. In this chapter we'll look at nuances of writing the IF function in Power Query and consider a few very interesting applications.

> **Note:** For this chapter, we'll be using the file if then else.xlsx (which you'll find in the if then else folder). As you work through this chapter, you'll be able to walk through the examples by using the queries provided in this file.

The IF Syntax

I'm assuming that you've worked enough with Excel to understand this IF syntax:

```
IF (Condition, Value_If_True, Value_If_False)
```

Now consider the if statement in Power Query:

```
if Condition then Value_If_True else Value_If_False
```

To avoid syntax errors, keep two things in mind:

- You must use all the three keywords if...then...else in lowercase, without any brackets or comma separators.
- The first input (i.e., condition) must return TRUE or FALSE as output.

The good thing is, you don't have to write the if because it is already built into the user interface (under Add Column → Conditional Column).

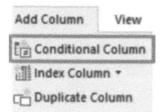

Figure 6-1 *Power Query lets you write an* if *in the user interface.*

However, the UI is restrictive and won't let you work with several nuances. For instance:

- You cannot write and, or within an if.
- if can only be written as a column in the UI and not as a step. (If you didn't think of this, you will be blown away when you see what I'm talking about here.)
- With the UI, if can only return a scalar value and not a table, a list, or a record.

Enough small talk. Let's write some if statements using M code.

Two if Examples

Both of the following examples can also be produced using Power Query's UI. However, we're just getting warmed up with more complex—or should I say more interesting—ways of writing if statements.

Example 1: Using Vanilla IF

> Refer to the query ClassGrades.

Consider this table, where each student has a numeric grade in the Marks column, an attendance percentage in the Attendance column, and a letter grade (A, B, or C) in the Conduct column.

AᴮC Student	1²₃ Marks	% Attendance	AᴮC Conduct
1 Roy	94	70.00% A	
2 Wilson	83	75.00% A	
3 Mike	39	72.00% C	
4 Bon	34	77.00% B	
5 Timmy	90	17.00% B	
6 Helen	50	31.00% C	

Figure 6-2 *A table with four columns.*

Let's start off by creating a simple `if` to mark each student as Fail if Marks < 40 and otherwise as Pass:

1. Create a new custom column (Add Column → Custom Column).

2. Name the new column Result.

3. Write this simple `if` statement in the formula bar:

```
= if [Marks] < 40 then "Fail" else "Pass"
```

4. Click OK. You now see either Pass or Fail in each row of the new Result column.

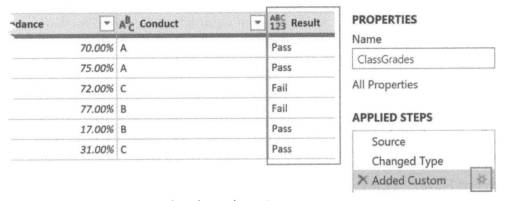

Figure 6-3 *Creating a Result column by using* `if`.

> **Note:** If you click on the gear icon for the Added Custom step, the Conditional Column dialog box opens, and not the Custom Column box. This is because the `if` function we wrote is simple enough to be translated back to the conditional columns user interface.

Example 2: Using a Complex if (with and)

Now say that we're working with the same data as in Example 1, and we'd like to add a new column called Teacher Grade. The logic for the contents of this column is as follows:

- If the value in the Conduct column is A and the value in the Marks column is greater than or equal to 90, the Teacher Grade column says Star.
- If the value in the Conduct column is C and the value in the Marks column is less than 40, the Teacher Grade column says Needs Work.
- For everything else, the Teacher Grade column says Meets Expectation.

Although we could kind of solve this by using the UI, I'd prefer to use the `if` statement with `and` to solve this problem with a single custom formula. Here's how:

1. Create a new column (Add Column → Custom Column).

2. Write the following M code in the formula bar:

```
if [Marks] >= 90 and [Conduct] = "A"
then "Star"
else if [Marks] <40 and [Conduct] = "C"
     then "Needs Work"
     else "Meets Expectation"
```

3. Click OK. This is the result:

Attendance	Conduct	Result	Teacher Grade
1	70.00%	A	Pass	Star
2	75.00%	A	Pass	Meets Expectation
3	72.00%	C	Fail	Needs Work
4	77.00%	B	Fail	Meets Expectation
5	17.00%	B	Pass	Meets Expectation
6	31.00%	C	Pass	Meets Expectation

Figure 6-4 *Using* `if` *and the* `and` *keyword to create a new column.*

Notes:

- In this formula, the `and` keyword is lowercase and does not use any comma separator.

- To compare more than two conditions, you have to write the `and` between two conditions, like this:

```
condition 1 and condition 2 and condition 3
```

- The formula uses nested `if` statements and starts with another `if` after the `else` keyword. If needed, you can also write the `if` keyword after the `then` keyword, like this:

```
if condition 1 then
    if condition 2 then "condition 2 is true"
    else "condition 2 is false"
else "condition 1 is false"
```

Note: The `or` keyword works just like `and` but looks for any one condition to be true instead of requiring both to be true.

Using if in Applied Steps

Refer to the query Users.

Now let's look at an edge case with a one-of-a-kind use of the `if` statement in applied steps rather than the conventional use to create conditional columns.

Consider these two tables:

Users1 Table

User	SecretKey
1	1	4154a00d-fda4-44cc-aac6-c6050baa998c
2	2	0fb4b249-1b84-44cd-a60c-17e6300d3d88
3	3	c7837f93-c837-477e-b505-8cae78001da3
4	4	9375fd59-b2b2-4c36-9598-fa0e723e4c55
5	5	cf049032-e82d-4965-b1fc-1bbb31f79ebd

Users2 Table

	A^B_C User	A^B_C SecretKey
1	1	4154a00d-fda4-44cc-aac6-c6050baa998c
2	2	0fb4b249-1b84-44cd-a60c-17e6300d3d88
3	3	c7837f93-c837-477e-b505-8cae78001da3
4	4	9375fd59-b2b2-4c36-9598-fa0e723e4c55
5	5	cf049032-e82d-4965-b1fc-1bbb31f79ebd

Figure 6-5 *Tables with User and SecretKey columns.*

Are they the same?

I know, it is a daunting task to try to exactly match the 36 characters of the SecretKey—even for only five rows of data. We need something more sophisticated than our eyes to sift through the alphanumeric characters.

All we need to do in this case is write a simple `if` as a new step:

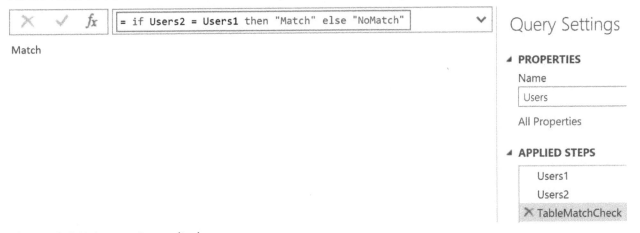

Figure 6-6 *Using `if` in applied steps.*

If the tables are the same, the formula returns `Match`; otherwise, the formula returns `NoMatch`. The `if` syntax remains the same as the syntax you've already seen, but using `if` at the step level opens possibilities for writing much more complex logic and referencing intermediate steps or other queries.

Using List.Contains Instead of or

Refer to the query Sales.

Since there is nothing more remarkable about `if` in Power Query, let's divert our attention toward alternative ways of solving problems. Consider this simple dataset:

	Date	A^B_C Sales Rep	A^B_C Region	1²₃ Sales
1	16-06-2005	Varsha	South	10450
2	06-07-2005	Roy	West	12300
3	23-08-2005	James	East	14650
4	20-09-2005	James	West	11400
5	07-01-2006	Aaron	North	12550
6	12-03-2006	Aaron	South	12350
7	18-03-2006	Bruce	North	12300
8	21-05-2006	Bruce	South	11050
9	17-07-2006	Varsha	North	10000
10	08-08-2006	Charley	North	12450
11	02-10-2006	Bruce	West	12350

Figure 6-7 *Sales data with four columns.*

The task is to create a new Region Group column based on the following logic:

- If the Region column says South or West, return `South-West`.
- If the Region column says North or East, return `North-East`.

		A^B_C Sales Rep	A^B_C Region	1²₃ Sales		ABC 123 Region Group
1	16-06-2005	Varsha	South		10450	South-West
2	06-07-2005	Roy	West		12300	South-West
3	23-08-2005	James	East		14650	North-East
4	20-09-2005	James	West		11400	South-West
5	07-01-2006	Aaron	North		12550	North-East
6	12-03-2006	Aaron	South		12350	South-West
7	18-03-2006	Bruce	North		12300	North-East
8	21-05-2006	Bruce	South		11050	South-West
9	17-07-2006	Varsha	North	Expected	10000	North-East
10	08-08-2006	Charley	North	output	12450	North-East
11	02-10-2006	Bruce	West		12350	South-West

Figure 6-8 *Expected output in the Region Group column.*

If you were to use the standard `or` logic coupled with `if` in your custom column formula, it would look like this:

```
if [Region] = "South" or [Region] = "West"
then "South-West" else
    if [Region] = "North" or [Region] = "East"
    then "North-East" else "NA"
```

There is not a single error in this code, and it would work just fine. But what if we were to add more regions in our condition? The `or` statement would surely become verbose.

Consider a slightly different approach that involves omitting the `or` and using the `List.Contains` function instead:

1. Create a new column (Add Column → Custom Column).
2. Name the new column Region Group.
3. Write the following M code in the Custom Column box:

```
if List.Contains({"South", "West"}, [Region])
then "South-West" else
    if List.Contains({"North", "East"}, [Region])
    then "North-East" else "NA"
```

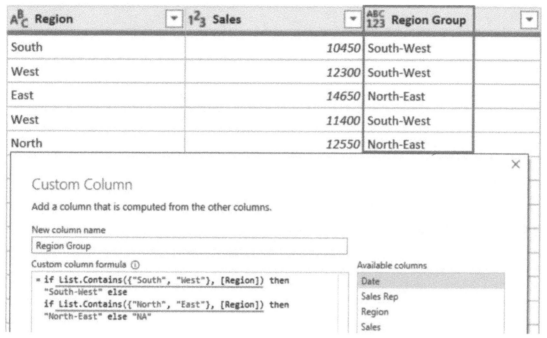

Figure 6-9 *Using* `List.Contains` *to omit the* `or` *keyword.*

Notes:

- `List.Contains` will return `true` if any of the list items match the region.
- Here `List.Contains` replicates the behavior of the `or` keyword. This can come in very handy when you're grappling with a lot of `or` conditions.

Using List.ContainsAll Instead of and

Further building on our example, let's say we need a new column, Season, based on the following logic:

- If the Date column value is between January and March and the Region Group column is South-West, return `Seasonal`.
- Otherwise, return `Non Seasonal`.

This is the expected output:

	Date	Sales Rep	Region	Sales	Region Group	Season
1	16-06-2005	Varsha	South	10450	South-West	Non Seasonal
2	06-07-2005	Roy	West	12300	South-West	Non Seasonal
3	23-08-2005	James	East	14650	North-East	Non Seasonal
4	20-09-2005	James	West	11400	South-West	Non Seasonal
5	07-01-2006	Aaron	North	12550	North-East	Seasonal
6	12-03-2006	Aaron	South	12350	South-West	Non Seasonal
7	18-03-2006	Bruce	North	12300	North-East	Seasonal

Figure 6-10 *The Season column shows the value Seasonal where the condition is met.*

We can obviously solve this by using the `and` function, but let's take a different approach and use `List.ContainsAll`. Before we start, let's look at an example of the `List.ContainsAll` function:

```
=List.ContainsAll (
    {A List to search in},
    {List of values to search for}
)

// The following example returns true
// because both of the values are found.
=List.ContainsAll (
  {"Boy", "Cat", "Horse"}, // List of values to search in
  {"Cat", "Boy"}           // List of values to search for
)
```

Notes:

- `List.ContainsAll` returns `true` if all the list values to search for are found.
- Both arguments are lists.

With the basics out of our way, let's see it in action:

1. Create a custom column (Add Column → Custom Column).
2. Enter the following M code in the Custom Column box:

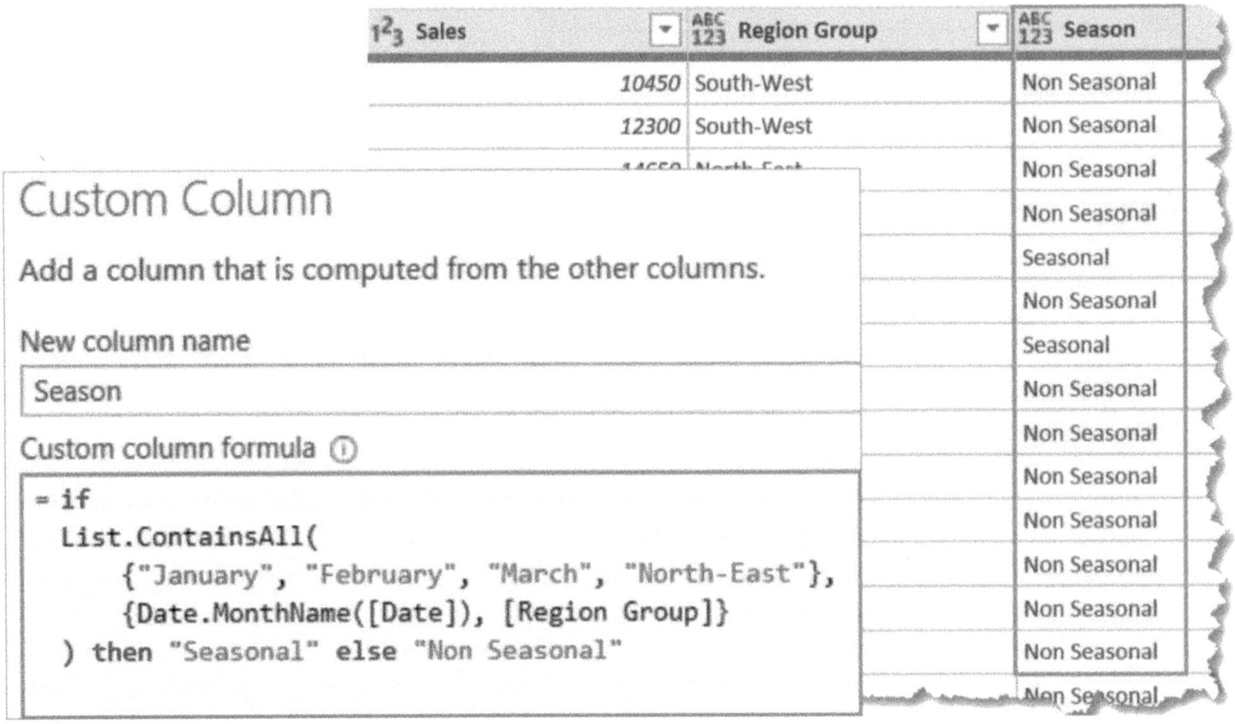

Figure 6-11 *Creating a custom column using* `List.ContainsAll`*.*

Note that:

- For the first argument of `List.ContainsAll`, we use all the values for the Month and Region Group columns as a list.
- Because the search values also need to be a list (in the second argument), we wrap both `Date.MonthName` and `Region Group` in curly brackets.

Exercise

Here is an exercise to test your understanding. Ready?

> **Note:** Open the Excel file if then else Exercises - Unsolved in the if then else folder and then use the Power Query Editor to work through this exercise.

Exercise 1: Replace OR with a List Function

Consider this simple data loaded in Power Query:

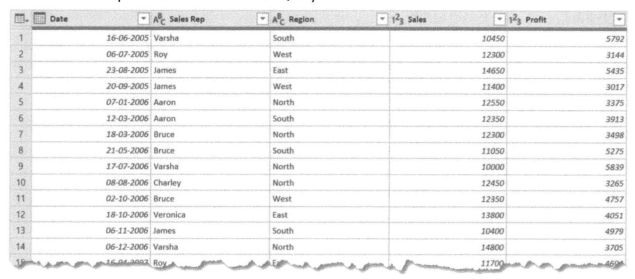

	Date	ABC Sales Rep	ABC Region	123 Sales	123 Profit	
1	16-06-2005	Varsha	South	10450	5792	
2	06-07-2005	Roy	West	12300	3144	
3	23-08-2005	James	East	14650	5435	
4	20-09-2005	James	West	11400	3017	
5	07-01-2006	Aaron	North	12550	3375	
6	12-03-2006	Aaron	South	12350	3913	
7	18-03-2006	Bruce	North	12300	3498	
8	21-05-2006	Bruce	South	11050	5275	
9	17-07-2006	Varsha	North	10000	5839	
10	08-08-2006	Charley	North	12450	3265	
11	02-10-2006	Bruce	West	12350	4757	
12	18-10-2006	Veronica	East	13800	4051	
13	06-11-2006	James	South	10400	4979	
14	06-12-2006	Varsha	North	14800	3705	
1	16-04-2003	Roy	E	11700	469	

Figure 6-12 *Sales data.*

Create a custom column to calculate commission based on the following logic:

- If Sales > 14,500 or Profit > 5,000, then calculate 10% commission on the Sales value.
- Otherwise, return 0.

In this exercise, you should not use the `or` keyword. Instead, use a list function to check whether either of the two conditions is true.

> **Note:** When you're done with this exercise, you can compare your answer against the one I provide in the Solutions chapter at the end of this book or refer to the Excel file if then else Exercises - Solved or do both. 😄

Chapter 7: Iteration

Iteration in the context of computer science means executing the same set of instructions repeatedly. I know, that isn't a very friendly way to start a chapter. More simply, iteration means "doing it again." 😄

> **Note:** For this chapter, we'll be using the file Looping.xlsx (which you'll find in the Iteration folder). As you work through this chapter, you'll be able to walk through the examples by using the queries provided in this file.

Iteration in English

If I were to ask my 7-year-old son, "Which of these numbers are equal to a 100"? I'm sure he'd start from the top, scanning one number at a time, and point to the fourth value, 100. I'm assuming that he'd stop checking as soon as he found the first 100, but I haven't tried his intelligence yet!

	ABC 123 Numbers
1	82
2	14
3	88
4	100
5	96
6	28
7	95
8	99
9	57
10	49
11	100
12	63

Figure 7-1 *A list of numbers where two values are equal to 100.*

In Power Query, we can use iteration to perform transformations or to check for conditions. Here are a few nuances:

- Iteration can be done on a table, a list, a record, or even more complex values like nested lists, lists containing tables,....pretty much anything that has multiple items to iterate through.
- Iteration can continue until the last item of a list or table is reached or can stop when the condition is met (just as my son would allegedly do 😄).
- There are a few M functions that inherently have the "stop when condition is met" kind of behavior, but often you'll be creating iterations that scan all items.
- Particular syntax is required to set up iteration.

Now please allow me to be slightly more technical and translate these thoughts into M.

Understanding each _ (underscore)

> Refer to the query ListofNumbers.

Let's pick up my son's "spot the 100" test again and write some M code to do it for us. This time, the numbers are a list in the Source step. I am sure you're now familiar with adding a new step, so I'll just skip to showing you the code for a new step named Is100Check:

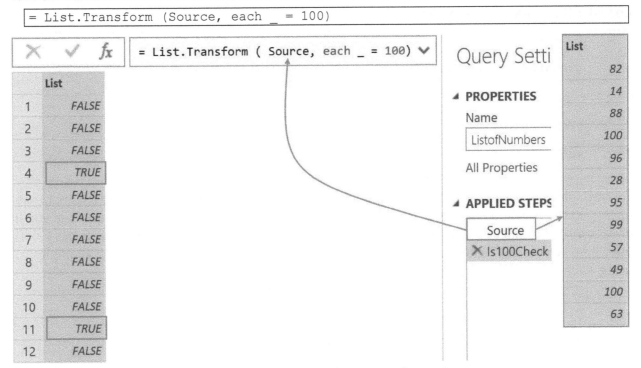

```
= List.Transform (Source, each _ = 100)
```

Figure 7-2 *Using* `each _` *to check whether each value is equal to 100.*

Note that:

- The first argument in the `List.Transform` function is a list (i.e., Source is a list of numbers).
- The second argument, `each _ = 100`, is a simple condition to determine whether each value is equal to 100 or not. As output we get `TRUE` if the number is 100; otherwise, we get `FALSE`.

This is not the first time in this book that we have seen `each _` (underscore). But what is it? Let me try explaining in English first. Consider this sentence:

"Each kid gets a candy."

Each refers to every single...what? In this case, kid—every single kid.

In conversation, we'd typically mention each boy or each girl or each car or each whatever to avoid confusion about what *each* refers to.

Similarly, in M, when iterating through a table or list (or any structured value), we write `each _`, where `each` means "every single," and the _ (underscore) is the value itself. So:

- If you're looping through a table, `each _` means each row of the table (i.e., each record).
- If you're looping through a list, `each _` means each value in the list.
- If you're looping through a record, `each _` means each column of the record (i.e., each field).

The underscore (_) is like a throwaway variable that stores the current value in the ongoing iteration. It is often used with the `each` keyword, but it can be used without the `each` keyword, too. (More on that later.)

The `each _` keyword is used in a lot of M functions. The problem is, there are 700+ functions in the M language, and I cannot possibly list the usage of `each _` in all of them. But I can give you a simple trick that'll help you identify which functions can possibly leverage the `each _` syntax.

Consider the syntax for these two functions:

```
= List.Transform (
    list as list,
    transform as function
)

= Table.AddColumn(
    table as table,
    newColumnName as text,
    columnGenerator as function,
)
```

For both of these functions, notice the argument that seeks a function as input. Usually, you can use each _ in the function argument. There are times, however, when each _ won't work, and you'll have to write an explicit function. I don't want to overload you with these complexities at this point, but I'll be sure to highlight this anomaly wherever applicable. For now, here are two examples of using each _:

```
// Example 1
=List.Transform(
    {1..5},
    each _ + 1.  // add 1 to each number in the list
)

// Example 2
=Table.AddColumn(
  #table(
    {"Num", "Letter"},
    {{"A", 1}, {"B", 2}, {"C", 3}}
  ), "No of Fields",
  each Record.FieldCount(_)) // Count columns for each row
```

There are also functions that do not explicitly declare the argument type as a function. One such function is Record.TransformFields. Here you can see its syntax and an example of the function in action:

```
// Syntax
= Record.TransformFields(
    record as record,
    transformOperations as list
)

// Example
= Record.TransformFields(
    [Name = "ALICE", Email = "Alice@sample.com"],
    {
        {"Name", each Text.Proper(_)},
        {"Email", each Text.AfterDelimiter(_, "@")}
    }
)
```

The Record.TransformFields function seeks the second argument as a nested list, but nothing explicitly hints to the use of the function to transform each column of the record. When you investigate the documentation, though, you'll notice the mention of a function as one of the arguments to transformOperations:

Syntax

```
Record.TransformFields(record as record, transformOperations as list, optional missingField as nullable numb
```

About

Returns a record after applying transformations specified in list transformOperations to record. One or more fields may be transformed at a given time.

In the case of a single field being transformed, transformOperations is expected to be a list with two items. The first item in transformOperations specifies a field name, and the second item in transformOperations specifies the function to be used for transformation. For example, {"Quantity", Number.FromText}

In the case of a multiple fields being transformed, transformOperations is expected to be a list of lists, where each inner list is a pair of field name and transformation operation. For example, {{"Quantity",Number.FromText},{"UnitPrice", Number.FromText}}

Figure 7-3 *A snapshot of the documentation on* `Record.TransformFields`.

Unfortunately, there is no other way to find these Easter eggs besides just reading the documentation and looking for examples. With those tough words, let's look at a few examples.

Example 1: Concatenating Text in a List

Refer to the query Qtrs.

Consider this list of four numbers:

```
= {1, 2, 3, 4}
```

As a simple task, we'd like to prefix each number with the string "Qtr". We can write a simple list transformation function like this:

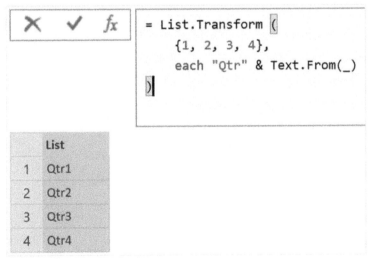

Figure 7-4 *Each number in the list is concatenated with the string* "Qtr".

Note that:

- _ (underscore) here references each number in the list.
- The Text.From function transforms the number to text so that it can be concatenated with the string "Qtr" using the & operator.

Example 2: Adding a Column

Refer to the query Adding Cost Column.

Consider this simple table, with Year and Sales columns:

	ABC 123 Year	ABC 123 Sales
1	2014	108000
2	2015	180000
3	2016	159000
4	2017	123000
5	2018	144000
6	2019	201000
7	2020	156000
8	2021	209000
9	2022	244000
10	2023	247000

Figure 7-5 *A table with two columns.*

We'd like to add a new column, Cost, whose fields show 35% of the value in the Sales column. This straightforward problem can be solved with the Power Query UI. Let's create a custom column (Add Column → Custom Column). In the Custom Column box, we can do this simple multiplication:

```
=[Sales] * 0.35
```

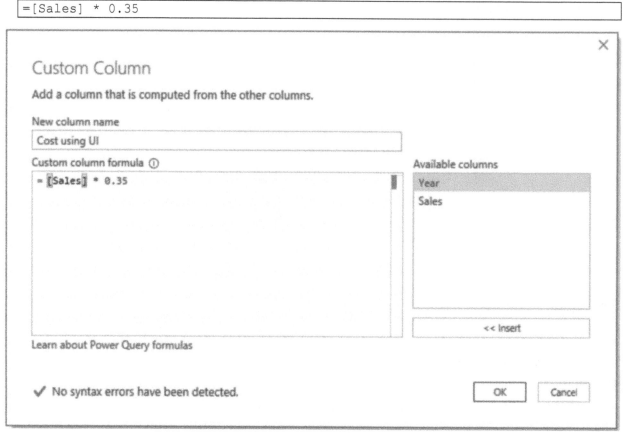

Figure 7-6 *Custom column formula.*

And boom! Here is the result:

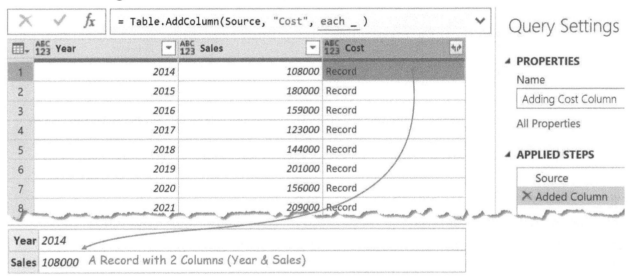

Figure 7-7 *The Cost column, created using the* `each` *keyword without the* _ *(underscore).*

Notice that `each` got inserted automatically. However, there's is no _ (underscore). Why is this so?

To figure this out, let's modify the Added Column step in the formula bar and write the M code our way, replacing `each [Sales] * 0.35` with `each _`. This results in a record value for each row. We can also change the column name to Cost.

Figure 7-8 *Modifying the M code for the Added Column step.*

Note that:

- In each row, we get a record value.
- Since we used `each` _ in the context of the table, it means each record (or each row).
- If you peek into the record, you'll see the Year and Sales columns and their respective values.

I hope you're starting to get comfortable with the `each` _ syntax. We're still a few steps away from the result, though. To get to the correct output for the Cost column, we'll modify the M code a bit, like this:

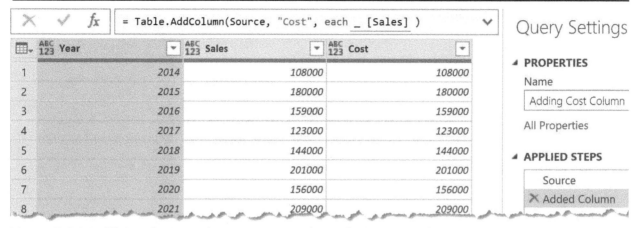

Figure 7-9 *Modifying the M code to extract a column from a record.*

Recall from Figure 7-8 that the underscore (_) returned a record with two columns, Year and Sales. We added the `[Sales]` column reference (after the underscore) to extract its value from the record. The final modification is to multiply the value by 35%:

```
each _ [Sales] * 0.35
```

Year	Sales	Cost
2014	108000	37800
2015	180000	63000
2016	159000	55650
2017	123000	43050
2018	144000	50400
2019	201000	70350
2020	156000	54600
2021	209000	73150

`= Table.AddColumn(Source, "Cost", each _ [Sales] * 0.35 )`

Figure 7-10 *Each sales value is multiplied by 35% to get the cost.*

At this point, you may be compelled to ask me, "So, what have we just accomplished?"

Nothing! The UI and our modified M code resulted in the same output:

```
// M code generated by Power Query UI.
= Table.AddColumn(Source, "Cost", each [Sales] * 0.35)

// Our modified M code (explicitly using each and _)
= Table.AddColumn(Source, "Cost", each _[Sales] * 0.35)
```

The only difference is that we used the underscore in the M code, and the UI didn't use the underscore. This means Power Query understands that when we create the new Cost column, we are referencing the Sales column for each record, so it is perfectly okay to entirely skip the underscore. Therefore, the Power Query UI writes more intuitive M code, like this (refer to Figure 7-7):

```
= Table.AddColumn(Source, "Cost", each [Sales] * 0.35)
```

I might have just confused you further. Heck, I was confused when I was new to this, and in all probability, you are, too! I think the most helpful thing to discuss at this point would be a few variations for writing each _.

each _ as Shorthand for Writing Functions

Refer to the query Adding Cost Using Fx.

We have used the function `Table.AddColumn` quite a bit. Here is what the official documentation shows as its syntax:

```
= Table.AddColumn(
    table as table,
    newColumnName as text,
    columnGenerator as function
)
```

The third argument, `columnGenerator`, requires a function, and as input, we used `each _` in the previous example. Recall that `each _` is shorthand for writing a function.

Although I have included a whole chapter on creating custom functions (see Chapter 8), for now you just need to know how to write the same M code using an explicit function rather than using `each _`:

```
// using each _
= Table.AddColumn(
    Source,
    "Cost",
    each _)      // using each and underscore _

// using a function
= Table.AddColumn(
    Source,
    "Cost",
    (x) => x)    // using a function instead of each _
```

Let me help you understand:

- **(x):** x is a variable (and it could be any text string; even an underscore would work). The variable x is declared in parentheses, and because it is used in the context of a table (in the `Table.AddColumn` function), it means each record.
- **=>:** Together, the equals sign and the greater than sign are the "goes to" symbol, which is used to initiate a function.
- **x:** After the => symbol, we simply return the x variable (i.e., the record).

The results now are the same as before (refer to Figure 7-8):

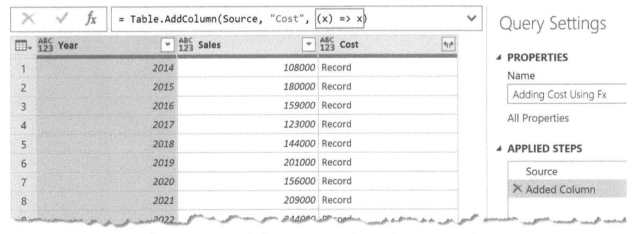

Figure 7-11 *Writing a function instead of* `each _` *produces the same result.*

If we want to carry out the same cost calculation as before but using a function this time, the M code would look like this:

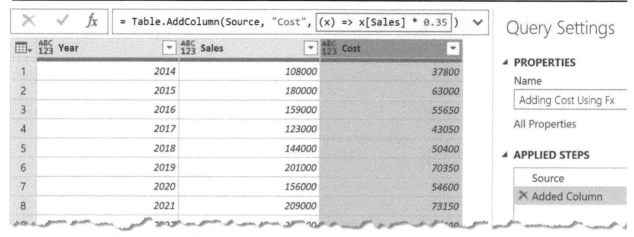

Figure 7-12 *The function produces the same result as* `each _`.

In summary, all of these options will return the same output and are just sugar syntaxes for writing a function in Power Query:

```
= Table.AddColumn(Source, "Cost", each [Sales])
= Table.AddColumn(Source, "Cost", each _[Sales])
= Table.AddColumn(Source, "Cost", (_) => _[Sales])
= Table.AddColumn(Source, "Cost", (_) => [Sales])
= Table.AddColumn(Source, "Cost", (x) => x[Sales])
```

Next, we'll discuss how we can use both the explicit functions (i.e., the `(x) => x` syntax) and `each _` to solve more practical problems. Don't worry: If you've gotten this far, I am sure you'll be able to handle the next logical step. 😊

Nested Iterations Using List.Transform

Refer to the query List Transform Nested Looping.

Remember that earlier in this chapter, when talking about `each _` in the context of a list example, we used the function `List.Transform` to concatenate "Qtr" with numbers (refer to Figure 7-4).

Now let's use the `List.Transform` function in a slightly more sophisticated way to perform nested iteration. Here is our query so far:

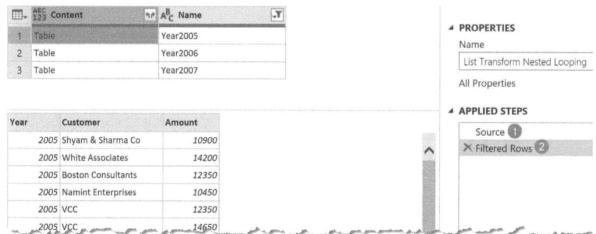

Figure 7-13 *A query with two applied steps.*

Note that:

- The Source step connects to an Excel file.
- Then a simple filter keeps three tables (Year2005, Year2006, and Year2007). You can even see a preview of the Year2005 table.

The problem: For each table in the Content column, we'd like to add a new column to calculate the max sales amount and eventually combine all tables. Here is our expected output:

	ABC 123 Year	ABC 123 Customer	ABC 123 Amount	ABC 123 Max Amount
1	2005	Shyam & Sharma Co	10900	14650
2	2005	White Associates	14200	14650
3	2005	Boston Consultants	12350	14650
4	2005	Namint Enterprises	10450	14650
5	2005	VCC	12350	14650
6	2005	VCC	14650	14650
13	2006	MNTL	13050	14800
14	2006	Sharma & Co	12300	14800
15	2006	MNTL	14800	14800
16	2006	VCC	12300	14800
17	2006	India Trotters	11050	14800
18	2006	MNTL	13800	14800
	2006	GoodFly	11050	148..
32	2007	VCC	12500	12750
33	2007	VCC	11700	12750
34	2007	White Associates	11850	12750
35	2007	White Associates	12750	12750
36	2007	White Associates	11950	12750
37	2007	Boston Consultants	12300	12750

Figure 7-14 *The expected output has a new Max Amount column with all three tables combined.*

Here is a visual way of thinking about the logic we're trying to build:

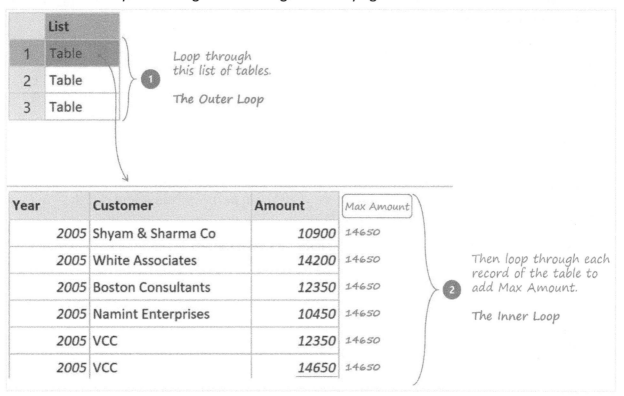

Figure 7-15 *For each table in the list, we need to add a Max Amount column.*

Note that:

- The outer loop iterates through a list of three tables.
- The inner loop iterates through the records of each table and adds a Max Amount column.

Step 1: Creating an Outer Loop and an Inner Loop

Consider the following code as a new step:

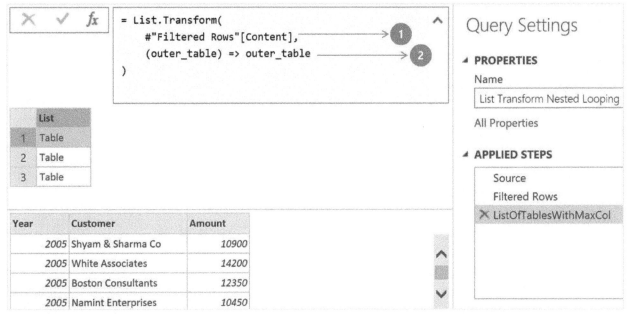

Figure 7-16 *Using* `List.Transform` *to create a function that returns the same tables.*

Let's take a minute to digest this:

1. Since `List.Transform` works with a list, referencing the table in the previous step and its column name (`#"Filtered Rows" [Content]`) will create a list of tables.

2. We declare an `outer_table` variable to store each table of the list and return it as is.

> **Note:** Let me take a quick detour. We could have written the same code using `each _`, like this:
>
> ```
> = List.Transform(
>     #"Filtered Rows"[Content],
>     each _
> )
> ```
>
> ...and it would have made no difference to the current output. Instead, we chose to create a function with the variable `outer_table` on purpose. You'll find out the reason as we continue to build the formula.

Now let's modify the M code further to add the Max Amount column:

```
= List.Transform(
    #"Filtered Rows"[Content],
    (outer_table) =>
    Table.AddColumn(outer_table, "Max Amount",
    each List.Max(outer_table[Amount]))
)
```

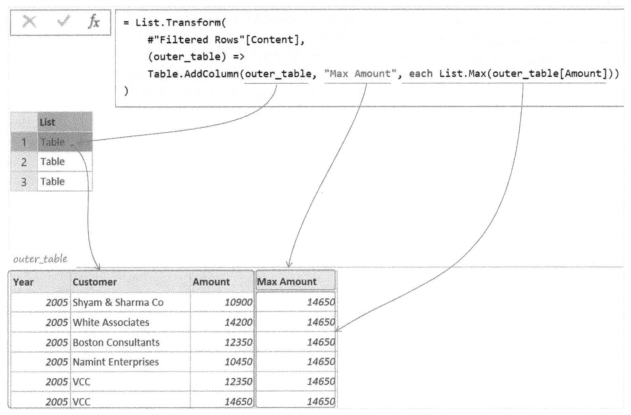

Figure 7-17 *Adding a column to each* `outer_table` *to calculate the max amount.*

Let's run through the formula together:

- For each `outer_table`, we create a new column (Max Amount) by using the `Table.AddColumn` function.

- In each row of the table, we reference the outer table's Amount column.

- Referencing a column from a table (i.e., `outer_table[Amount]`) produces a list, and `List.Max` retrieves the max value from that list. Remember to feed Power Query what it eats!

Note: It's only because we used a variable (`outer_table`) that we were able to reference it in each row of the inner loop. This wouldn't be possible using `each _` because we have two nested iterations going on: The first iteration is through the list of tables, and the second iteration is through each row of the nested table (refer to Figure 7-15). Therefore, this code wouldn't work:

```
= List.Transform(
    #"Filtered Rows"[Content],
    each Table.AddColumn(_, "Max Amount",     // 1
    each List.Max(_[Amount]))                 // 2
)
```

Why wouldn't it work?
- The first `each _`, used in `Table.AddColumn`, references each table. So far, so good. No problem.
- The second `each _`, used in `List.Max`, ideally should reference the Amount column of each table in the list, but since `each _` by default means the current item in the iteration, it references each value in the Amount column.

Because we need to feed the `List.Max` function a list and not a single value, it returns an error. A gentle reminder: Feed Power Query what it eats! 😄

```
= List.Transform(
      #"Filtered Rows"[Content],
      each Table.AddColumn(_, "Max Amount",
      each List.Max(_[Amount]))
)
```

	List
1	Table
2	Table
3	Table

Returns an error!

Year	Customer	Amount	Max Amount
2005	Shyam & Sharma Co	10900	Error
2005	White Associates	14200	Error
2005	Boston Consultants	12350	Error
2005	Namint Enterprises	10450	Error

Figure 7-18 *Using* `each _` *twice returns and error.*

Step 2: Combining All Tables

Once we have a Max Amount column created for each of the nested tables, all we need to do is combine them. Consider this M code as a new step:

```
= Table.Combine(ListOfTablesWithMaxCol)
```

	ABC 123 Year	ABC 123 Customer	ABC 123 Amount	ABC 123 Max Value
1	2005	Shyam & Sharma Co	10900	14650
2	2005	White Associates	14200	14650
3	2005	Boston Consultants	12350	14650
4	2005	Namint Enterprises	10450	14650
5	2005	VCC	12350	14650
6	2005	VCC	14650	14650
7	2005	MNTL	12600	14650
8	2005	Sharma & Co	13650	14650
9	2005	Namint Enterprises	13600	14650
10	2005	Shyam & Sharma Co	14350	14650

Query Settings

▲ PROPERTIES
Name
List Transform Nested Looping
All Properties

▲ APPLIED STEPS
Source
Filtered Rows
ListOfTablesWithMaxCol
✕ CombinedAllTables

Figure 7-19 *List of three tables combined using the* `Table.Combine` *function.*

Since we have a list of tables in the previous step, we can simply wrap it in the `List.Combine` function as a new step, and—voila!—we've got a value in the Max Amount column for each year.

	ABC 123 Year		ABC 123 Customer		ABC 123 Amount		ABC 123 Max Amount	
1	2005		Shyam & Sharma Co		10900		14650	
2	2005		White Associates		14200		14650	
3	2005		Boston Consultants		12350		14650	
4	2005		Namint Enterprises		10450		14650	
5	2005		VCC		12350		14650	
6	2005		VCC		14650		14650	
13	2006		MNTL		13050		14800	
14	2006		Sharma & Co		12300		14800	
15	2006		MNTL		14800		14800	
16	2006		VCC		12300		14800	
17	2006		India Trotters		11050		14800	
18	2006		MNTL		13800		14800	
	2006		Goodfly		11050		148..	
32	2007		VCC		12500		12750	
33	2007		VCC		11700		12750	
34	2007		White Associates		11850		12750	
35	2007		White Associates		12750		12750	
36	2007		White Associates		11950		12750	
37	2007		Boston Consultants		12300		12750	

Figure 7-20 *The output after combining all the tables.*

> **Note:** What we've done here could also be done using the UI. The Group operation in the Transform tab is meant to add aggregation columns (like sum, min, and max columns) to nested tables. Although the logic is pretty much the same, you've learned to write an explicit function, and you can do a lot more than find the max value with a function.

Understanding List.Accumulate

So far in our examples, we have iterated through all the items in a list or table. But there are going to be advanced scenarios where we would not only iterate through a list or a table but also save, capture, and work with the result of the previous iteration—that is, accumulate the results of the iteration.

In such scenarios, we can use an incredibly powerful function, List.Accumulate. I'm assuming that nothing I've just said has made sense, so let's start with the basics. 😄

List.Accumulate Syntax

The List.Accumulate function takes three arguments:

```
= List.Accumulate(
    list as list,            // 1
    seed as any,             // 2
    accumulator as function  // 3
)
```

Note that:

1. The first input is a list that we want to iterate through.

2. The second input, the seed, is a starting point. A starting point could be a single value, a null value, a list, a record, or even a table or a more complex object, like a nested list or list of tables.

3. The accumulator enables us to accumulate the results of each iteration. For this argument, you cannot use `each _`, and you need to create an explicit function because the function requires two mandatory input parameters (i.e., state and current).

Example 1: Understanding List.Accumulate

Refer to the query ListAccumulateEg1.

Let's look at a simple example of how accumulation works. In the column shown below, each row holds one of the letters in my name: Chandeep.

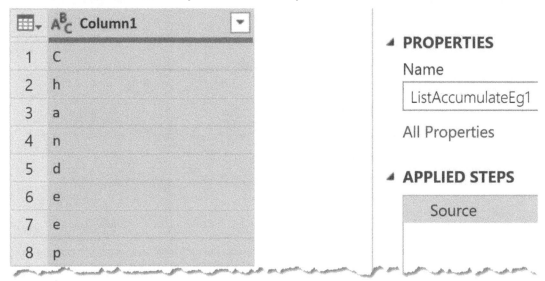

Figure 7-21 *Each row contains a letter in my name.*

How can we concatenate these letters to get Chandeep as a result? Let me stop you right here before you mock me with this simple solution:

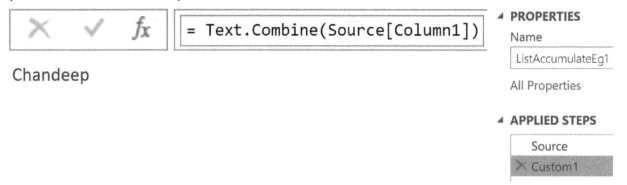

Figure 7-22 *One solution could be to combine the letters.*

For the purpose of explaining `List.Accumulate`, let's solve it differently. For `List.Accumulate` to work, we need to feed our data to its three arguments. Here is how the formula would look:

```
// The logical way of thinking about List.Accumulate
= List.Accumulate(
    Letters as a list,
    Start with a Blank,
    concatenate each letter with the previous letter
)

// Here is how the actual formula would look like
= List.Accumulate(
    Source[Column1],      // list of letters
    "",                   // start with a blank string
    (s, c) => s & c       // accumulating logic
)
```

When this formula is executed as a new step, we get the desired output:

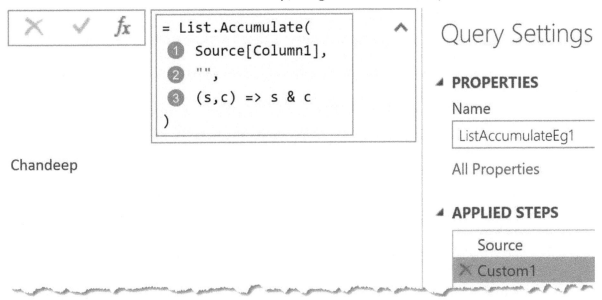

Chandeep

Figure 7-23 *Using* `List.Accumulate` *to concatenate the letters.*

But the question is, how did this work?

1. **`Source[Column1]`:** In the first argument, we fed the list of letters. Recall the syntax `table reference[column reference]` to extract the column as a list.

2. **"":** We start the accumulation from a blank string as our starting point.

3. **`(s, c) => s & c`:** This suddenly starts to look foreign. What is this?

Let me show a visual of how this accumulation works:

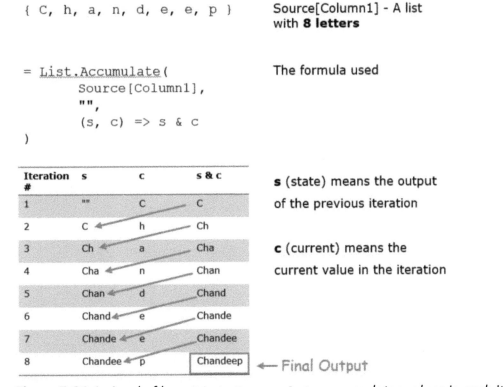

Figure 7-24 *A visual of how* `List.Accumulate` *accumulates values in each iteration.*

Here are a few important points to note:

- The first argument of `List.Accumulate` will always be a list.

- The second argument can be a string, a number, a date, or even a complex structured value like a list or a table. **Very important:** The output of the `List.Accumulate` function will be the value type declared as a starting/seed value. For instance, in this scenario, we declared the seed (starting value) as a blank string, so the final output will also be a string. In future examples, we'll declare the starting value as a table, so the final output will also be a table.

- We declared a function with state and current parameters (which can be labeled differently). In this case, we called them `s` and `c`. Note that:

  - The state parameter (`s`) captures the output value of the previous iteration. For example, in this case, `s` in the first iteration will be a blank string (because that is our starting point). Thereafter, `s` holds the value of the previous iteration and can be used in the next iteration.

  - The current parameter (`c`) refers to the current value in the iteration. In this case, as the iteration moves forward, the value of `c` keeps changing to reference each letter in the list.

  - The first parameter (no matter the label) will always play the role of state, and the second parameter will play the role of current.

- Because we've concatenated `s & c` (state and current), the result is the accumulated value of all iterations.

I understand that this is a convoluted way of solving a simple problem, but the idea here was to help you understand how the `List.Accumulate` function works.

Example 2: Finding a Running Total with List.Accumulate

> Refer to the query List Accumulate - Running Total.

Please allow me to show one more semi-entertaining and semi-useful example of the `List.Accumulate` function before we take a big leap. In this case, we'd like to use the input list of numbers shown on the left to create the expected output shown on the right—a list of running total values.

Input

	List
1	1
2	2
3	3
4	4
5	5

Expected Output

	List
1	1
2	3
3	6
4	10
5	15

Figure 7-25 *The input list and the expected output list.*

If you compare the expected output in this example against the output in the previous example (refer to Figure 7-24), you'll notice that here we want to return a list of running total values rather than a single text value, Chandeep, as returned in the previous example.

You might think, "So what is the big deal?" This means that:

- Our starting point, or seed value, needs to be a list because our output is also a list.
- This change will add slight complexity while we're accumulating values.

As we explore these nuances and build the solution, we'll look at the subtleties of `List.Accumulate`. It's very important to understand these subtleties in order to understand how this function works.

Running Total Logic

On the face of it, the running total logic is just adding the previous accumulated values to the current value. In Excel, it can be written like this:

	B	C
5	1	1
6	2	3
7	3	6
8	4	=C7+B8
9	5	15

Figure 7-26 *Running total formula in Excel.*

But in our case, we're not expecting a single value as output, as shown here (i.e., 15, the total of all numbers). Instead, we want a list of all the running total values as they build up.

Running Total Logic Using List.Accumulate

Let's hit the ground running with this loosely written `List.Accumulate` logic:

```
=List.Accumulate(
    {1,2,3,4,5},       // 1   list of numbers
    {0},               // 2   Start with a 0 in a list
    (s, c) => s &      // 3   Concatenate s (prev total) with
    s + c.             //     s + c (current value)
)
```

A few things to note:

1. We start off with a list of numbers.

2. Next, our seed value is a zero within a list: {0}. This is because we want the output to be a list as well, and unless we start with a list, we won't get the output as a list.

3. The accumulation function (s, c) => s & s + c means the previous value (s) is concatenated with the sum of the previous value and the current value (s + c). If you compare this with the Excel formula in Figure 7-26, you see that the only new thing here is the concatenation—and that is because we want to show the previous values in our list as well.

Here is what happens if this code is executed as a new step:

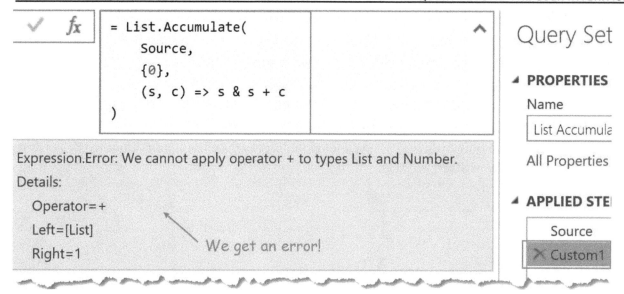

```
= List.Accumulate(
    Source,
    {0},
    (s, c) => s & s + c
)
```

Expression.Error: We cannot apply operator + to types List and Number.

Details:

  Operator=+

  Left=[List]

  Right=1   *We get an error!*

Query Set

PROPERTIES

Name

List Accumula

All Properties

APPLIED STEI

    Source

  ✕ Custom1

Figure 7-27 *List.Accumulate shows an error.*

For someone trying to work through only the second example of `List.Accumulate` in their life, this error seems like a scary dark room with no way out. 🙀

If we turn on the metaphorical lights, you'll see that this is not as scary as it seems. Consider this illustration of the workings of `List.Accumulate` and why the error happened:

```
= List.Accumulate(
    Source,         // list of num
    {0},            // seed value
    (s, c) => s & s + c
)
```

Source (list)

List	
1	1
2	2
3	3
4	4
5	5

Seed value

List	
1	0

1ˢᵗ Iteration

```
= List.Accumulate(
    Source,
    {0},
    (s, c) => s & s + c
)
```

$s = \{0\}$

$c = 1$

$s \& s + c$ is not possible because
$s = \{0\}$ and $c = 1$.

A number cannot be added or concatenated to a list.

Figure 7-28 *Workings of List.Accumulate.*

Notice that the error occurred in the first iteration, and the query was terminated because of incompatible value types. In this case, for the first iteration, we have:

- Seed = `{0}` (i.e., a list with 0).
- Variables in accumulator function = `(s, c)`, where:
  - s = a list (always)
  - c = 1 (i.e., the first number from the Source step)

The logic for the accumulator function (=> s & s + c) is correct, but we have to manipulate the formula in such a way that the values of s and c become compatible. If you go back and once again read the scary error in Figure 7-27, it will make more sense now.

We need to further modify the formula so it looks like this:

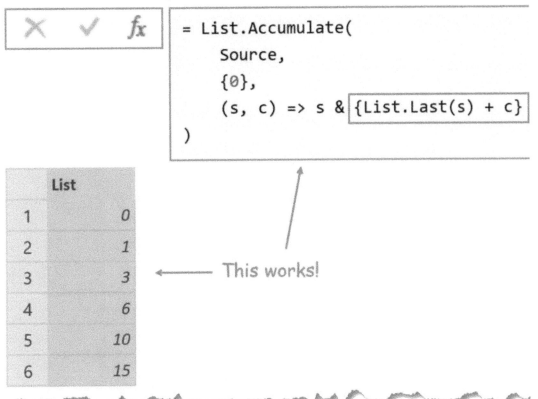

Figure 7-29 *Manipulating the values of* s *and* c *to make them compatible with each other.*

Notice the changes:

- s + c is now changed to List.Last(s) + c. Why? Because the List.Last(s) function extracts the last (single) value from the list (i.e., s), and c is also a single value, the two are compatible for the operation s + c.

- This addition is wrapped in curly brackets, like this: {List.Last(s) + c}. Why? Because the addition is concatenated to s (which is a list), and a list can only be concatenated to another list—hence the curly brackets.

I still feel your fear. This image should calm you down 😊:

```
= List.Accumulate(
    Source,              // list of num
    {0},                 // seed value
    (s, c) => s & s + c
)
```

Source (list)   Seed value

1st Iteration

```
= List. Accumulate(
    Source,
    {0},
    (s, c) => s & {List.Last(s) + c}
)
```

List.Last(s)
= 0
c = 1

2nd Iteration

```
= List. Accumulate(
    Source,
    {0},
    (s, c) => s & {List.Last(s) + c}
)
```

List.Last(s)
= 1
c = 2

3rd Iteration

```
= List. Accumulate(
    Source,
    {0},
    (s, c) => s & {List.Last(s) + c}
)
```

List.Last(s)
= 3
c = 3

And so on!

Figure 7-30 *Iterative workings of* `List.Accumulate`.

Note: Before we do anything further, it is very important to note a couple things that summarize the essence of this example:

- The seed value can be anything—a table, a list, a record, a single value, etc. We're going to base our next two examples on variations of the seed and state values.
- The accumulator function needs to be compatible with the value types for the state and current variable; otherwise, the formula won't work. And yet again, I repeat: "Feed Power Query what it eats!" 😄

At this stage in our query, we have two lists (source and running total, as two steps) and two problems:

- The running total list shows the unwanted 0 at the start (refer to Figure 7-29).

- What exactly do we do with these two lists? Shouldn't it be a table with two columns, Numbers and Running Total?

To solve the first problem, we can simply wrap the `List.Skip` function around the `List.Accumulate` formula to skip the first value in the list, like this:

```
= List.Skip( List.Accumulate(
     Source,
     {0},
     (s, c) => s & {List.Last(s) + c}
))
```

	List
1	1
2	3
3	6
4	10
5	15

Figure 7-31 *Using `List.Skip` to skip the first value in the list.*

To tackle the second problem, we can wrap the two lists in the `Table.FromColumns` function in a new step, like this:

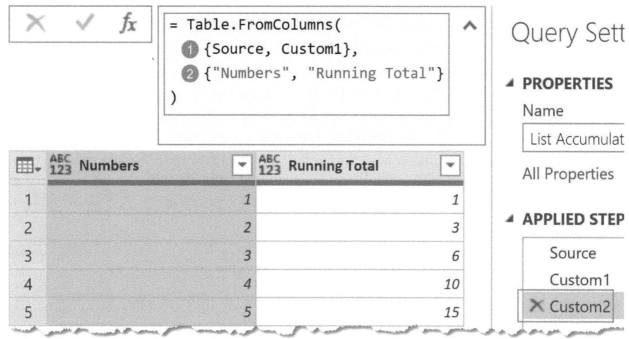

Figure 7-32 *Creating a table with two lists.*

Note that:

1. We've created a list and fed Source (the numbers list) and Custom1 (the running total list) into it. These two lists will be used to create two columns.

2. As the optional input, we've declared the column names in a list. Yes, it's hard-coded, but we can live with that for now. 😎

> **Note:** Although this is reasonable output to make this example legit, this is not the most efficient way to calculate a running total. I used this method just to demonstrate the workings of the state and current variables in the `List.Accumulate` function.

Example 3: Replacing Multiple Values by Using List.Accumulate

Refer to the query ListAccumulateEg2.

Now let's take a leap and apply `List.Accumulate` in a more practical use case. Consider this table, which has five columns that represent some sort of market data:

Product	MarketSh%	Sales	Distribution Score	Brand Score
FreshJuice	25%	100000	85	70
SpringWater	?	80000	75	65
SnackBars	15%	60000	65	?
CoconutOil	10%	**	70	55
NutriCereal	30%	120000	90	75
AlmondMilk	18%	72000	68	63
BerrySmoothie	22%	88000	**	67
GreenTea	28%	112000	88	72
ProteinShake	12%	48000	58	57
VitaMix	16%	64000	73	

Figure 7-33 *Notice the junk values ? and **.*

Alongside the above table we also have a supplementary table that explains the junk characters:

Mark	Explains
?	Not available
**	System Busy

Figure 7-34 *Supplementary table that explains the special characters used in* **Figure 7-33**.

Our requirement is simple: No matter what the special characters mean and in which columns they appear, replace each of them with a null. The expected output looks like this:

	Product	MarketSh%	Sales	Distribution Score	Brand Score
1	FreshJuice	0.25	100000	85	70
2	SpringWater	null	80000	75	65
3	SnackBars	0.15	60000	65	null
4	CoconutOil	0.1	null	70	55
5	NutriCereal	0.3	120000	90	75
6	AlmondMilk	0.18	72000	68	63
7	BerrySmoothie	0.22	88000	null	67
8	GreenTea	0.28	112000	88	72
9	ProteinShake	0.12	48000	58	57

Figure 7-35 *Expected output with all special characters replaced with the null value.*

Tinkering with the UI

Let's act naïve and tinker with the Replace Values feature in the Power Query UI to see what code we get and how we can mash it with the `List.Accumulate` function.

As a first step, let's do what any UI expert would do: Select the MarketSh% and Brand Score columns → Transform → Replace Values and replace the ? with null. Doing this results in the following code and table:

```
= Table.ReplaceValue(Source,"?",null,Replacer.ReplaceValue,{"MarketSh%", "Brand Score"})
```

ABC 123 MarketSh%		ABC 123 Sales		ABC 123 Distribution Score		ABC 123 Brand Score	
0.25		100000		85		70	
null		80000		75		65	
0.15		60000		65		null	
0.1	**			70		55	
0.3		120000		90		75	
0.18		72000		68		63	
0.22		88000	**			62	

Figure 7-36 *Replacing ? with null.*

Cool, but let's take a moment to dissect the `Table.ReplaceValue` function used and also take a look at its official documentation:

```
// Our UI Generated Code
= Table.ReplaceValue(
    Source,                           // 1
    "?",                              // 2
    Null,                             // 3
    Replacer.ReplaceValue,            // 4
    {"MarketSh%", "Brand Score"}      // 5
)

// Documentation
= Table.ReplaceValue(
    table as table,                   // 1
    oldValue as any,                  // 2
    newValue as any,                  // 3
    replacer as function,             // 4
    columnsToSearch as list           // 5
) as table                            // 6
```

Note that:

1. The first argument is a table (in this case, the Source step).
2. Did you notice the `as any` part of `oldValue as any`? This means there could be multiple value types that could go in there. In this case, we fed a single value as ?, but we should tinker with this more in a bit.
3. Again, the `newValue as any` argument could be any value type. In this case, we want to replace every special character with null, so this works fine for now.
4. This function input replaces the values.
5. This is a list of all the columns to be fed as a list where the replacement will happen—in this case, `{"MarketSh%", "Brand Score"}`.
6. The output value will be a table.

Notice the `oldValue` argument of the `Table.ReplaceValue` function. The value type is `any`—that is, it could be a single value, a list, a record, or anything else, but we can't say for sure which value types will fit in here just by looking at the documentation.

So, we've got to tinker. Consider this slightly revised code:

wrapped in { }

```
= Table.ReplaceValue(Source, {"?"} , null,Replacer.ReplaceValue, {"MarketSh%", "Brand Score"})
```

ABC 123 MarketSh%	ABC 123 Sales	ABC 123 Distribution Score	ABC 123 Brand Score
0.25	100000	85	70
? not null	80000	75	65
0.15	60000	65 ? not null	
0.1 **		70	55

Figure 7-37 *Editing the second argument as a list.*

Because the `oldValue` argument could accept any value type, we tried a list, but clearly it didn't work; the ? is not replaced with a null. It also didn't return any errors.

> **Tip:** If this code had worked, we'd be sitting with a hand of aces 😎, and our fully modified code would look like this:
>
> ```
> = Table.ReplaceValue(
>     Source,
>     {"?", "**"} , null,
>     Replacer.ReplaceValue,
>     Table.ColumnNames(Source)
> )
> ```
>
> I encourage you tinker like this often. You have nothing to lose, and you'll often win—even though we didn't today! 😟

Sorry I digressed. At this stage, with the help of the UI, we don't know how to modify the `Table.ReplaceValue` function to make it dynamic so that it replaces as many junk characters as shown in Figure 7-34 with null values.

For now, let's keep the process manual and add one more Replaced Value step to replace the ** with a null. We can select the other two columns Sales and Distribution Score → Transform → Replace Values and replace the ** with null. Our query looks like this:

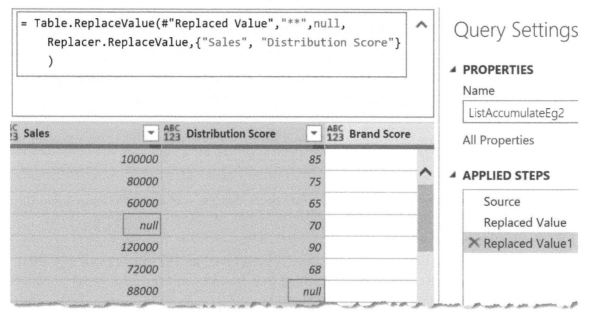

Figure 7-38 *Adding the Replaced Value step twice to replace two junk characters.*

Let's see if we can rewrite the two Replaced Value steps as a single step by using `List.Accumulate`.

List.Accumulate Logic

If you peek into the Advanced Editor (View → Advanced Editor), you'll see this code (though it may not look as organized because I formatted this a bit 😊):

```
1   let
2     ①  Source = Excel.CurrentWorkbook(){[Name="MarketData"]}[Content],
3
4     ②  #"Replaced Value" =
5             Table.ReplaceValue(
6                 Source, "?",null,
7                 Replacer.ReplaceValue,
8                 {"MarketSh%", "Brand Score"}
9             ),
10
11    ③  #"Replaced Value1" =
12             Table.ReplaceValue(
13                 #"Replaced Value",
14                 "**",null,
15                 Replacer.ReplaceValue,
16                 {"Sales", "Distribution Score"}
17             )
18   in
19    ④  #"Replaced Value1"
20
```

Figure 7-39 *The M code generated so far using the Power Query UI.*

In this code, note that:

1. First, the Source step produces a table to work with.
2. That table is fed into the Replaced Value step and replaces ? with null.
3. The resulting table is fed again into the second Replaced Value step, which replaces ** with null.
4. Finally, the second Replaced Value table is returned.

This behavior exactly mimics the functionality of `List.Accumulate`. Consider this loosely written logic for the `List.Accumulate` function, and you'll see the connection:

```
= List.Accumulate(
    Special Characters List,    // 1
    Starting Value,             // 2
    (s, c) =>                   // 3
    Table.ReplaceValue (
        s,                      // 4
        c, null,                // 4
        Replacer.ReplaceValue,
        List of All Columns
    )
)
```

No, didn't get it? Let me explain:

1. Let's say we start with a list of special characters like {"?", "*"}. At this point, it's a hard-coded list, but please bear with the mediocrity for a while. 😊
2. Our seed (starting) value is the Source step table. (That is where we'd like to start replacing values.)
3. Then come the two mandatory arguments, state and current (s, c), where s means the result of the previous iteration, and c is the list item in the current iteration. In this case, s

will denote the table produced in the previous iteration, and `c` will be the special character in the current iteration.

4. `s` and `c` are then used in the `Table.ReplaceValue` function, and it takes two iterations to replace both of the special characters with null in all the columns.

I know, it's a lot to imagine. Perhaps this visual will help you understand better:

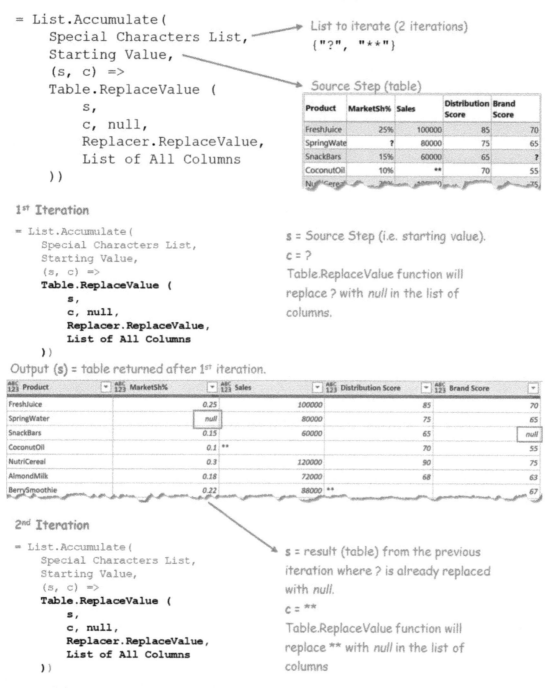

Figure 7-40 *Iterative workings of* `List.Accumulate`*.*

Using List.Accumulate

With that swirling logic out of way, we hit the final nail with a ticked-and-tied ListAccumulate step that works like {M}agic:

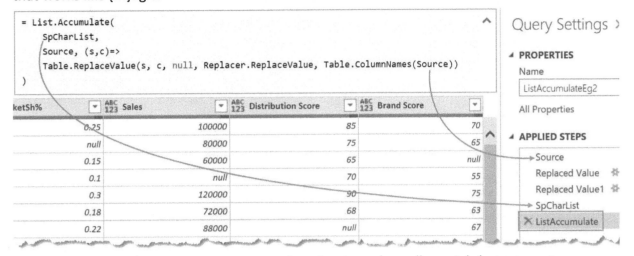

Figure 7-41 *Using the* `List.Accumulate` *function to replace all special characters at once.*

In this code, we've made a jump that I believe will be apparent by now:

```
=List.Accumulate(
    SpCharList,                          // 1
    Source, (s,c)=>
    Table.ReplaceValue(
      s, c, null,
      Replacer.ReplaceValue,
        Table.ColumnNames(Source)    // 2
      )
)
```

Note that:

1.   The list of hard-coded special characters has been replaced with a dynamic list from the previous SpCharList step. It's not hard to imagine that the SpCharList step results in a list like this but that is not hard-coded: `{"?", "**"}`. 😊

2.   The column names that were hard-coded are now dynamic, thanks to the `Table.ColumnNames` function.

Technically, we could delete the two Replaced Value steps, but let's keep them for your perusal.

Example 4: Adding Multiple Columns with List.Accumulate

Refer to the query ListAccumulateExampleEg3.

Let's solve another practical problem using `List.Accumulate`. Consider this two-column table, which lists each product and the number of leads:

Products	Leads
Consulting	800
IT	700
Staffing	400
Training	600
Media	900
Contact Work	500

Figure 7-42 *Products with numbers of leads.*

We need to build a sales funnel by adding three more columns to this table, using the following logic:

- **Calls column:** 25% of the value in the Leads column.
- **Meetings column:** 25% of the value in the Calls column.
- **Sales column:** 25% of the value in the Meetings column.

When the numbers are rounded, the output table should look like this:

	Products	Leads	Calls	Meetings	Sales	
1	Consulting	800	200	50	12	
2	IT	700	175	44	11	
3	Staffing	400	100	25	6	
4	Training	600	150	38	10	
5	Media	900	225	56	14	
6	Contact Work	500	125	31	8	

Figure 7-43 *This is the expected output.*

Now, this isn't an edge case that cannot be solved using the UI. Here are three simple custom column steps to solve it:

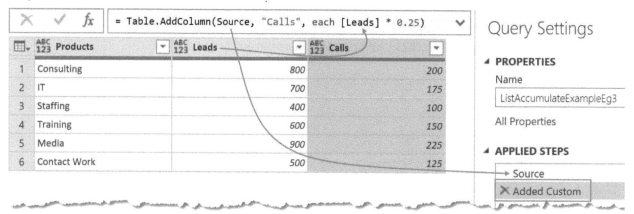

Figure 7-44 *Using the Power Query UI to add a Calls custom column.*

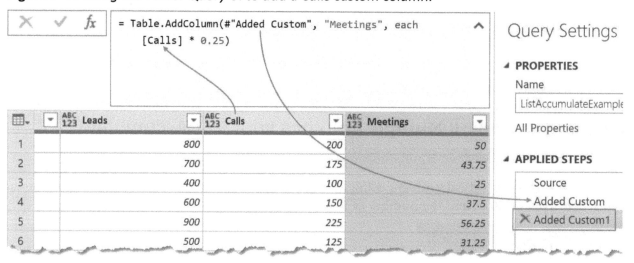

Figure 7-45 *Using the Power Query UI to add a Meeting column.*

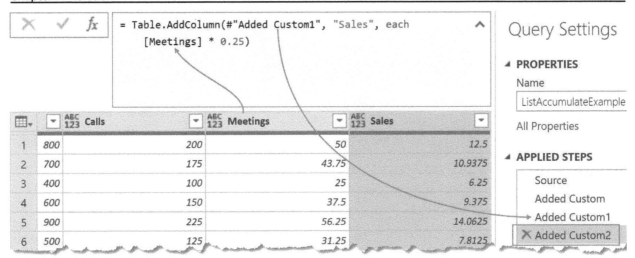

Figure 7-46 *Using the Power Query UI to add a Sales column.*

There are two problems with this approach:

- The smaller problem is that this approach is a bit verbose, and we've repeated the Added Custom step three times.

- The big problem is that it's not scalable. That is, we cannot add more columns dynamically if the number of steps in the funnel increases.

Look closely at Figures 7-44, 7-45, and 7-46, and you'll see that there are three iterations of the Added Custom step that create new columns, each based on the previous step (i.e., table). This behavior is like accumulating the result of the previous step to create a new column, and it is very similar to what `List.Accumulate` does.

The Logic of List.Accumulate

Let's go through the syntax of the `Table.AddColumn` function and then try to combine it with `List.Accumulate`. Here's the syntax:

```
= Table.AddColumn(
      table as table,                // 1 Table Reference
      newColumnName as text,         // 2 New column name
      columnGenerator as function)   // 3 Function to create
                                     //   column values
```

Before we go down the path of writing dynamic M code, let's talk about the logic involved in combining the functions. Here is how we can think about the three arguments of `List.Accumulate` shown in the syntax above:

1. **List:** We iterate through the list of values `{"Calls", "Meetings", "Sales"}` (i.e., columns to be created).

2. **Seed value:** The starting value is the Source step table (refer to Figure 7-42).

3. **Accumulator function:** In each iteration, we create a new column by using the `Table.AddColumn` function.

Step 1: Creating a List of Columns

Let's start by creating a new step with a hard-coded list for all the columns we want to create:

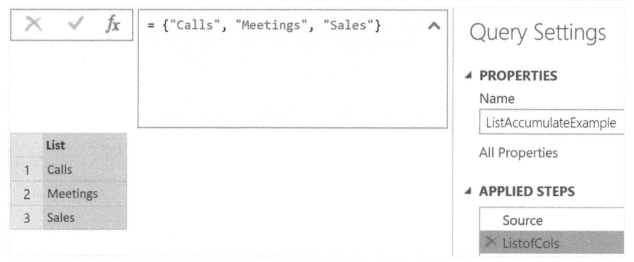

Figure 7-47 *Creating a hard-coded list as a new step.*

This list could instead be user input from an Excel table, but for now we're hard-coding the values in the list.

Step 2: Using List.Accumulate

We can now use List.Accumulate to iterate through ListofCols, like this:

```
=List.Accumulate(
    ListofCols,                                     // 1
    Source,                                         // 2
        (PvStp, ColNm) =>                           // 3
        Table.AddColumn(PvStp, ColNm, each 1)   // 3
)
```

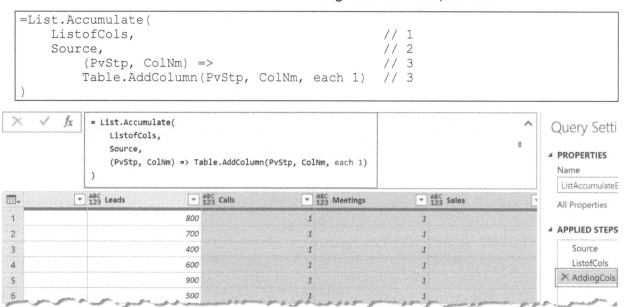

Figure 7-48 *Using List.Accumulate to add multiple columns.*

Here is how the formula works:

1. **ListofCols:** As the first argument, we feed in the list of column names.

2. **Source:** In the second argument, the Source step becomes the seed (or the starting table) to start adding more columns.

3. **(PvStp, ColNm) => Table.AddColumn(PvStp, ColNm, each 1):** In the accumulator function, PvStp acts as the state variable, ColNm acts as the current variable, and we use the Table.AddColumn function as the accumulation logic. At this point, recall the syntax of the Table.AddColumn function, which has three arguments:

   - **Table reference:** In this case, it is the output of the previous step (i.e., PvStp).

   - **Column name as text:** In this case, it is the current value of the list (i.e., ColNm).

   - **Column generator function:** For now we've used the pseudo value 1 for each row.

Although we have created three new columns, we've fed a dummy number in those columns (i.e., 1). To feed the correct value, we need to reference the last column created in the previous step (i.e., table) and multiply that by 25%. Take a look at this revised code, especially the part after the `each` keyword:

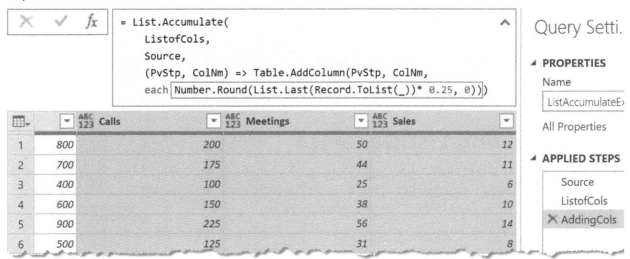

Figure 7-49 *Modifying the code to multiply the last column of the previous table by 25% and round the result.*

In this code, we have replaced the pseudo value 1 with a bunch of code. Let's explore it from the inside out:

- `_` (underscore) fetches the record from the underlying table. Recall the use of the underscore in the context of a table (refer to Figure 7-8).

- `Record.ToList(_)` converts the record to a list.

- `List.Last(Record.ToList(_)) * 0.25` returns a single last value from the list (which is the last column's value of the table in the previous step) and then multiplies that by 25%.

- `Number.Round(List.Last(Record.ToList(_))* 0.25, 0))` rounds the value obtained above to zero decimal places.

Is This Dynamic?

The genius of this code is that it is dynamic. Let's test it out by adding the new value `Repeat Sales` to the hard-coded list:

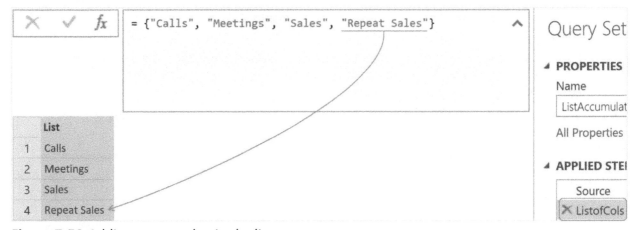

Figure 7-50 *Adding a new value in the list:* `Repeat Sales`.

We should now automatically get a new column added to our output from the `List.Accumulate` function in the next step:

		ABC 123 Meetings		ABC 123 Sales		ABC 123 Repeat Sales	
1	200		50		12		3
2	175		44		11		3
3	100		25		6		2
4	150		38		10		2
5	225		56		14		4
6	125		31		8		2

All Properties

◢ APPLIED STEPS

     Source

     ListofCols

     ✕ AddingCols

Figure 7-51 *The new column has automatically been added to our query output.*

This is awesome! 🍴

Understanding List.Generate

The `List.Generate` function is a perfect example of a function that does do...while looping. Let's explore its syntax and then jump into a few interesting examples. First, the syntax:

```
List.Generate(
    initial as function,                          // 1
    condition as function,                        // 2
    next as function,                             // 3
    optional selector as nullable function        // 4
) as list                                         // 5
```

Note that:

1. The first argument defines the first value of the list.
2. The second argument is a condition function that must return a TRUE value for the function to keep running and generate the next value. When the condition returns FALSE, it stops executing.
3. The third argument is a function that defines the logic for generating each value of the list.
4. The fourth argument is optional but can be very handy if we want to modify each value of the list that is being generated.
5. The as list at the end means this function will always produce a list as output.

Notice a few things in the syntax:

- Every argument is a function.
- That means for each argument, we'll either declare an explicit function or use each `_`. (I'll explain the nuances of this in the upcoming examples.)
- The most interesting part: The `List.Generate` function produces a list, and the values of the list can be numbers, text, or even structured values like lists, tables, or records. It may seem like an out-of-reach concept for now, but this is what makes the function truly {M}agical. We'll explore a complex example of this a bit.

Example 1: Generating Even Numbers with List.Generate

Refer to the query ListUntil20.

Let's say we'd like to generate a list of even numbers from 0 to 20. In this scenario, `List.Generate` will look like this:

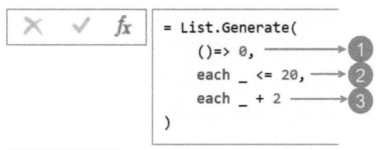

```
         X    ✓    fx     = List.Generate(
                              ()=> 0, ─────────► 1
                              each _ <= 20, ───► 2
                              each _ + 2 ──────► 3
                          )
```

	List
1	0
2	2
3	4
4	6
5	8
6	10
7	12
8	14
9	16
10	18
11	20

Figure 7-52 *Using* `List.Generate` *to generate a list of even numbers from 0 to 20.*

In this example, we've only used the first three mandatory arguments of the function. Let's look at each of them:

1. **()=> 0:** Since the first argument must be declared as a function, we create an empty function (like this: `()=>`) and pass the fixed value `0`. This simply means the starting value of the list is `0`. You might be tempted to use `each _` in the first argument (like this: `each _ = 0`), but this is not acceptable. **You must declare an explicit function as the first argument.**

2. **each _ <= 20:** The second argument is the condition that says when to stop generating the list. For now, we've used `each _`, but you can instead use an explicit function (e.g., `(val) => val <= 20`).

3. **each _ + 2:** The third argument is self-explanatory, but I'll be explicit in telling you that `each _` in this case does not mean the current value of the list; rather, it means the previous value (already generated), so you're adding 2 to the previous value. This can also be written as an explicit function, like this: `(PreviousValue) => PreviousValue + 2`. If you haven't noticed it, yes, you can declare different variable names for the explicit functions in the second and third arguments.

That was a lot of text. Now take a look at how this function will be executed:

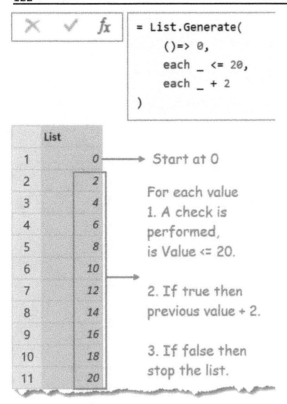

```
= List.Generate(
    ()=> 0,
    each _ <= 20,
    each _ + 2
)
```

Start at 0

For each value
1. A check is performed,
is Value <= 20.

2. If true then previous value + 2.

3. If false then stop the list.

Figure 7-53 *Workings of the* `List.Generate` *function.*

For the sake of satisfying your curiosity, I want to point out that we can do the same thing by using explicit functions in the second and third arguments. Here is how it looks:

```
= List.Generate(
    ()=> 0,
    (val) => val <= 20,
    (PreviousValue) => PreviousValue + 2
)
```

	List
1	0
2	2
3	4
4	6
5	8
6	10
7	12
8	14
9	16
10	18
11	20

Figure 7-54 *Using* `List.Generate` *with explicit functions as arguments.*

Example 2: Generating a List of Dates Until Today with List.Generate

Refer to the query ListUntilToday.

As a slightly more useful example, say that we have to generate all dates between, for example, January 1, 2024 and today (i.e., April 2, 2024, at this writing 😊). The `List.Generate` function in this case would look like this:

```
= List.Generate(
    () => #date(2024, 1, 1),
    each _ <= Date.From(DateTime.LocalNow()),
    each Date.AddDays(_, 1)
)
```

	List
1	01-01-2024
2	02-01-2024
3	03-01-2024
4	04-01-2024
5	05-01-2024
6	06-01-2024
7	07-01-2024
8	08-01-2024

Figure 7-55 *Using* `List.Generate` *to generate dates until today.*

A few notes:

- The first argument is a static date created using `#date` (with year, month, and the day number as three arguments).
- The second argument checks whether each date is less than or equal to today's date. Notice the use of the `DateTime.LocalNow()` function, which returns today's date as a `datetime` data type. To have a date being compared to a date, we further wrap it in the `Date.From` function, which returns a date value instead of a `datetime` value.
- In the third argument, we're adding 1 day to the previous date by using the `Date.AddDays` function.

While this example does provide a bit more clarity about `List.Generate`, it's rare that you'll ever produce a list like this. To increase the utility of `List.Generate`, consider this table in the Changed Type step of the query:

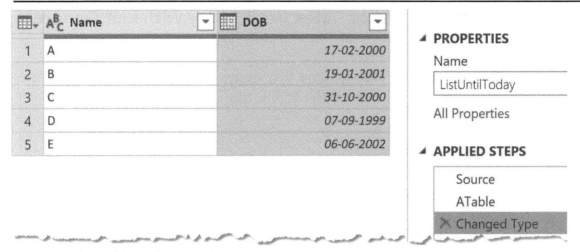

Figure 7-56 *A table with two columns.*

How about adding a new column to this table that can list all the dates in between the DOB (date of birth) date and today's date?

Let's start by creating a new custom column with the following code:

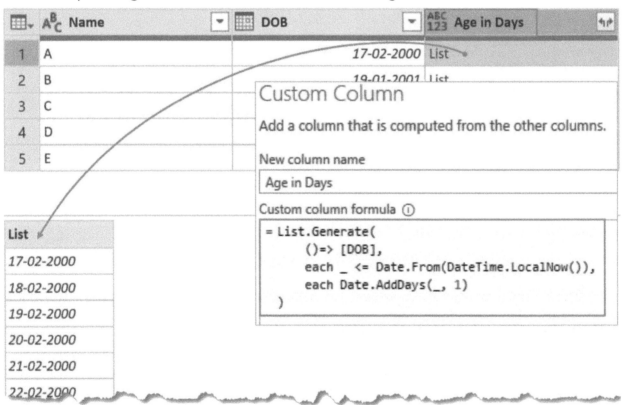

Figure 7-57 *Using* `List.Generate` *to create a list of dates until today.*

If you compare the code in the custom column and the code in Figure 7-55, you see that very little has changed. Perhaps the only thing that has changed is the reference to the DOB column instead of the hard-coded date.

As expected, this produces a dynamic list of dates between the DOB and today. At this point, we can just count the items in the list by wrapping the existing function in `List.Count`, like this:

	Name	DOB	Age in Days
1	A	17-02-2000	8812
2	B	19-01-2001	8475
3	C		
4	D		
5	E		

Custom Column

Add a column that is computed from the other columns.

New column name

Age in Days

Custom column formula ⓘ

```
= List.Count(
      List.Generate(
            ()=> [DOB],
            each _ <= Date.From(DateTime.LocalNow()),
            each Date.AddDays(_, 1)
      )
)
```

Figure 7-58 *The column now shows the count of days.*

> **Note:** This code returns the age in days. I used this example to demonstrate the use of `List.Generate`, but the same output can be achieved by using this simple custom column formula:
> ```
> =Duration.Days(Date.From(DateTime.LocalNow()) - [DOB]) + 1
> ```
> There is even a UI option available: Select the DOB column → Add Column → Date → Age. You'll need to add 1 to the resulting value to ensure that both the DOB and today's date are included in the count.

Example 3: Listing Completed Months Between Start and End Dates with List.Generate

Refer to the query ListMonths.

Now let's consider an example that goes a bit further. In this case, we have a table with three columns: Company, Purchase Date, and Selling Date.

	Company	Purchase Date	Selling Date
1	MSFT	20-11-2023	01-01-2024
2	GOOG	15-01-2024	15-03-2024
3	AMZN	01-10-2023	10-02-2024
4	AAPL	08-09-2022	02-04-2024
5	NVDA	06-06-2023	10-01-2024

Figure 7-59 *A table with three columns.*

We'd like to expand this table and add all the completed months between the purchase date and the selling date. The expected output looks like this:

#	Company	Purchase Date	Selling Date	Months
1	MSFT	20-11-2023	01-01-2024	20-11-2023
2	MSFT	20-11-2023	01-01-2024	20-12-2023
3	GOOG	15-01-2024	15-03-2024	15-01-2024
4	GOOG	15-01-2024	15-03-2024	15-02-2024
5	GOOG	15-01-2024	15-03-2024	15-03-2024
6	AMZN	01-10-2023	10-02-2024	01-10-2023
7	AMZN	01-10-2023	10-02-2024	01-11-2023
8	AMZN	01-10-2023	10-02-2024	01-12-2023
9	AMZN	01-10-2023	10-02-2024	01-01-2024
10	AMZN	01-10-2023	10-02-2024	01-02-2024
11	AAPL	08-09-2022	02-04-2024	08-09-2022
12	AAPL	08-09-2022	02-04-2024	08-10-2022
13	AAPL	08-09-2022	02-04-2024	08-11-2022

Figure 7-60 *The new Months column shows the completed months.*

To explain the output a bit:

- For MSFT, the purchase date is 20-Nov-2023, and there is one completed month between the purchase date and the selling date (i.e., 20-Dec-2023), so we get two rows generated for MSFT.
- Similarly, for GOOG, we have three rows generated. The purchase date is 15-Jan-2024, and we have two completed months after that.

A rough version of the List.Generate function to solve this problem would look like this:

```
// Create a new column with the following Logic
= List.Generate(
    Start with: Purchase and Selling Date,
    Condition: Purchase Date <= Selling Date,
    Each Value Calculation : Purchase Date + 1 Month,
    Output : Incremented Purchase Dates by 1 Month
)
```

Let's start with creating a new column (Months) with the following List.Generate formula:

```
= List.Generate(
    () => [p = [Purchase Date], s = [Selling Date]],    // 1
    each [p] <= [s],                                     // 2
    each [p = Date.AddMonths([p], 1), s = [s]],         // 3
    each [p]                                             // 4
)
```

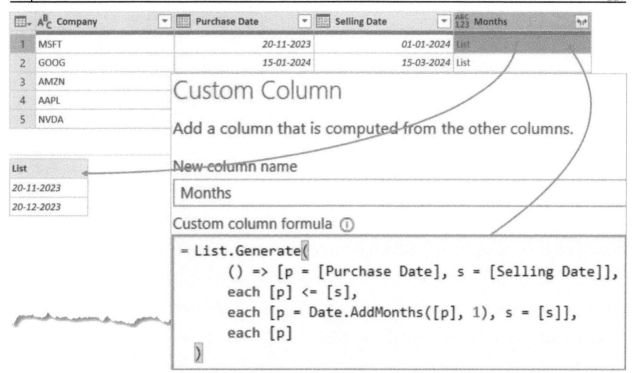

Figure 7-61 *Using* `List.Generate` *to create a list of dates.*

Yes, I know it looks a bit intimidating, but hear me out:

- **() => [p = [Purchase Date], s = [Selling Date]]:** We start off with a blank function for the starting value, but this time, rather than having text or a number, we create a record instead. Notice the use of square brackets ([ ]) to declare two fields:
  - **p = [Purchase Date]:** References the current row's purchase date value
  - **s = [Selling Date]:** References the current row's selling date value
- **each [p] <= [s]:** The condition that needs to be true to keep generating the list is [p] (i.e., purchase date) <= [s] (i.e., selling date).
- **each [p = Date.AddMonths([p], 1), s = [s]]:** The first thing to notice is the use of square brackets ([ ]) after the each keyword. Why do we do this? Since our starting point is a record with two columns, we can now only work with a record value to perform any transformation. So, it's like saying, from the record created in the first step:
  - **p = Date.AddMonths ([p], 1):** Go to column [p] and add one month to the previous purchase date by using the Date.AddMonths function.
  - **s = [s]:** This means there is no transformation done to the selling date, and we just want to refer to the previous selling date as is.

  Important: Since our first argument was a record with two columns, we must also define how the next value will be generated for both of those columns. Missing any of the columns defined in the first argument will result in an error.
- **each [p]:** This is an optional parameter that we haven't used so far. In this case, we are extracting the value of the column ([p]) from the record that contains two columns ([p] and [s]). If you skip this argument, the output will be a record (with two columns) in the list generated.

And that is it. Once the list has been generated, we can happily expand it and set the data types to get the final output, like this:

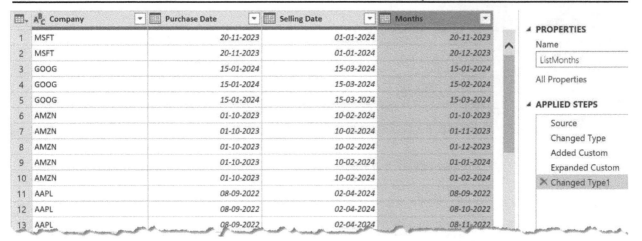

Figure 7-62 *The expanded table now contains the completed Months column.*

Exercises

Here are a few exercises to test your understanding. Ready?

> **Note:** Open the Excel file Looping Exercises - Unsolved in the Iteration folder and then use the Power Query Editor to work through these exercises.

Exercise 1: Use each _

Use each _ to transform each letter in the following list to uppercase.

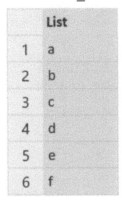

	List
1	a
2	b
3	c
4	d
5	e
6	f

Figure 7-63 *Transforming each letter to uppercase.*

Exercise 2: Use a Function

Use a function (and not each _) to add 10 to each value in the following list.

	List
1	2
2	4
3	6
4	8
5	10

Figure 7-64 *Using a function to add 10 to each value in the list.*

Exercise 3: Calculate a Factorial

Transform each value of the list on the left below into its factorial.

	List			List
1	1		1	1
2	2		2	2
3	3		3	6
4	4		4	24
5	5		5	120

List of 5 numbers   Factorial value for each number.

Figure 7-65 *Transforming each value as a factorial, with the expected output on the right.*

> **Note:** When you're done with these exercises, you can compare your answers against the ones I provide in the Solutions chapter at the end of this book or refer to the Excel file Looping Exercises - Solved or do both. 😄

Chapter 8: Custom Functions

Before I start throwing around fancier lingo, it's important that you understand what the heck a function really is. A function takes one or more inputs and transforms them into a single output. If we add the word "custom" before the word "function," we still have something that takes one or more inputs, but the transformation can be customized beyond the capabilities of the user interface.

Consider this native Power Query function: `Text.Proper("POWER QUERY")`. You already know that it capitalizes the first letter of each word and returns `Power Query` as output. Sometimes you need to accomplish something that isn't built in to Power Query as a native function. For such situations, welcome to this chapter on custom functions.

> **Note:** For this chapter, we'll be using the file Custom Functions.xlsx (which you'll find in the Custom Functions folder). As you work through this chapter, you'll be able to walk through the examples by using the queries provided in this file.

The Syntax

Refer to the query InputAsOutput.

When you're creating your own custom functions, you need to use a ridiculously simple syntax that involves using the "goes to" operator: => (which I often call the "rocket sign" because it looks like one, but let's not be swayed away by my imagination and call it what it is). 😄

Here is an example of a function that returns the input as output (i.e., it does nothing). In this case, we write the following M code in the Advanced Editor of a blank query.

Figure 8-1 *Creating a custom function in the Advanced Editor.*

Note a couple of syntactical things:

- We start by declaring a variable in parentheses: `(inputsomething)`
- Then we add the => operator, and everything after the operator becomes a function. In this case, we are just calling the same variable as output (although it would also be possible to use a complex multi-step query after the =>).

After creating the function, we can try it out by entering `Hello` and clicking Invoke:

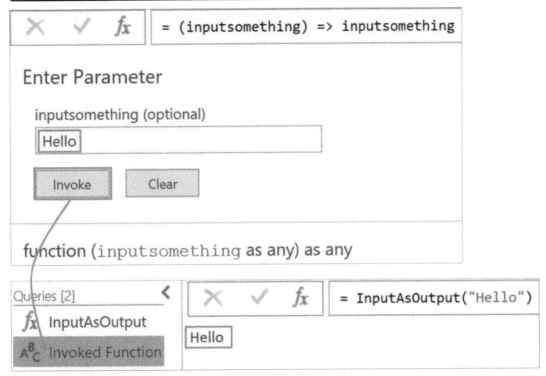

Figure 8-2 *Invoking the function.*

As you can see, a new query is created that returns the same `Hello` as output. This is nothing spectacular, and it's not especially useful, but it is your first custom function. Congratulations!

A few more details on the syntax:

- A function in the Power Query window is denoted by the fx symbol.
- You can declare as many variables as you'd like.
- You can also declare the type of a variable.
- If there are any optional variables, they come at the end.
- You can also declare the type of output for the function.
- You can also create nested functions.

In the following examples we'll create a few custom functions and explore these syntax details in action.

A Slightly Useful Function: Calculating PMT

Refer to the query Loans.

For this example, we have a few people with loans. For each one, we know the loan amount, rate, and tenure, and we need to calculate the annual installment payment.

	A^B_C Name	1²₃ Loan	% Rate	1²₃ Tenure Yrs
1	A	115000	6.01%	11
2	B	314000	3.65%	6
3	C	388000	4.50%	10
4	D	163000	6.95%	6
5	E	309000	4.31%	12
6	F	315000	5.54%	11

Figure 8-3 *A table with loan amounts, rates, and tenures.*

There's a slight hiccup: Excel has a =PMT function, but there is no such function in Power Query. This is a good place to create a custom function. I am sure you know it, but here is a quick rundown on the financial math (formula) we'll be using to create a PMT function:

$$P = \frac{Pv \times R}{1 - (1 + R)^{-n}}$$

$P = \frac{Pv \times R}{1-(1+R)^{-n}}$

Where:

- P is the payment amount.

- Pv is the present value (or principal amount).

- R is the interest rate per period.

- n is the number of periods.

Figure 8-4 *Formula for calculating PMT.*

To create a custom PMT function, we follow these steps:

1. Create a new blank query (Home → New Source → Other Sources → Blank Query).
2. Navigate to the Advanced Editor (View → Advanced Editor).
3. Replace the existing M code with the following code:

```
(PV, Rate, Tenure) =>
let
    PMT=(Rate * PV)/(1 - Number.Power(1 + Rate, - Tenure))
in
    PMT
```

Note that:

- The user input consists of three variables: PV (present value, or the loan amount), Rate (annual rate of interest), and Tenure (loan duration, in years).

- The => operator in the first row converts the query into a function, and the rest is simple math.

Once you click OK in the Advanced Editor, the query turns into a function. Here I have taken the liberty of renaming the function PMT:

Enter Parameters

PV (optional)

Rate (optional)

Tenure (optional)

[Invoke]   [Clear]

PROPERTIES

Name

PMT

All Properties

APPLIED STEPS

PMT

function (PV as any, Rate as any, Tenure as any) as any

Figure 8-5 *The PMT function.*

Let's head back to our Loans query and put this function to use. We can start by creating a new custom column (Add Column → Custom Column).

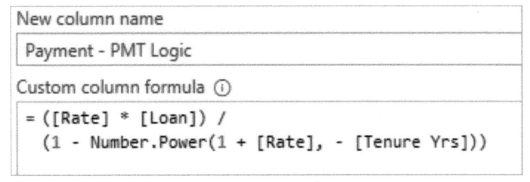

▼	1²₃ Tenure Yrs	▼	ABC 123 Payment	▼
6.01%	11		14588.64625	
3.65%	6		59218.48842	
4.50%	10		49034.98284	
6.95%	6		34143.94831	
4.31%	12		33519.54909	
5.54%	11		39005.48981	

PROPERTIES

Name

Loans

All Properties

APPLIED STEPS

Source

Changed Type

✕ Added Custom

New column name

Payment

Custom column formula ⓘ

`= PMT ( [Loan], [Rate], [Tenure Yrs] )`

Figure 8-6 *Creating a custom column to call the call PMT function.*

Note that:

- We name the custom column Payment.
- We use the custom function = PMT.
- As we type the parenthesis after the PMT function, Power Query prompts us with the variables that we declared: PV, Rate, and Tenure.
- So, the function looks like this:

```
= PMT ([Loan], [Rate], [Tenure Yrs])
```

- Once we commit this code, we get the periodic payment calculated as a new column.

You might argue that in this scenario, we could have instead written the PMT calculation logic directly in the custom column—something like this:

New column name

Payment - PMT Logic

Custom column formula ⓘ

```
= ([Rate] * [Loan]) /
  (1 - Number.Power(1 + [Rate], - [Tenure Yrs]))
```

Figure 8-7 *PMT calculation without the use of a function.*

This produces the same (correct) result, but it cannot be used as a plug-and-play solution, which means we'll have to rewrite this long formula again if we want to use it in any other query.

Important Note: At this writing, a custom function that you create is only available in Power Query in the current Excel/Power BI file and not globally across all Excel/Power BI files.

Practical Example 1: Calculating Fiscal Quarters

Refer to the query FiscalQuarter.

Let's say you have a few dates for which you want to find the appropriate fiscal quarter. In this example, the fiscal year starts in April and ends in March (of the next year). The output should look like this:

⊞	▦ Dates	dd/mm ▼	AᴮC Fiscal Quarter	▼
1		01-01-2020	Q4	
2		01-02-2020	Q4	
3		01-03-2020	Q4	
4		01-04-2020	Q1	
5		01-05-2020	Q1	
6		01-06-2020	Q1	
7		01-07-2020	Q2	
8		01-08-2020	Q2	
9		01-09-2020	Q2	
10		01-10-2020	Q3	
11		01-11-2020	Q3	
12		01-12-2020	Q3	
13		01-01-2021		

Figure 8-8 *Fiscal quarters for a year that starts in April and ends in March.*

While we're at it, let's ensure that the function is dynamic, making it possible to adjust the start of the fiscal year so that anyone with a different fiscal year (let's say July to June) can use the same function with a little tweak.

The Logic to Solve This Problem

Consider this intermediate query as an attempt to build some logic:

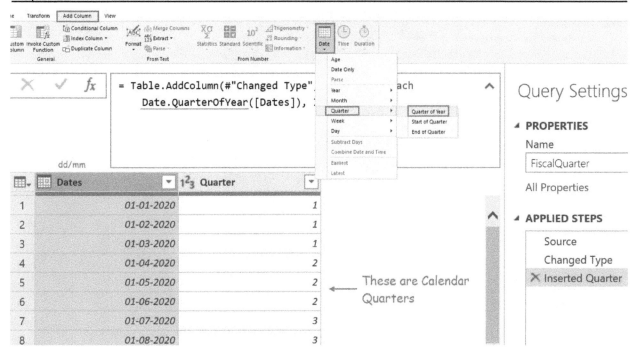

Figure 8-9 *Using the Power Query UI to calculate calendar quarters.*

Note that:

- We have month start dates, and we use them to calculate calendar quarters (Add Column → Date → Quarter → Quarter of Year).

- We also use the function `Date.QuarterofYear`, which we can use later when creating our custom function.

Unfortunately, this produces calendar quarters. Here is a possible solution to transform this output into fiscal quarters:

1. In our case, the fiscal year starts in April, after three months (January, February, and March) have passed. To allow for this delay, we can push the date back by three months. So, for example, the date April 20 will become January 20, January 15 will become October 15, and so on. We just go back three months. Simple.

2. We can use the `Date.QuarterofYear` function to find the quarter of the three-month delayed date. So:

   - April 20, which is now January 20, is in Q1.

   - January 15, which is now October 15, is Q4.

If we were to implement this formula as a new column in our query, the M code would look like this:

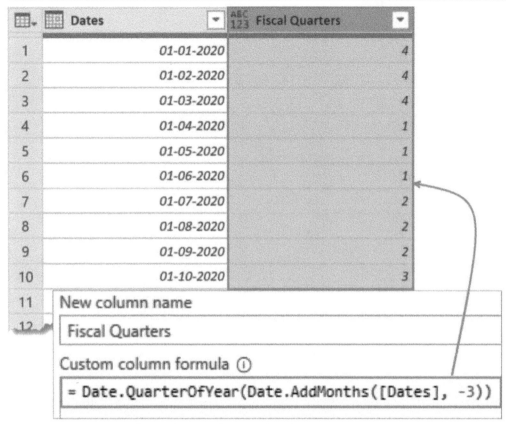

Figure 8-10 *Using a formula to calculate fiscal quarters.*

The formula seems to be working, but there are two more problems:

- There should ideally be a Q prefix before each quarter number.
- We should be able to change the start of the fiscal year, which currently is static (i.e., April).

Creating a Custom Function

To make our solution scalable and easy to use, let's put together a custom function:

1. Create a blank query (Home → New Source → Other Sources → Blank Query).
2. Navigate to the Advanced Editor (View → Advanced Editor).
3. Write the following M code and then click Done:

```
1   (Dates as date, optional #"Year End Month Num" as number) as text =>
2   let
3       YearEndingMonth =
4           if #"Year End Month Num" = null
5           then 12
6           else #"Year End Month Num",
7       Qtr = "Q" & Text.From ( Date.QuarterOfYear (
8               Date.AddMonths(Dates, - YearEndingMonth ) ) )
9   in
10      Qtr
```

Figure 8-11 *A custom function for calculating fiscal quarters.*

Notes:

- Notice the syntax used for the two variables (in row 1):
    - The `Dates` variable should only accept the date data type as input.
    - `#"Year End Month Num"` is optional and therefore is prefixed with the `optional` keyword, but if it is used, the data type should be a number.
    - Also notice that the entire function will return the output as a text data type.
- The M code is not far from the logic we built earlier, but to make the function robust, we've made a couple of tweaks:
    - The `if` function sets the month ending number to 12 (i.e., December) in case the user doesn't input a value.

> **Tip:** Our code in lines 3 to 6 could've been made shorter by replacing the `if` with a coalesce operator (`??`), like this:
>
> `YearEndingMonth = #"Year End Month Num" ?? 12`
>
> But for now, let's roll with the standard `if` statement. I'll share more about the coalesce operator later in the book.

    - A little "Q" concatenation will make the output a lot more presentable (e.g., Q1 or Q2).

We can name this function `FQ`. It looks like this in my Power Query window:

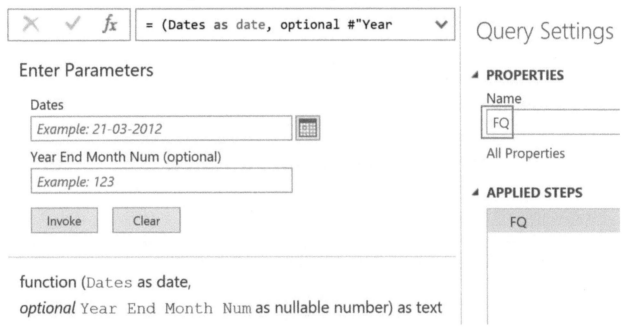

Figure 8-12 *The `FQ` custom function in Power Query.*

Using the Custom Function

Refer to the query FiscalQuarter.

Let's create a new custom column so we can use put our `FQ` function to use. In the Custom Column box, we can write the M code like this:

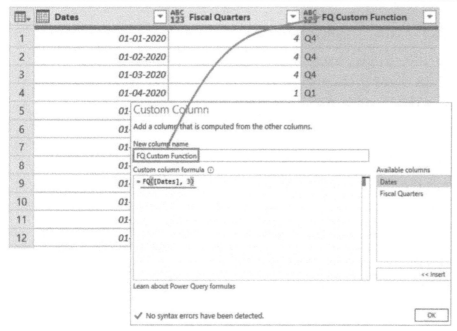

Figure 8-13 *Custom function used to calculate fiscal quarters.*

Notice that:

- All the logic that we built is packed into a neat and tidy `FQ` function that takes two input parameters: `Dates` and `Year End Month Num`.

- The user will have a far easier and better experience using this function than writing the M code (refer to Figure 8-10).

- The parameter `Year End Month Num` could be omitted, but if it were, the function would calculate the regular calendar quarter (January to December) rather than allowing the user to tweak the fiscal year start month.

Practical Example 2: A Custom Function Like Excel's TRIM

Refer to the query Names.

Excel's `TRIM` is awesome. It can remove not only leading and trailing spaces but also any extra spaces within a string while retaining one space between two words. Consider this example:

Figure 8-14 *Excel's TRIM function in action.*

The Excel `TRIM` function removed all leading, trailing, and extra in-between spaces from the names in this example, leaving one standard space between each pair of words.

This is not how Power Query works. If we select the Names column and add a new column (Add Column → Format → Trim), unfortunately Power Query can only remove leading and trailing spaces and not the extra spaces in between words.

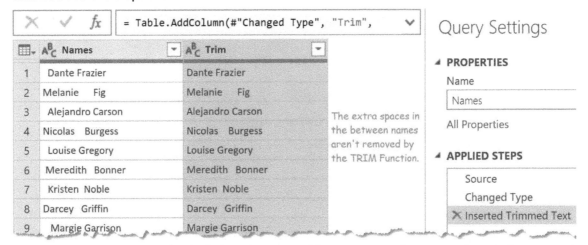

Figure 8-15 *Power Query's `Trim` function is unable to remove the spaces from in between the words.*

It's time to roll up our sleeves and make a custom function that behaves like Excel's `TRIM` function.

The Logic to Solve This Problem

Here is a three-step method to solve this problem:

1. Split the text string into multiple words based on the space delimiter and return a list of words.
2. Remove all the blanks from the list, keeping only the words.
3. Combine the list of words so there is one standard space between each pair.

Splitting by the Space Delimiter

Instead of jumping to create a function right at the start, let's solve this problem by writing a bit of M code to mimic Excel's `TRIM` function and then translate that into a custom function.

We can start by modifying the code in the Trim custom column to split based on a space delimiter, like this:

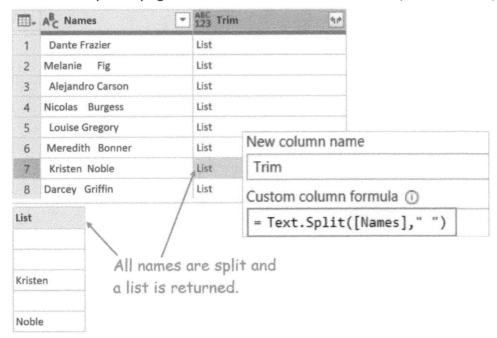

Figure 8-16 *The names are split by the space delimiter, and the output is a list.*

From this list we can remove the blank values (which resulted from the split at each occurrence of the space) by using the `List.Select` function, like this:

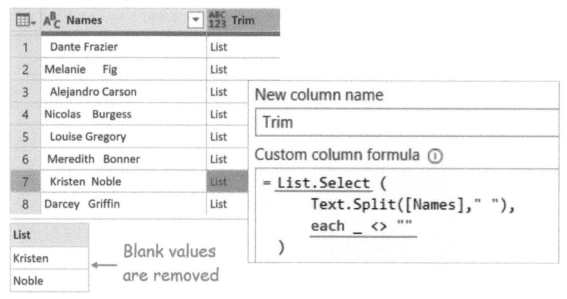

Figure 8-17 *List.Select selects only the non-blank values from the list.*

Let's take a closer look at this code (so we can feed Power Query what it eats!):

```
= List.Select(
    list as list,              // 1
    selection as function      // 2
) as list
```

Note that:

1. In our code in Figure 8-16, `Text.Split ([Names], " ")` returns a list, and therefore it fits perfectly in the first argument of the `List.Select` function.

2. As a second argument, for each value of the list, we are performing a simple check to filter out values that are not equal to a blank (i.e., `each _ <> ""`).

As the last part of our logic, let's insert a standard space between the words. To do that, we use a text-combining function, like this:

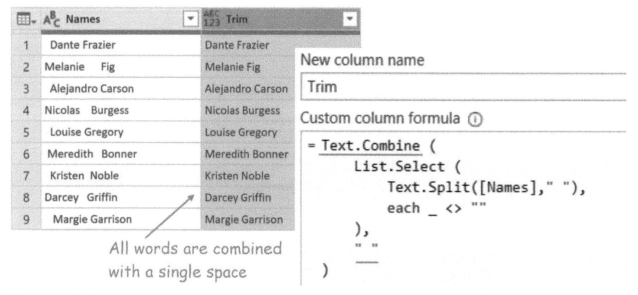

Figure 8-18 *The text of each name is combined, with one standard space in between.*

Again, it's worth noticing that we are feeding Power Query what it eats:

```
= Text.Combine(
    texts as list,                              // 1
    optional separator as nullable text         // 2
) as text                                       // 3
```

Note that:

1. `Text.Combine` accepts a list in the first argument, and that is the output of the `List.Select` function, which makes it a nice fit.

2. As the second argument, the delimiter is a space (as a text input).

3. The final output is a text value.

Creating a Function

So far, we've written the following custom column code to solve the problem:

```
= Text.Combine (
    List.Select (
        Text.Split([Names]," "),
        each _ <> ""
    ),
    " "
)
```

But this code isn't a function yet. Let's make a new query (Home → New Source → Other Sources → Blank Query) and modify our existing M code to transform it into a function.

Consider this code in the Advanced Editor of our new query (renamed ExcelTrim):

ExcelTrim ⟶ Renamed the function Query

```
1    ( InputText as text ) =>
2    Text.Combine(
3        List.Select(
4            Text.Split(InputText, " "),
5            each _ <> ""
6        ),
7        " "
8    ) as text
```

Figure 8-19 *Creating a custom function as a new query.*

Notice the subtle changes that we've made:

- In row 1, the code starts with a variable (i.e., `InputText`) to prompt the user to input a text value.

- In row 4, the `Text.Trim` function now references the `InputText` variable.

- In row 8, the function output type is `text`.

Calling the Function

Refer to the query Names.

Let's put the function to use in our Names query. We can start off by creating a custom column (Add Column → Custom Column) and calling the function with the Names column as input, like this:

Figure 8-20 *Calling the* `ExcelTrim` *custom function.*

And it works!

Scaling Our Custom Function

Refer to the query NamesAddress.

If you were to apply a trim to multiple columns in a query, would you be creating multiple custom columns?

In this query, we have three columns, two of which have junk spaces:

Both the Names and Address Columns have junk spaces

Figure 8-21 *Two columns containing junk spaces.*

Let's bulk transform the Names and Address columns. We can do this by using the `Table.TransformColumns` function. But first, let's get some help from the UI so we can understand how the `Table.TransformColumns` function works.

We can select the two columns Names and Address → right-click → Transform → Trim. This generates a new step that uses the `Table.TransformColumns` function. Nice!

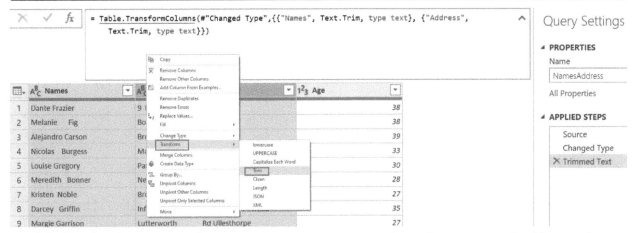

Figure 8-22 *Using Transform → Trim in the UI to trim spaces from the Names and Address columns.*

The trim transformation here is useless because we have already created our own custom function, but this gives us a head start so we can see the `Table.TransformColumns` function in action.

Let's dive into the `Table.TransformColumns` function a bit:

```
= Table.TransformColumns(
    #"Changed Type,                           // 1
    {                                         // 2
        {"Names", Text.Trim, type text},      // 3
        {"Address", Text.Trim, type text}
    }
)
```

Note that:

1. The first argument is the table from the previous step.

2. In the second argument, all column transformations are packed into a list.

3. Each column transformation is a nested list with three arguments: column name, function used, and data type.

It is very very important to note that the syntax used for creating multiple column transformations is a nested list. Whatever M code we write needs to return a dynamic nested list with three parts:

*   The column name as a text value

*   The function (which is where we can use our custom function)

*   The data type applied to the column (which we'll add even though it is not a mandatory input)

The next part is so crucial that I've decided to take you on a short detour and revisit a few concepts from the previous chapter. Ready?

> Refer to the query TransformationList.

Take a close look at the following M code. It's nothing significant so far. We have a list with two text strings, and we return the same values as output.

Figure 8-23 *Using* `List.Transform` *to return the input values as output.*

Recall that to make our `Table.TransformColumns` function work, we need to produce a nested list with three parts: column name, function, and data type (refer to Figure 8-22). Let's make a small tweak in our code to produce a nested list structure:

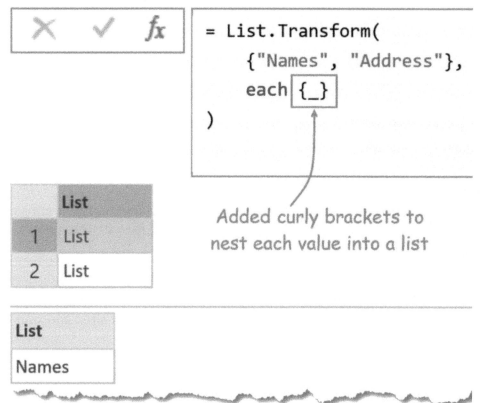

Figure 8-24 *Wrapping the _ in curly brackets creates a nested list structure.*

So far, we have one item on the list, and we need to add two more: the function and the data type. Let's edit the code a bit more:

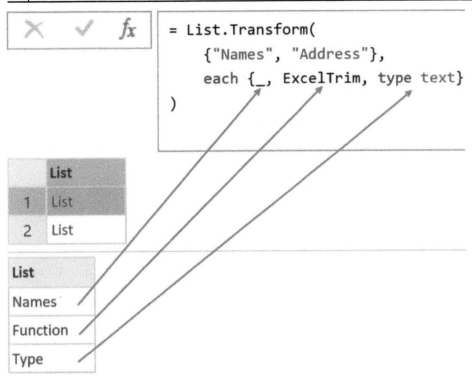

Figure 8-25 *A nested list with names, function, and data type.*

Refer to the query NamesAddress.

Well, now that we have our syntax right, the only logical thing left to do is to replace the part of the old `ExcelTrim` function with our modified code in the NamesAddress query.

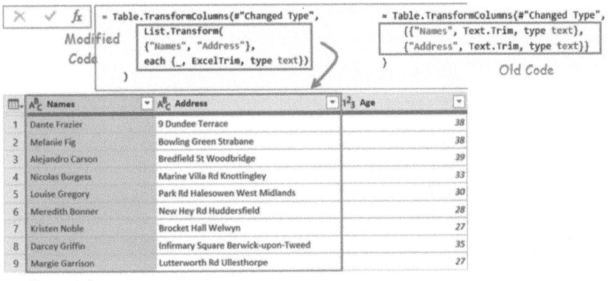

Figure 8-26 *Replacing the old code with the modified code.*

> **Gotcha!** 😐 There's a slight catch. Although it's a small problem, it's worth noting that the code isn't fully dynamic yet because the names of the columns are still hard-coded: `{"Names","Address"}`. Power Query wouldn't know which columns to apply the `ExcelTrim` function to without a pattern to identify column names with extra spaces or without a user's input of a list of such columns.

Exercises

Here are a few exercises to test your understanding. Ready?

Note: Open the Excel file Custom Functions Exercises - Unsolved in the Custom Functions folder and then use the Power Query Editor to work through these exercises.

Exercise 1: Use the Fiscal Year Function

Consider this table with dates (in dd-mm-yyyy format). Write a custom function to calculate fiscal year (from April to March) for each date value.

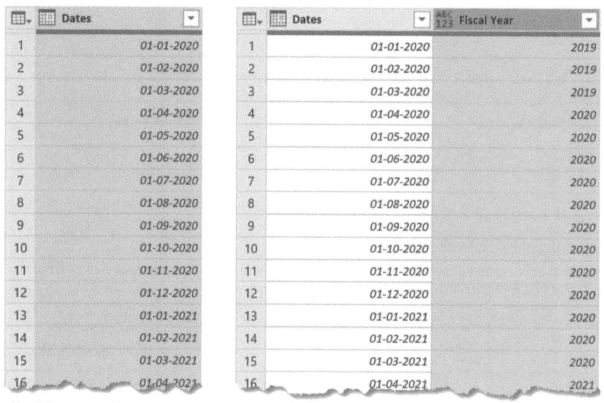

Table with Dates   Fiscal year added

Figure 8-27 *A table with dates and the expected output on the right.*

Keep in mind that the user should be able to change the fiscal year if needed.

Exercise 2: Remove Null Columns

The table below has a few null columns. Write a dynamic custom function to remove the null columns.

	Letter	Column1	Value	Blank
1	A	null	10	null
2	B	null	20	null
3	C	null	30	null
4	D	null	40	null
5	E	null	50	null

Figure 8-28 *The table contains null columns that are to be removed.*

The custom function should accept table input and remove all columns that contain only null values.

Note: When you're done with these exercises, you can compare your answers against the ones I provide in the Solutions chapter at the end of this book or refer to the Excel file Custom Functions Exercises - Solved or do both. 😄

Chapter 9: Errors

Errors are a way for computer applications to talk to you (at least until the time computers can literally talk, as we do). Unfortunately, errors in Power Query are nasty, just as they are in most other programming languages. They always make me say out loud, "What now??"

In this little chapter, we'll explore interesting ways to handle and possibly capture errors. You ready?

> **Note:** For this chapter, we'll be using the file Errors.xlsx (which you'll find in the Errors folder). As you work through this chapter, you'll be able to walk through the examples by using the queries provided in this file.

Row-Level and Step-Level Errors

Refer to the queries StepError and RowError.

There are two places where an error can occur in Power Query: at the step level or at the row level. Let's look at both.

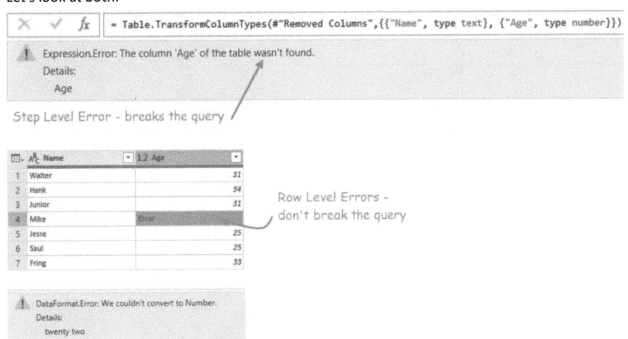

Figure 9-1 *Step-level (StepError query) and row-level (RowError query) errors.*

I am sure you've experienced this type of pain several times. There are two key things to keep in mind:

- A step-level error breaks further execution of the query.
- A row-level error is contained at the row level and generally doesn't break the query.

IFERROR in Power Query: try and otherwise

Everyone frets about errors, but let's try to handle them—literally "try." I mean, the keywords used to handle errors are `try` and `otherwise`. 😶 They work a lot like Excel's `IFERROR` function.

Here's how you write a `try...otherwise`:

```
= try a function or a value
  otherwise a function or a value
```

Note that:

- Both `try` and `otherwise` are written in all lowercase.
- After the `try` keyword, you can write a function or a value, and if it returns an error, the input after the `otherwise` keyword is returned.

Let's look at a few examples.

Example 1: Mitigating Row-Level Errors

Refer to the query TryOtherwise.

Consider this simple table, which has inconsistent data in the Units column and where we'd like to add a Cost Per Unit column (i.e., Cost / Units) like the one shown on the right:

	Shift	Units	Cost		Cost Per Unit
1	A	25	1430		57.2
2	B	25	1750		70
3	C	10	1100		110
4	E	35	1050		30
5	F	Nil	1300		null
6	G	20	1630		81.5

Existing Table   New Column to be added

Figure 9-2 *A table with three columns and the soon-to-be-added Cost Per Unit column.*

The only challenge is that the formula in row 5 (= `1300 / Nil`) is going to return an error, and we would rather show a null value than an error. To handle the error, let's use `try` and `otherwise`:

1. Add a new column(Add Column → Custom Column).
2. Name the new column Cost Per Unit.
3. Write the following formula, which uses `try...otherwise`, and click OK:

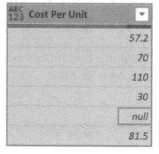

New column name

Cost Per Unit

Custom column formula ⓘ

```
= try [Cost]/[Units] otherwise null
```

Figure 9-3 *Using* `try` *and* `otherwise`.

Now, any value that returns an error will be replaced with a null value.

Example 2: Mitigating Step-Level Errors

Refer to the query TryOtherwise.

Consider this step error in the same query, where we can see that the query broke because the Cost Per Unit column wasn't found:

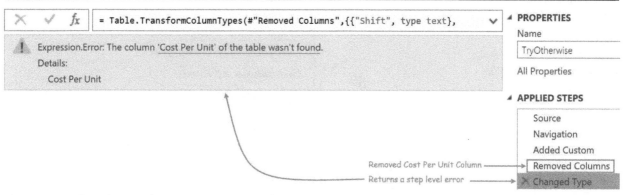

Figure 9-4 *The Changed Type step returned an error.*

A patchy solution to this problem would look like this:

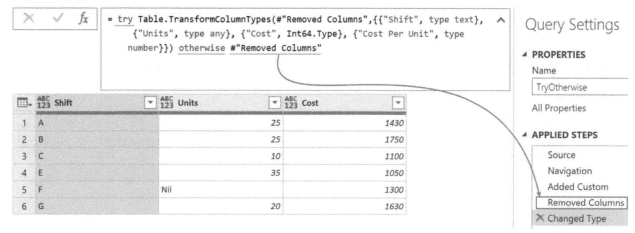

Figure 9-5 *Using* `try` *and* `otherwise` *in a step.*

Here we have the existing formula between the `try` and `otherwise` keywords and reference the previous step (i.e., `#"Removed Columns"`) in case the step returns any errors.

Although the query starts to work again, there are a couple caveats to keep in mind with this approach:

- When an error occurs, the query no longer applies correct data types because it is referring to the previous step.

- This means any further steps that rely on the output of the Changed Type step might break.

  Note: You're probably thinking that this is like a bandage that doesn't heal but merely covers the wound. My intention with this example is to show you that the `try...otherwise` keywords can also be used with step-level errors.

Query Termination by Errors

Let me start this concept by saying that you cannot work on top of errors in Power Query. I'll say the same thing a bit more technically toward the end of the section, but for now, look at this semi-entertaining meme between Mr. User and Mr. Try. Read it carefully!

Figure 9-6 *Some code snippets that explain the chat between Mr. User and Mr. Try.*

Refer to the query TryOnErrors.

First, let's consider what's happening in Scene 1. As soon as the `Table.TransformColumns` function encounters an existing error (from the Changed Type step), it doesn't trigger the `try` keyword but simply terminates, retaining the error as is.

```
= Table.TransformColumns(
        #"Changed Type",
        {"Column", each try Number.From(_) otherwise 0}
    )
```

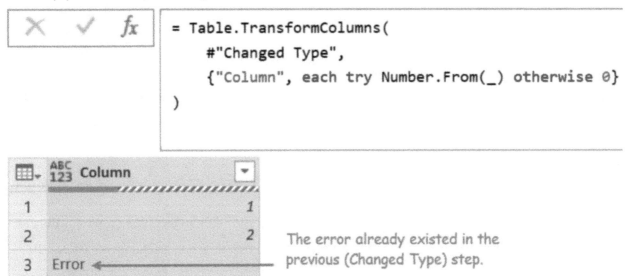

The error already existed in the previous (Changed Type) step.

Figure 9-7 *Using the `try` keyword on the Changed Type step, which already contained an error.*

Now let's look at what's happening in Scene 2. If we instead use the `Table.TransformColumns` function on the Source step (which doesn't contain errors), the `try` keyword evaluates and replaces the error with 0. This is because the error occurred during the evaluation and did not exist before the evaluation started.

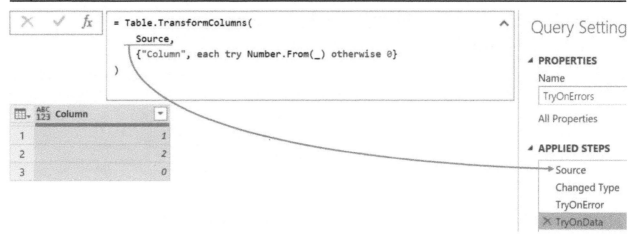

Figure 9-8 *Using the* `try` *keyword on the Source step, which is error free.*

In summary, `try` cannot transform existing errors. In other words, an error has to happen after the `try` keyword and not before (e.g., in the previous step). However, there are two subtleties that I'll leave you with:

- We could also use the `Table.ReplaceErrorValues` function (or right-click and select Replace Errors) to replace each error with a 0. This function is perfectly capable of replacing existing errors (as in Scene 1), but I wanted to show pitfalls of using the `try` keyword.

- The `try` keyword works perfectly when used in a new column that is trying to evaluate the column with errors. Consider this new column, for instance:

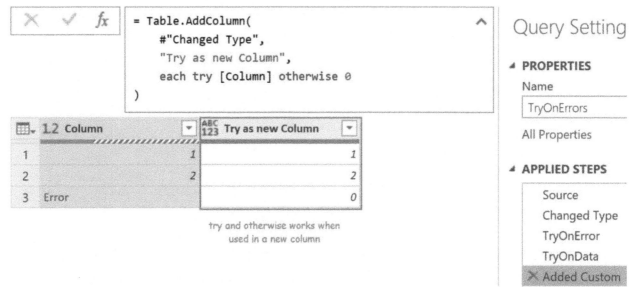

Figure 9-9 *Using* `try` *in a new column.*

Why? The `Table.AddColumn` function doesn't see an existing error in the new column being created, so it genuinely tries to evaluate the column with errors, and `try` works as expected.

Using Only try

Have you ever caught yourself or people around you "shooing" away errors by clicking OK or Cancel impulsively? Yeah, you know what I am talking about.

By popping errors on the screen, Power Query is trying to talk to you. I know the language it uses isn't human, but until Excel is able to speak in some other way, errors are an important way to help you understand what's going on. On that note, let's catch some errors.

Exploring try (Without otherwise)

Refer to the query Try.

You have already seen the keyword `try` used with `otherwise`, but `try` can also be used without `otherwise` to catch errors. You can see that this query has errors in the Cost Per Unit column (Cost / Units):

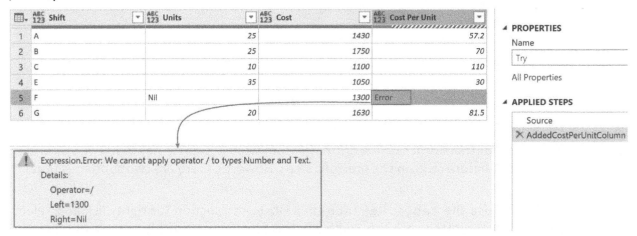

Figure 9-10 *One of the values shows an error in the Cost Per Unit column.*

Previously, we used `try` and `otherwise` to take an else action in the event of an error, but how do we capture and report the error itself? We can use the `try` keyword without `otherwise`.

As you can see here, if we precede the exiting Cost Per Unit column formula with only the `try` keyword, it results in a record:

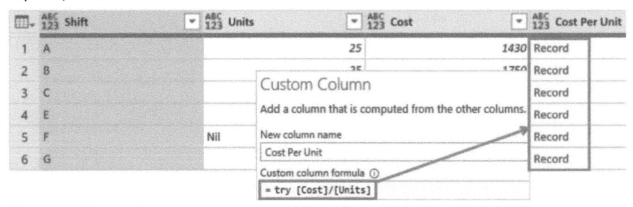

Figure 9-11 *The* `try` *keyword returns a record for each row of the Cost Per Unit column.*

Further peeking into a record, we can see that it has either one of the two field/value pairs:

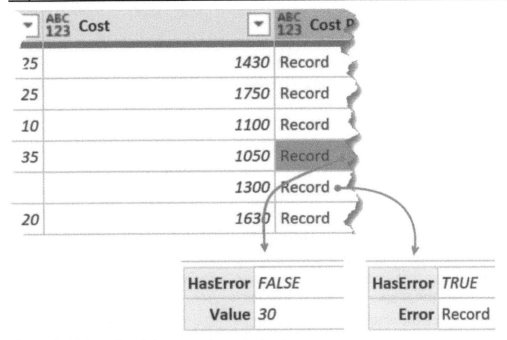

Figure 9-12 *Details of the record created using* `try`.

For rows that have errors:

- The `HasError` field shows TRUE because it returns an error.
- The Error field has a record containing the details of the error.

For rows that don't have errors:

- The `HasError` field shows FALSE because no errors were found.
- The Value field shows the evaluated output.

The rows that don't contain the errors aren't as enticing, so let's click on the record that contains the error to see what's inside.

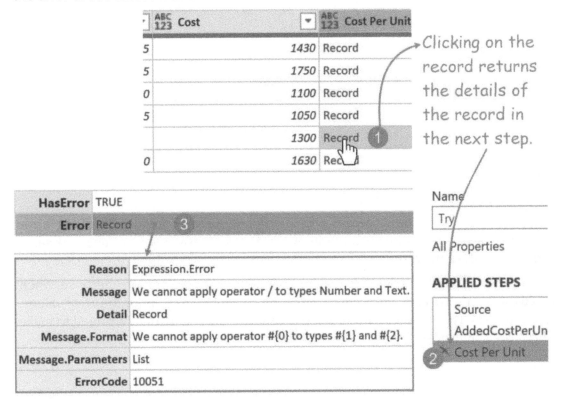

Figure 9-13 *Exploring the record containing the error.*

Note that:

1. We click on the erroneous record (with Nil in the Units column) to drill into the record.
2. A new step, Cost Per Unit, is created with the details of that record.
3. The record shows that the error is made up of five fields. This is always the case, as an error is made up of these fields:
   - **Reason:** Displays the reason for the error.
   - **Message:** Displays a semi-friendly message about the error.
   - **Detail:** Displays the values that produced the error as a record.
   - **Message.Format:** Displays the error message.
   - **Message.Parameters:** Contains a few parameters (as a list) that are inserted into the Message.Format field.

I know this is quite a bit to digest. It's time to close our exploration loop.

If we compare the error message that we typically see in Power Query with the error record details, we find that they are precisely the same—and that is how these error messages are created.

This image will help you visualize the errors:

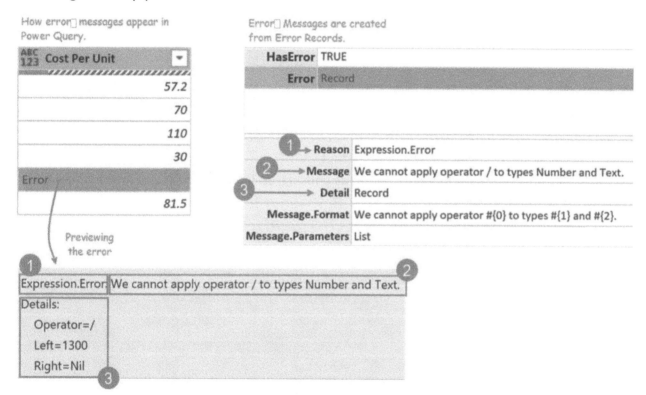

Figure 9-14 *Error messages are made from error records.*

An error message is made from an error record, which holds three key components of the error message: reason, message (which in turn is made of the fields Message.Format and Message. Parameter), and the details of the error.

Big question: So why did we "try" (pun intended) all this hassle of error exploration? Because, when you close and load the query, the error messages vanish, and you get blank cells for the error values. Wouldn't it be nice to capture what these errors are and report them? To do that, we need to make our formula a bit more sophisticated. Let's add a new step and reference it back to Source.

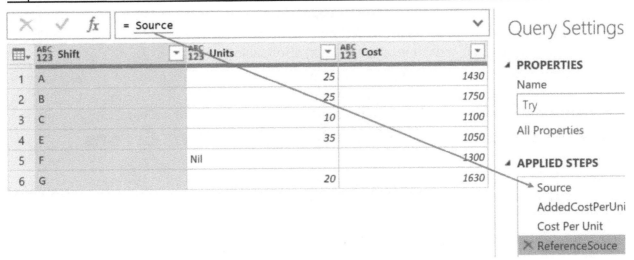

Figure 9-15 *Adding a new step and referencing it back to Source.*

Next, we create a new custom column (Add Column → Custom Column) and use the `try` keyword a bit differently this time. Here is the code:

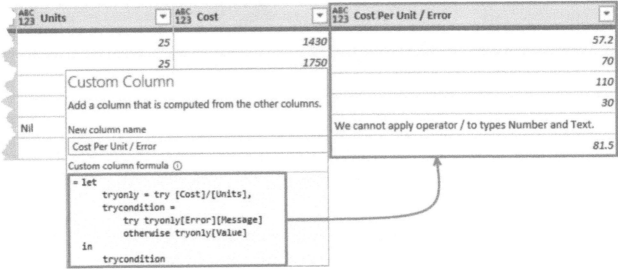

Figure 9-16 *Using* `try` *to extract the error message and otherwise return the value.*

We've used two steps in the `let...in` keywords in the custom column:

1. In the first step, `tryonly`, we evaluate a record that may or may not contain an error. (Recall our use of `try` in Figure 9-11.)

2. In the second step, `trycondition`, we use `try` to extract the error message; otherwise, we display the value calculated:

   - If there is an error, the step `tryonly` creates a record with the Error field. The Error field also contains a record where one of the five fields is Message (refer to Figures 9-12 and 9-13).

   - If there is no error, `tryonly` has a field named Value, which contains the value calculated.

	Shift	Units	Cost	Cost Per Unit / Error
1	A		25	1430	57.2
2	B		25	1750	70
3	C		10	1100	110
4	E		35	1050	30
5	F	Nil		1300	We cannot apply operator / to types Number and Text.
6	G		20	1630	81.5

Figure 9-17 *The Cost Per Unit / Error column shows either the error message (as text) or the value.*

Although it looks awesome, this isn't going to be very helpful because the column contains both the error message (as text) and numbers, and a simple Changed Type step would break it. In addition, any aggregations (like sum, max, min, average, etc.) also wouldn't work.

We keep hitting points where I'm sure you want more. Here again, I am going to ask you to read further. 😄 In the forthcoming chapters, I provide elaborate examples of capturing and reporting errors not just from one column but dynamically from all the columns of a table. Stay with me.

try and catch: An Easier Way to Capture Errors

Refer to the query Try&Catch.

One of the recent additions to the M language is the `catch` keyword, which makes it a tad bit easier to capture errors. Let's repeat the previous example by using `try` and `catch`.

Here is the M code to calculate the values for the Cost Per Unit column:

```
try [Cost]/[Units] catch (e)=> e[Message]
```

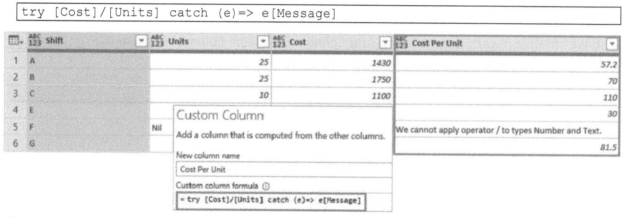

Figure 9-18 *Using* `try` *and* `catch` *to calculate cost per unit and otherwise display an error message.*

Notice that the formula is much shorter than before, but it returns the same result. Let's spend some time understanding how this works:

- Recall that `try` written in isolation returns a record (refer to Figure 9-11), which further nests a record with the field name Error in the event that `try` returns an error (refer to Figure 9-12).

- The `catch` keyword can capture the Error field from the record returned by `try` and return one or more of the five fields from the record (refer to Figure 9-13).

Consider this quick variation of the same code:

```
try [Cost]/[Units]
catch (e)=> e[Message] & " | " & e[Reason]
// In case of an error it will return a concatenation
// of the Error Message and Error Reason.
```

Now let's look at some peculiarities of writing `try` and `catch`, like this:

```
try a function or a value catch (e)=> e[Field Name]
```

Note that:

- The e variable used in the `catch` function refers to the record output of the `try` keyword. We can use any variable name; for instance, `try...catch (err) => err[Field Name]` is also valid.

- The Field Name value can only be one of five fields returned by `try` (i.e., Reason, Message, Detail, Message.Format, or Message.Parameters).

- The `catch` keyword cannot be referenced from elsewhere but must be defined inline:

```
// this is not allowed
let
  ACustomError = error "crazy",
  TryCatch = try ACustomError catch ACustomError
in
  TryCatch
```

- You cannot replace the parameter with the each keyword. It must be defined within the brackets:

```
// this is also not allowed.
try...catch each _[Message]
```

Exercises

Here are a few exercises to test your understanding. Ready?

> **Note:** Open the Excel file Errors Exercises - Unsolved in the Errors folder and then use the Power Query Editor to work through these exercises.

Exercise 1: Use try and otherwise

In the following table, calculate the sales amount (i.e., Units x Price$). If the formula results in an error, show a null value; otherwise, display the sales amount.

	Product	Units	Price$
1	A	25	8
2	B	25 Error	
3	C	10	6
4	E	35	7
5	F	Nil	10
6	G	20	9

Figure 9-19 *A table with products, units, and prices.*

Exercise 2: Use try and catch

In the same table calculate sales, but this time, if the formula results in an error, show the error message; otherwise, display the sales amount.

	Product	Units	Price$	Error or Sales
1	A	25	8	200
2	B	25 Error		Invalid cell value '#N/A'.
3	C	10	6	60
4	E	35	7	245
5	F	Nil	10	We cannot apply operator * to types Text and Number.
6	G	20	9	180

Table with 3 columns

Expected output - with Error Message or Sales Value

Figure 9-20 *Adding a new column to the table showing the error message or the sales value.*

> **Note:** When you're done with these exercises, you can compare your answers against the ones I provide in the Solutions chapter at the end of this book or refer to the Excel file Errors Exercises - Solved or do both. 😄

Chapter 10: Nested Tables

I feel you're now ready to understand the nuances and magic of working with nested tables. I wanted us to get through the core concepts of lists, records, looping, and functions before expanding on nested tables (pun intended). 😌

> **Note:** For this chapter, we'll be using the file Nested Tables.xlsx (which you'll find in the Nested Tables folder). As you work through this chapter, you'll be able to walk through the examples by using the queries provided in this file.

What Are Nested Tables?

Nested tables are hard to miss. They look like this:

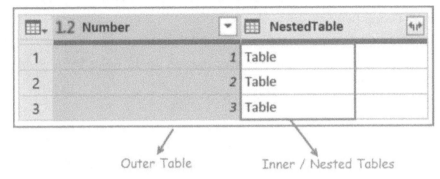

Figure 10-1 *Nested tables in Power Query.*

A nested table can appear directly from the source (e.g., when you're combining data from multiple Excel/CSV files) or can be created by using the Group By option or while manipulating lists and records. Let's look at a few interesting applications.

Nested Tables Example: Concatenating Customers

Refer to the query TableContenation.

Let's start with an interesting example of concatenation. Consider this table:

Year	Customer	Sales Value $Mn
2020	C	19
2020	D	10
2020	B	16
2021	A	16
2021	B	11
2022	E	16
2023	D	12
2023	E	13
2023	D	16
2023	C	14
2023	D	15
2023	F	19
2023	E	18
2023	C	18

Figure 10-2 *A table with three columns: Year, Customer, and Sales Value.*

We'd like to summarize this table by year and add two columns, Total Sales and Customers, where the Customers column has all unique values separated by commas:

1²₃ Year	1²₃ Total Sales	A⁸C Customers
1	2020	45	B, C, D
2	2021	27	A, B
3	2022	16	E
4	2023	125	C, D, E, F

Figure 10-3 *Expected output.*

The Group By feature is handy for summarizing data. Here's how we use it in this case:

1. Group the table (Transform → Group By).
2. Select Basic → Year.
3. Add a new column called Total Sales by performing a Sum operation on the Sales Value $Mn column.

Here is what we get as output:

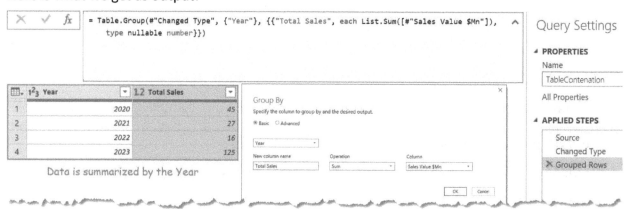

Figure 10-4 *Using the Group By option to summarize the data.*

The only problem is that we don't yet have a Customers column. Before we solve for that, let's examine the M code for the Grouped Rows step that got us here:

```
= Table.Group(
    #"Changed Type",  // 1
    {"Year"},         // 2
    {                 // 3
        {"Total Sales",
        each List.Sum([#"Sales Value $Mn"]),
        type nullable number}
    }
)
```

Here is how this works:

1. The `Table.Group` function accepts a table as the first argument (i.e., `#"Changed Type"`, which is the table in the previous step; refer to Figure 10-2).
2. The second argument is the list of the columns that need to be summarized. In our case, we have `"Year"` wrapped in curly brackets to form a list.
3. The third argument is a nested list, and each inner list is a column added to the summarized table. Each inner list has three arguments: the column name, the function to add a column, and a data type. In our case, these three arguments look like this:

- **"Total Sales":** The column name, as text
- **each List.Sum([#"Sales Value $Mn"]):** The function used
- **type nullable number:** The data type applied (as an optional input)

To add a new Customers column, let's feed another inner list and update the code so it looks like this:

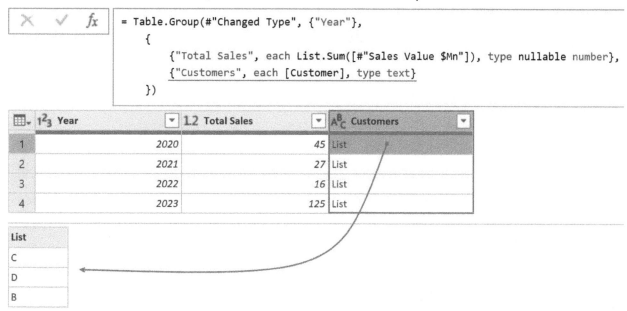

Figure 10-5 *A new Customers column is added with a list in each row.*

What just happened? We added a new list with three arguments:

```
{"Customers", each [Customer], type text}
```

In the second argument, we used each [Customer] to return a list of all customers in that year. But we don't want a list; we want to concatenate all unique customers in the list. So we need to further revise the code so that it looks like this:

```
= Table.Group(#"Changed Type", {"Year"},
    {
        {"Total Sales", each List.Sum([#"Sales Value $Mn"]), type nullable number},
        {"Customers", each Text.Combine(List.Distinct([Customer]), ", "), type text}
    })
```

▦	1²₃ Year	1.2 Total Sales	A⁸c Customers
1	2020	45	C, D, B
2	2021	27	A, B
3	2022	16	E
4	2023	125	D, E, C, F

Figure 10-6 *The customers' names are concatenated.*

Note that:

- The List.Distinct function removes the duplicates from the list.
- Text.Combine accepts a list in the first argument and combines the values with the comma separator in the second argument.

Nested Tables: Comparing Columns Between Expanded and Nested Tables

Refer to the query Nested Tables Compared.

Here is some simple sales data we are working with:

▦ ▾	🗓 Date	▾	A^B_C Sales Rep	▾	1²₃ Sales	▾
1	30-05-2005		Mark			14900
2	31-05-2005		Rajat			12400
3	05-06-2005		Rajat			14150
4	07-06-2005		Abhay			11100
5	09-06-2005		Rajat			12650
6	12-06-2005		Bruce			10800
7	13-06-2005		Rajat			12950
8	14-06-2005		James			11950
9	16-06-2005		Varsha			10450
10	18-06-2005		Anshika			13900
	2005		Swati			14900

Figure 10-7 *Sales data with Date, Sales Rep, and Sales columns.*

We'd like to add a column to check whether each sales value is greater than the average sales of the sales rep for the entire year. Here is the expected output:

▦ ▾	ABC 123 Date	▾	ABC 123 Sales Rep	▾	ABC 123 Sales	▾	ABC 123 Avg Check	▾
1	30-05-2005		Mark			14900		TRUE
2	08-08-2005		Mark			13650		TRUE
3	08-08-2005		Mark			12050		FALSE
4	13-09-2005		Mark			11650		FALSE
5	21-09-2005		Mark			12400		FALSE
6	12-10-2005		Mark			12050		FALSE
7	16-10-2005		Mark			13300		TRUE
8	16-11-2005		Mark			13400		TRUE
9	27-11-2005		Mark			11750		FALSE
10	21-12-2005		Mark			15000		TRUE
11	2005		Rajat			12400		FALSE

Figure 10-8 *Expected output with a new column, Avg Check.*

> **Note:** The output doesn't contain the average sales value, but it should be used as an intermediate calculation for the new Avg Check column.

The Logic to Solve This Problem

To solve this problem, we need to do three things:

- We need to find the average sales value for each sales rep for the year (which we get by summarizing the data using the Group By option).

- Then we compare each sales value with the average sales to get TRUE or FALSE as output.
- If there is any junk created in the process, we remove it.

Using Group By

Let's start by adding a Year column: Select the Date column → Add Column → Date drop-down → Year → Year.

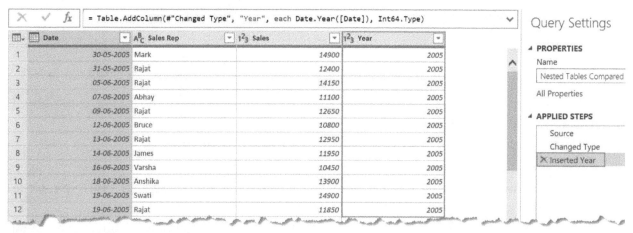

Figure 10-9 *Adding a Year column.*

Next, we use Group By (Transform → Group By) to summarize by Year and Sales Rep columns and add a calculated column, AllRowsTable (to keep all matching rows for the sales rep and year), that uses the All Rows operation.

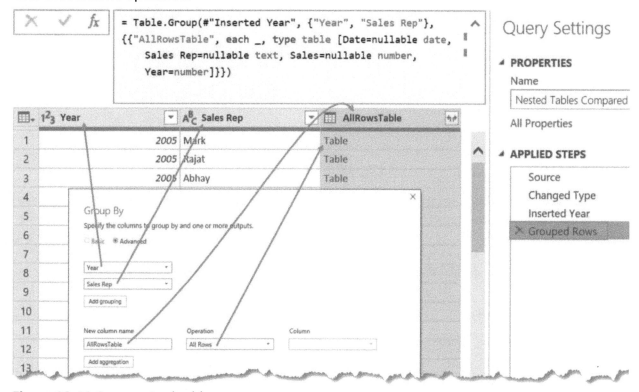

Figure 10-10 *Summarized table.*

> **Tip:** The All Rows operation allows us to create a nested table for each combination of year and sales rep.

Here is the `Table.Group` function generated using Group By:

```
= Table.Group(
    #"Inserted Year",                    // 1
    {"Year", "Sales Rep"},               // 2
    {{"AllRowsTable", each _,            // 3
    type table [Date=nullable date,
        Sales Rep=nullable text,
        Sales=nullable number, Year=number]}}
)
```

Note that:

1. The first argument here is the table (i.e., the previous step).

2. In the second argument we have a list of the two columns by which the table is summarized (i.e., Year and Sales Rep).

3. Next, we have a nested list where each inner list has three arguments:

    • The name of the calculated column (i.e., `AllRowsTable`) as text

    • The function to generate the column (in our case, it's `each _`, which returns a table in a row of the summarized table)

    • The data type for all the columns in the table (created using `each _`), which is optional

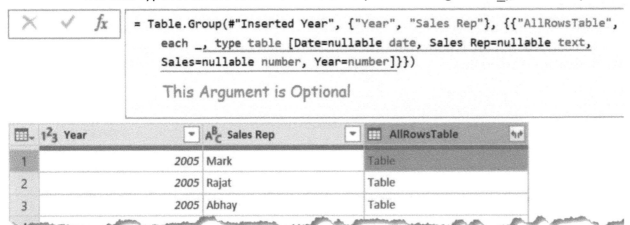

Figure 10-11 *M code generated using Group By.*

Because the AllRowsTable column will be thrown away after some transformations, we can remove the optional data types declared in the Grouped Rows step, and we still get more or less the same output:

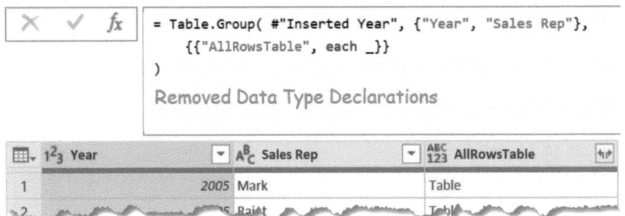

Figure 10-12 *Removed data types.*

Note: Removing data types only makes the code a bit less intimidating. Everything we do from here on will work just as well even if we don't remove the data types.

Calculating the Average

Our query at the current stage returns the AllRowsTable column with nested tables, and within each table we have to create a new column with the following logic:

1. Calculate average sales.
2. Compare each sales value with the average sales to get TRUE or FALSE.

1²3 Year	A⁸C Sales Rep	ABC 123 AllRowsTable
1	2005 Mark	Table
2	2005 Rajat	Table
3	2005 Abhay	Table
4	2005 Bruce	Table
5	2005 James	Table

Date	Sales Rep	Sales	Year	Avg Check Column
30-05-2005	Mark	14900	2005	The Logic
08-08-2005	Mark	13650	2005	
08-08-2005	Mark	12050	2005	1. Calculate Average of Sales
13-09-2005	Mark	11650	2005	Column
21-09-2005	Mark	12400	2005	2. Check if each
12-10-2005	Mark	12050	2005	Sales Value >
16-10-2005	Mark	13300	2005	Average
16-11-2005	Mark	13400	2005	
27-11-2005	Mark	11750	2005	
21-12-2005	Mark	15000	2005	

Figure 10-13 *Preview of the nested table and the Avg Check column logic.*

Let's modify our M code a bit to first find the average sales value:

```
= Table.Group(#"Inserted Year", {"Year", "Sales Rep"},
    {{"AllRowsTable", each
    let
        avg = List.Average([Sales])
    in
        avg}}
)
```

```
        ✕    ✓    fx   = Table.Group( #"Inserted Year", {"Year", "Sales Rep"},
                            {{"AllRowsTable", each
                                let avg = List.Average([Sales])
                                in avg }}
                        )
```

1²₃ Year	A^B_C Sales Rep	ABC 123 AllRowsTable
1	2005 Mark	13015
2	2005 Rajat	12776.92308
3	2005 Abhay	12406.25
4	2005 Bruce	12755
5	2005 James	12812.5
	2005 Varsha	11338.88889

Figure 10-14 *Modified code to calculate average sales.*

What just happened?

1. We used `each` _ to return a nested table for each row in the AllRowsTable column (refer to Figure 10-12).

2. We modified the code by adding an `avg` step (variable) between `let` and `in` to calculate the average sales.

> **Note:** You may find the code perplexing. Even though I don't physically see your mental discomfort, I sense these questions coming 😄:
>
> **How did we transition from `each` _, which returned a table, to finding the average sales?**
>
> Refer to Figure 10-12, and you'll see that our code looked something like this, where `each` _ meant the summarized table in each row of the AllRowsTable column:
>
> ```
> = Table.Group(
>     #"Inserted Year", {"Year", "Sales Rep"},
>     {{"AllRowsTable", each _}}
> )
> ```
>
> At this stage, to calculate the average, we can modify the code to look like this:
>
> ```
> = Table.Group(
>     #"Inserted Year", {"Year", "Sales Rep"},
>     {{"AllRowsTable", each List.Average(_[Sales])}}
> )
> ```
>
> Recall the syntax for extracting a column as a list from the table (refer to Figure 1-5 in Chapter 1). In this case, the _ (underscore) represents a table, and `[Sales]` represents the column. Therefore, `each List.Average(_[Sales])` returns the average value of the list (i.e., the Sales column). To simplify even further, we can remove the underscore:
>
> `each List.Average([Sales])`
>
> The output will be the same as shown in Figure 10-14.
>
> Your next question:
>
> **If finding the average is so straightforward, why the hell did we use the `let...in` keywords and make the code complex?**
>
> You're right: Right now it does nothing! But for now, it has allowed us to store the average value in the `avg` step—and later we will compare each sales value to the value in this `avg` step instead of recalculating average sales for each row. Think of this as an optimization technique. I'll come back with more notes on this in a bit.

Let's create a second step, `tbl`, to add a column to the inner table and compare each sales value with the `avg` step (i.e., average sales). We can further revise the code so it looks like this:

```
= Table.Group(#"Inserted Year", {"Year", "Sales Rep"},
    {{"AllRowsTable", each
    let
        avg = List.Average([Sales]),
        tbl = Table.AddColumn(
                _,
                "Avg Check",
                each [Sales] > avg
            )
    in
        tbl}}
)
```

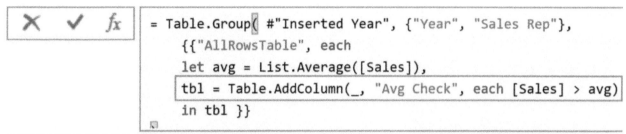

<table>
<tr><td>🔲▾</td><td>1²₃ Year</td><td>▾</td><td>A^BC Sales Rep</td><td>▾</td><td>ABC
123 AllRowsTable</td><td>↕⋕</td></tr>
<tr><td>1</td><td colspan="2">2005</td><td>Mark</td><td></td><td>Table</td><td></td></tr>
<tr><td>2</td><td colspan="2">2005</td><td>Rajat</td><td></td><td>Table</td><td></td></tr>
<tr><td>3</td><td colspan="2">2005</td><td>Abhay</td><td></td><td>Table</td><td></td></tr>
<tr><td>4</td><td colspan="2">2005</td><td>Bruce</td><td></td><td>Table</td><td></td></tr>
</table>

Date	Sales Rep	Sales	Year	Avg Check
30-05-2005	Mark	14900	2005	TRUE
08-08-2005	Mark	13650	2005	TRUE
08-08-2005	Mark	12050	2005	FALSE

Figure 10-15 *Adding a check column to the nested table.*

Let's spend some time on the code above:

- We created the `tbl` step and used the `Table.AddColumn` function.
- In the first argument of the `Table.AddColumn` function, we used an underscore (_) to refer to the underlying table (again refer to Figure 10-12) where the column needs to be added.
- The second argument is the new column name as text (i.e., `"Avg Check"`).
- The third argument is the function to generate each row (i.e., `each [Sales] > avg`). Note the reference of the `avg` step; it's not being recalculated for each row of the inner table but just once for the outside table. This is the precise reason we created the steps between the `let` and `in` keywords.

> **Note:** As a thought experiment, we can also do the same thing without the `let` and `in` keywords, calculating average sales for each row of the nested table. This method might be slower, but it works (see the query Nested Tables Compared - Alternative):
>
> ```
> = Table.Group(#"Inserted Year", {"Year", "Sales Rep"},
>     {{"AllRowsTable", (nested_tbl)=>
>     Table.AddColumn(
>         nested_tbl, "Avg Check",
>         each [Sales] > List.Average(nested_tbl[Sales]))
>     }})
> ```

We have the output ready, but it's kinda stuck within those nested tables. Let's combine all those tables in the AllRowsTable column. We can create a new step named CombinedTables with the following code:

```
= Table.Combine(#"Grouped Rows"[AllRowsTable])
```

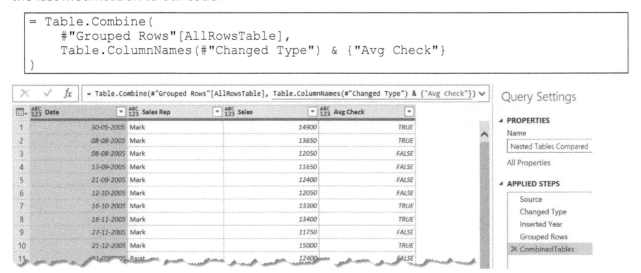

All the tables are combined along with the Avg Check Column

Figure 10-16 *All nested tables are combined.*

The code is straightforward:

- We extracted the column as a list from the previous step by using `#"Grouped Rows"[AllRowsTable]`.
- We fed that list of tables into the `Table.Combine` function.

The only problem left is that we don't need the Year column. We can use a new step to delete it or modify our existing function to combine only the relevant columns rather than all of them. Here is the last modification to our code:

```
= Table.Combine(
    #"Grouped Rows"[AllRowsTable],
    Table.ColumnNames(#"Changed Type") & {"Avg Check"}
)
```

Figure 10-17 *The Year column is removed.*

Note that:

- As the second argument of the `Table.Combine` function, we fed a list of columns by using the `Table.ColumnNames` function from one of our initial steps (Changed Type) to restore the original columns.
- We concatenated to our list the new Avg Check column that we created in the previous step.

And it looks like we've reached our output.

Nested Tables: Determining Employee Stint Duration

Refer to the query Counting Stints.

Another interesting example of grouping is consecutive counting. Consider this data, where each month an employee (in the EmpCode column) is assigned to a role. By default, this data is sorted in ascending order based on the EmpCode and Date columns. (This sorting is automatic, and you'll understand why as you read through this section. If it didn't occur automatically, we'd have added a step to sort the data.)

	Date	EmpCode	Role
1	01-01-2018	EMPC105782	Zone Manager
2	01-02-2018	EMPC105782	Zone Manager
3	01-03-2018	EMPC105782	Branch Manager
4	01-04-2018	EMPC105782	Branch Manager
5	01-05-2018	EMPC105782	Branch Manager
6	01-06-2018	EMPC105782	Branch Manager
7	01-07-2018	EMPC105782	Branch Manager
8	01-08-2018	EMPC105782	Branch Manager
9	01-09-2018	EMPC105782	Branch Manager
10	01-10-2018	EMPC105782	Branch Manager
11	01-11-2018	EMPC105782	Branch Manager
12	01-12-2018	EMPC105782	Branch Manager
13	01-01-2019	EMPC105782	Branch Manager
14	2019	EMPC105782	Branch Manager

Figure 10-18 *A table with three columns: Date, EmpCode, and Role.*

From this data, we'd like to calculate the duration of each stint—where a stint is defined as an unbroken period of months an employee was assigned to a particular role. Our output should look like this:

	EmpCode		Role		Stint Duration Months	
1	EMPC105782		Zone Manager		2	
2	EMPC105782		Branch Manager		30	
3	EMPC105782		Team Supervisor		3	
4	EMPC105782		Branch Manager		10	
5	EMPC105782		Team Supervisor		3	
6	EMPC10783		Customer Support		5	
7	EMPC10783		Team Member		27	
8	EMPC10783		Regional Manager		16	
9	EMPC110		Central Team		48	
10	EMPC12477		Regional Manager		33	
11	EMPC12477		Facilities Team		1	
12	EMPC12477		Branch Manager		14	
13	EMPC13881		Team Supervisor - COE		32	
14	EMPC13881		Regional Manager		16	
15	EMPC143018		Ops Member		12	
16	EMPC143018		Regional Manager		16	

Figure 10-19 *The expected output shows the employee code and stint duration in months for each role.*

At least on the face of it, this seems to be a simple grouping pattern. So let's start off by grouping the data (Transform → Group By) by employee code and role, like this:

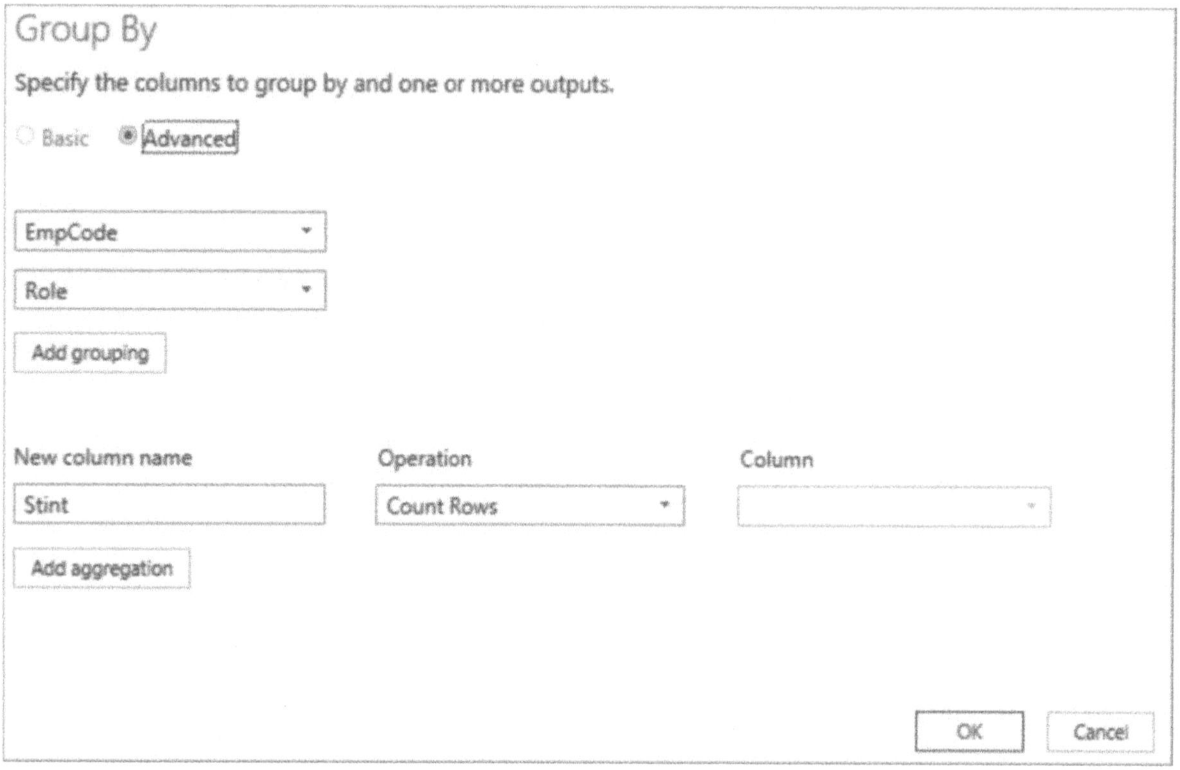

Figure 10-20 *Using the Group By feature in Power Query.*

The result looks like this:

Figure 10-21 *The data is summarized by employee code and role.*

The Stint Duration Months column shows the count of rows (where 1 row = 1 month) that match the EmpCode and Role columns, but this output is wrong. Why? Look at this summary for EMPC105782, who's had five stints:

Start	End	Role	Stint
01-Jan-18	01-Feb-18	Zone Manager	1
01-Mar-18	01-Aug-20	Branch Manager	2
01-Sep-20	01-Nov-20	Team Supervisor	3
01-Dec-20	01-Sep-21	Branch Manager	4
01-Oct-21	01-Dec-21	Team Supervisor	5

Figure 10-22 *Summary of EmpCode = EMPC105782.*

Note that:

- The first three stints as zone manager, branch manager, and team supervisor are unique roles.
- In the final two stints, earlier roles are repeated.

The summarized data in Figure 10-21 shows only three rows for EMPC105782 (which is wrong in this case) because the employee moved back to earlier roles (branch manager and team supervisor).

The default Group By feature in Power Query summarizes the data by all matching rows, and that is why we saw only three roles for EMPC105782 (refer to Figure 10-21). However, we'd like to do consecutive counting (i.e., count a new stint when the combination of the employee code and role changes in the next row and compared to the current row).

The problem is, the Power Query UI doesn't support this type of grouping. However, a minor tweak in `Table.Group` can give us the desired output.

Here is a small modification we can make to the Grouped Rows M code in the formula bar by adding `GroupKind.Local` in the `groupKind` parameter:

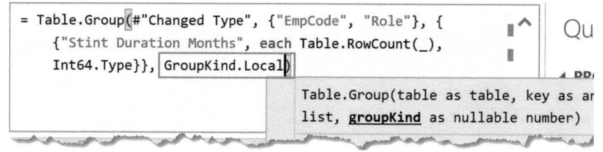

```
= Table.Group(#"Changed Type", {"EmpCode", "Role"}, {
    {"Stint Duration Months", each Table.RowCount(_),
    Int64.Type}}, GroupKind.Local)
```

Table.Group(table as table, key as an
list, **groupKind** as nullable number)

Figure 10-23 *Adding* `GroupKind.Local` *as the* `groupKind` *parameter.*

What does this do? `GroupKind.Local` groups the data by consecutively comparing the first row of the current group with the next row. It forms a new group as soon as the grouping conditions (i.e., EmpCode and Role) change in the next row.

This tiny change produces the expected output:

	A^B_C EmpCode	A^B_C Role	1²₃ Stint Duration Months
1	EMPC105782	Zone Manager	2
2	EMPC105782	Branch Manager	30
3	EMPC105782	Team Supervisor	3
4	EMPC105782	Branch Manager	10
5	EMPC105782	Team Supervisor	3
6	EMPC10783	Customer Support	5
7	EMPC10783	Team Member	27
8	EMPC10783	Regional Manager	16

Figure 10-24 *EMPC105782 now shows five stints along with stint duration.*

And this solves our problem.

Food for Thought

In the example we just walked through, the modified M code in the formula bar looks like this:

```
= Table.Group(
    #"Changed Type",
    {"EmpCode", "Role"},
    {{"Stint Duration Months",
      each Table.RowCount(_),
      Int64.Type}},
    GroupKind.Local
)
```

For the Stint Duration Months column, we've used the `Table.RowCount` function to count the number of rows (i.e., months).

But if we were to remove the row count function and just return the underlying table as is, we'd be able to peek into the inner table. For instance, consider this slightly modified M code with no row count done:

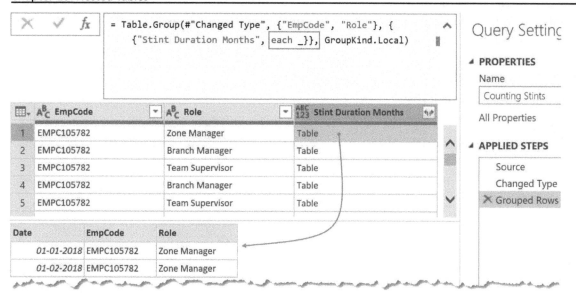

Figure 10-25 *Using* `each _` *to return the underlying grouped table.*

`each _` returns the underlying table as per the grouping conditions—in this case, EmpCode and Role.

Since the _ represents a table, we can perform any action that fits a table input. It could be finding a row count (by using `each Table.RowCount(_)`) or even extracting the list of months from the table (by using `each _[Date]` or `each [Date]`).

Once you understand the core concept that the grouping parameters result in table output by using `each _`, what you can do with the underlying table is limited only by your imagination.

Customizing Local Grouping

> Refer to the query WinLossStreak.

A few paragraphs ago, while explaining the `GroupKind.Local` parameter, I wrote "`GroupKind.Local` groups the data by consecutively comparing the first row of the current group with the next row." What does this mean?

To better understand how local grouping really works, let's consider another example. In the table below, we have two columns that show wins and losses and the date of each one.

WinLoss	Date
Win	01-Jan-24
Loss	01-Jan-24
Loss	02-Jan-24
Win	04-Jan-24
Win	05-Jan-24
Win	06-Jan-24
Win	07-Jan-24
Win	09-Jan-24
Loss	10-Jan-24
Loss	11-Jan-24

Figure 10-26 *Data showing wins and losses and their dates.*

From this data, we'd like to calculate the length of each win or loss streak, keeping in mind that a streak is only counted if the next win or loss happens on a consecutive day. For instance, in row 2, the loss streak that begins on January 1, 2024 ends on January 2, 2024 (i.e., losses on January 1 and 2 that occurred consecutively), and so the streak length is 2.

Our final output should look like this:

	AB_C WinLoss	Date	1²₃ Streak Length
1	Win	01-01-2024	1
2	Loss	01-01-2024	2
3	Win	04-01-2024	4
4	Win	09-01-2024	1
5	Loss	10-01-2024	2

Figure 10-27 *The data showing wins and losses, dates (in dd-mm-yyyy format), and streak lengths.*

Let's try grouping using `GroupKind.Local` and see what happens:

1. Group the data shown in Figure 10-26 by selecting Transform → Group By.
2. Group by the WinLoss column and use the Count Rows operation for the Streak Length column. We get this table as a result:

Figure 10-28 *Grouping rows for all Win and Loss values and counting them up in the Streak Length column.*

Based on the default grouping, all the data is summarized into Win and Loss rows, with their respective counts. Let's modify the M code in the formula bar and add `GroupKind.Local` as the `groupKind` parameter to see what happens.

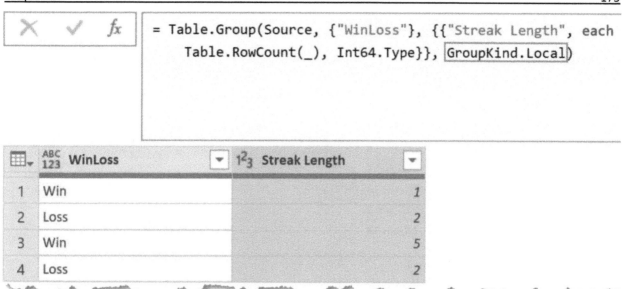

Figure 10-29 *Using* `GroupKind.Local` *as the* `groupKind` *parameter.*

We get some output, but it's clearly not the output we want. Let's take a moment to understand how this output is evaluated. At this stage, nothing can beat illustrations to help understand the inner workings of `GroupKind.Local`.

We can see in the image below that the value Win in the first row doesn't match with the value Loss in the second row, so the grouping breaks, and the `Table.Group` function starts a new group from the second row onward (i.e., where the grouping broke).

Figure 10-30 *How* `GroupKind.Local` *generates the first row of the output shown in* **Figure 10-29**.

The `Table.Group` function reinitiates the grouping starting with the second row, comparing the second row's value (i.e., Loss) to the value in the next row. If the values match, the row is retained in the same group. If they don't match, the grouping breaks. In this case, the grouping breaks in the fourth row because the value in the second row (Loss) doesn't match the value in the fourth row (Win).

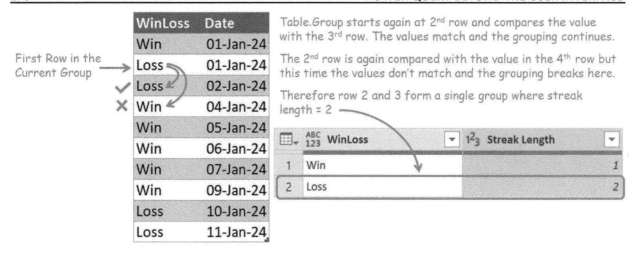

This process continues until all rows in the table are scanned and groups are formed.

Figure 10-31 *How* `GroupKind.Local` *generates the output for the second row and onward in* **Figure 10-29**.

Remember that I said this earlier: "`GroupKind.Local` groups the data by consecutively comparing the first row of the current group with the next row." By now you should be able to visualize what I mean by this.

There are still two problems to deal with:

- The win or loss streak calculation is based on consecutive date. The win streak that starts on January 4 breaks after January 7, 2024 in Figure 10-26 because even though the next outcome is a win, it happens two days later, not the next day. The output in Figure 10-29 shows the win streak length as 5, but it should 4 (refer to the expected output in Figure 10-27).

- In our attempt to understand how local grouping works, we completely forgot that the Date column also needs to be used to check whether the dates are consecutive in order to generate output like the expected output in Figure 10-27.

Custom Logic for Local Grouping

Merely adding `GroupKind.Local` to our formula (as shown in Figure 10-29) won't work. We need to modify the formula so that it can also check whether the dates are consecutive. This means we need to explore the fifth parameter of the `Table.Group` function, which allows us to customize two available parameters—the parameter for the first row in the current group and the parameter for the next row—to make this formula a lot more versatile. Let's look at the full syntax of the `Table.Group` function and cover some theory (I promise to keep it short 😄). Here's the syntax:

```
Table.Group(
  table as table,
  key as any,
  aggregatedColumns as list,
  optional groupKind as nullable number,
  optional comparer as nullable function, // 5th argument
) as table
```

Since we've already discussed the first four arguments, I'll explicitly talk about the fifth argument of the `Table.Group` function here. As we can see, the official documentation says it is a function, but as of this writing, there is no further explanation about how it works. That's okay because I've tinkered with this enough to share my two cents about what is happening.

This function argument must be declared explicitly with two parameters, like this:

```
= (x, y) => ...
// the output of this function must be a 0 or 1
```

Note that:

- x means the first row in the current group.
- y means the next row.
- The output of this fifth argument must be 0 or 1, where 0 means continue the grouping and 1 means break and start a new group.

Applying the Logic for the Fifth Argument

Before we go down a rabbit hole and start writing crazy M code, let's map out the logic to solve this problem. In summary, we need to check for two conditions:

- The value Win or Loss in the first row of the current group should be equal to the next row.
- The date in the first row of the current group should increment by 1 when compared to the next row.

Here is how this looks visually for the first group:

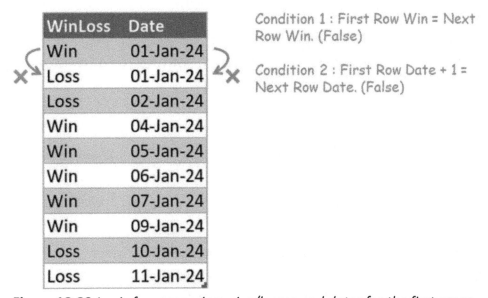

Figure 10-32 *Logic for comparing wins/losses and dates for the first group.*

Because the conditions don't match in Figure 10-32, a group should be formed with streak count equal to 1. Here's how the same two conditions look for the second group:

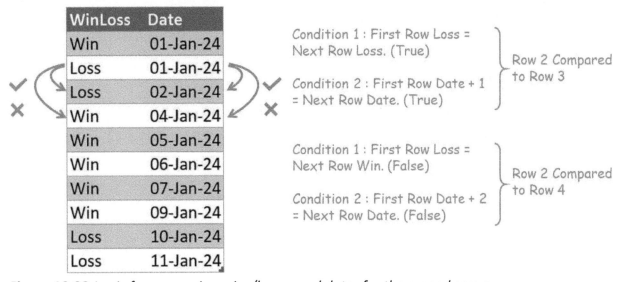

Figure 10-33 *Logic for comparing wins/losses and dates for the second group.*

This is where things get interesting. Note that:

- The two conditions between row 2 and row 3 match. Therefore, the grouping will continue to check whether row 2 also matches with the next row (i.e., row 4), but here the two conditions do not match, and so the grouping breaks.

- Another interesting observation is that when the date in row 2 is compared with the date in row 3, it should increment by 1 (i.e., 02-January-24 should become 03-January-2024), but when the grouping continues and the date in row 2 is again matched to row 4, this time it should increment by 2 (i.e., 02-January-2024 should become 04-January-2024). To solve for this anomaly, we'll need to create an Index column and then write the custom logic for local grouping.

Creating an Index Column

Let's create an Index column (Add Column → Index Column drop-down → From 1) in between the Source and Grouped Rows steps.

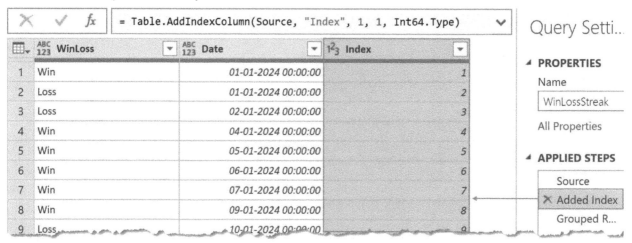

Figure 10-34 *Creating an Index column in between the Source and Grouped Rows steps.*

Why do we need to do this? Allow me a few more sentences and images to show its utility.

Customizing Local Grouping by Using the Fifth Parameter

We can now start modifying the code in the Grouped Rows step. It should look like this:

```
= Table.Group(
    #"Added Index",                                     // 1
    {"WinLoss", "Date", "Index"},                       // 2
    {"Streak Length", Table.RowCount, Int64.Type},
    GroupKind.Local,
    (ftrow, nxtr) => Number.From(                       // 3
        ftrow[WinLoss] <> nxtr[WinLoss] or
        Duration.Days(nxtr[Date] - ftrow[Date]) <>
        nxtr[Index] - ftrow[Index])
)
```

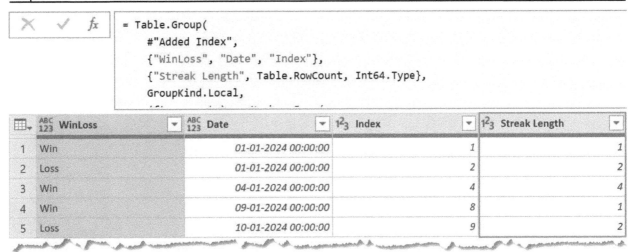

```
= Table.Group(
    #"Added Index",
    {"WinLoss", "Date", "Index"},
    {"Streak Length", Table.RowCount, Int64.Type},
    GroupKind.Local,
```

	ABC 123 WinLoss	ABC 123 Date	1²₃ Index	1²₃ Streak Length
1	Win	01-01-2024 00:00:00	1	1
2	Loss	01-01-2024 00:00:00	2	2
3	Win	04-01-2024 00:00:00	4	4
4	Win	09-01-2024 00:00:00	8	1
5	Loss	10-01-2024 00:00:00	9	2

Figure 10-35 *Adding the fifth parameter to the Grouped Rows step.*

- This might seem horrifying or at least hard to digest. Let's break it down and see what changed from the code in Figure 10-29:

1. The `Table.Group` function now refers to the Added Index step and not the Source step.

2. Since we've also added the Index column and want it to be considered in the calculation, we've added that in the list in the second argument as a grouping condition.

3. The fifth argument is where the magic begins. Here is how it works:

   - **(ftrow, nxtr) =>:** The two parameters we've declared are `ftrow` and `nxtr`, which represent the first row in the current group and the next row, respectively.

   - **ftrow[WinLoss] <> nxtr[WinLoss]:** The first condition checks whether the value in the WinLoss column (i.e., the value in the first row of the current group) matches with the next row. Notice the subtlety: We used the <> sign rather than the = sign because a new group is formed only if the output is 1 (meaning true), and a <> sign will return a true value if the values don't match (and form a new group).

   - **or Duration.Days(nxtr[Date] - ftrow[Date]) <> nxtr[Index] - ftrow[Index]):** The next condition starts with an `or` keyword so if any of these conditions don't match, we form a new group. In the second condition, we check whether the difference between the next row and first row dates is the same as the next row and first row index values. Look again at Figure 10-34 and think about it: The difference (in days) between dates in row 3 and row 4 is the same as the difference between the Index values in row 3 and row 2. When the difference is not the same, we form the new group.

   - **Number.From:** Although the logic discussed so far is correct, it doesn't produce a 0 or 1 as output. Therefore, we wrap the entire logic in the `Number.From` function, which transforms a true value to a 1 and a false value to a 0.

This argument creates a Streak Length column that returns the correct values. 😎

We can take two more tiny steps to remove the Index helper column and apply the data types to clean up our output:

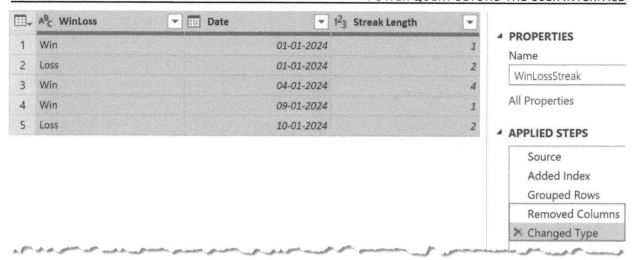

Figure 10-36 *Deleting the Index column and applying the data types.*

If you understand this, I'm giving myself a big pat on the back. If you don't, you probably understand why there is no documentation on this. 😄

Chapter 11: Patterns and Recipes

In this chapter, we'll put our learning to use and solve a variety of simple to complex problems by using M. I highly encourage you to fire up Power Query and follow along.

> **Note:** For this chapter, we'll be using the files that you'll find in the Patterns and Recipes folder. As you work through this chapter, you'll be able to walk through the examples by using the queries provided in this file.

Example 1: The Double Headers Problem

Consider this data, which is available on Sheet1 in the Excel file Double Headers - Problem. There are two header rows, and some of the main headers in row 1 span multiple subheaders in row 2.

	A	B	C	D	E	F	G	H
1	**Store**	**Customer**			**Sales**			**Order**	
2	**Num**	**Code**	**Name**	**Units**	**MRP**	**Value**	**Date**	**Ship Date**
3	Store1	M1	Mike	3	160	480	12-Dec-21	17-Dec-21
4	Store1	B1	Bobbie	2	210	420	12-Dec-21	17-Dec-21
5	Store1	M1	Mike	1	100	100	02-Dec-21	05-Dec-21
6	Store1	B1	Bobbie	3	130	390	02-Dec-21	05-Dec-21
7	Store1	R1	Rehet	2	220	440	02-Dec-21	04-Dec-21
8	Store1	M1	Mike	2	200	400	04-Dec-21	10-Dec-21
9	Store1	B1	Bobbie	3	220	660	09-Dec-21	17-Dec-21
10	Store 2	R2	Rob	1	70	70	06-Dec-21	12-Dec-21
11	Store 2	M1	Mike	1	70	70	11-Dec-21	21-Dec-21
12	Store 2	B1	Bobbie	1	90	90	05-Dec-21	13-Dec-21
13	Store 2	R1	Rehet	3	110	330	02-Dec-21	05-Dec-21

Figure 11-1 *The data has two header rows, and the cells are merged.*

We'd like to combine the headers from the first two rows into a single row, like this:

Figure 11-2 *Combining the first two header rows into a single row.*

This isn't a very difficult problem to solve using the Power Query UI, but it involves transposing the data, which can take a lot of time on large datasets. Here is how we would attempt to solve this using the UI:

1. Transpose the data so that rows become columns and columns become rows.
2. Fill down the first column to fill in the null values.
3. Merge the first two columns to concatenate the headers.
4. Transpose the data again.
5. Promote the headers.

Transposing the entire dataset just to fix the headers is a bad idea. It would probably kill our query on a large dataset. Instead, we need to selectively transpose only the two header rows and put the table back together.

The Logic to Solve This Problem

This solution is not very different from a UI solution, but it doesn't involve transposing the entire dataset. Here's what we need to do:

1.   Split the table (refer to Figure 11-1) at the second row so we end up with two tables: a table with the headers (the first two rows) and a second table with the rest of the rows.

2.   Transpose the first table (the one with only the headers), fill down the rows, merge the columns, and transpose it back. It's important to note that the transposing happens only for the first table (with only two header rows), so it won't be an expensive operation.

3.   Combine the two tables and promote the headers.

With the logic laid out, let's start the action!

Splitting the Table

Refer to the query Double Headers.

The table loaded in the Source step needs to be split into two parts: one table with only the header rows (the first two rows) and another table with the rest of the rows.

Figure 11-3 *The data is loaded in Power Query.*

We can create a new step called SplitTables to split the table (Source) into two parts, like this:

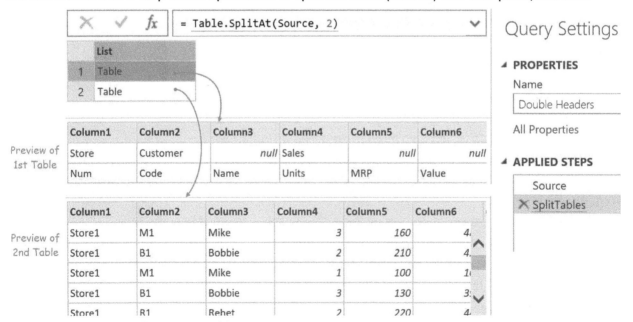

Figure 11-4 *Splitting the source table into two parts.*

The `Table.Split` function accepts a table as the first input and the row count where the split should happen as the second input. It returns a list with two split tables.

Transposing the Headers Table

The previous step resulted in two tables nested in a list. For now, we can work with only the first table, the headers table, and transpose it. We can create a new step called HeadersTbl with the following code:

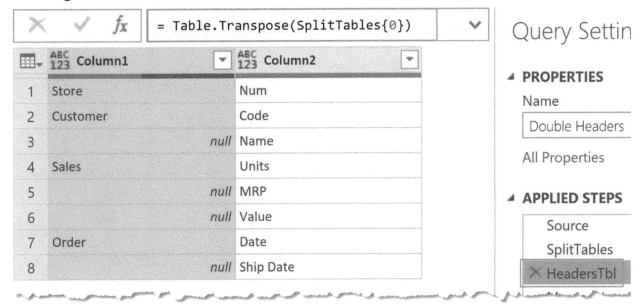

Figure 11-5 *The first table is extracted and transposed.*

In this code:

- `SplitTables{0}` extracts the first table from the list (in the previous step).
- `Table.Transpose` accepts a table as input and transposes it. Transposing allows the next vital transformation: filling down.

Filling Down and Transposing Transformations

We need to create a new step called MergedHeaders and use the `Table.FillDown` function like this:

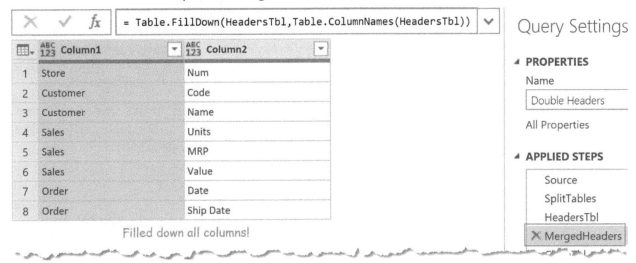

Figure 11-6 *Filling down all columns.*

In this code, note that:

- The `Table.FillDown` function accepts a table as the first argument (i.e., the table in the previous step, HeadersTbl).

- The second argument is the list of column names that will be filled down. We could hard-code a list (i.e., `= {"Column1", "Column2"}`), but why do that when we can make it dynamic by using the `Table.ColumnNames` function?

Recall from the expected output in Figure 11-2 that we need a single header row. We face two challenges:

- We need to merge the filled-down columns to get a single column.
- Then we need to transpose it to create a single row of headers.

Let's further enhance the code in the same step. First, we merge the columns:

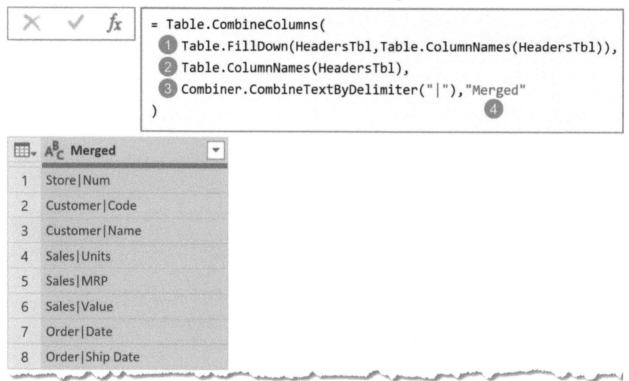

Figure 11-7 Using `Table.CombineColumns` to combine columns.

The `Table.CombineColumns` function comes in handy here. Note that:

The first argument is the table to work with.

The second argument is the list of columns to combine. Again, this could have been a hard-coded list like `= {"Column1", "Column2"}`, but we have the `Table.ColumnNames` function to make it dynamic.

The third argument is a combiner function to combine the column values. In this case, we've used `Combiner.CombineTextByDelimiter("|")` with a pipe symbol (|) as the delimiter. (I'll share some interesting notes on this argument in a bit, but let's keep going for now.)

The last argument is the merged column name as text (in this case, `"Merged"`).

Detour: Using Table.CombineColumns

I want to take a detour, but if you have the urge to finish the current example, you can skip this detour for now and come back to it later. Let's consider the `Table.CombineColumns` function once again. Here is its syntax:

```
= Table.CombineColumns(
    table as table,            // 1
    sourceColumns as list,     // 2
    combiner as function,      // 3
    column as text             // 4
) as table
```

Arguments 1, 2, and 4 are pretty straightforward (refer to Figure 11-7), but I want to focus on the third argument, `combiner as function`. What does it mean exactly, and why do we use the mysterious `Combiner.CombineTextByDelimiter` in this example?

Let's solve this mystery by rewriting the function a bit differently.

> Refer to the query TableCombineColumns, which includes all the steps created in our existing query so far.

We can make a slight tweak to our formula, as shown here:

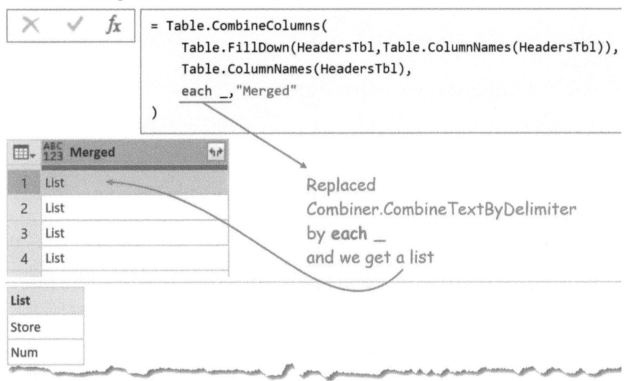

Figure 11-8 *Replacing* `Combiner.CombineTextByDelimiter` *with* `each _`

Why do we do this? Because the third argument needs a function input, and `each _` is the shorthand for writing a function.

Now the burning question: Why do we only use the `Combiner.CombineTextByDelimiter` function and not any other record or a table function? To answer this, let's explore the workings of `Combiner.CombineTextByDelimiter` in the official M documentation from Microsoft:

Syntax

```
Combiner.CombineTextByDelimiter(delimiter as text, optional quoteStyle as nullable number) as function
```

About

Returns a function that combines a list of text values into a single text value using the specified delimiter.

Example 1

Combine a list of text values using a semicolon delimiter.

Usage

Power Query M	Copy

```
Combiner.CombineTextByDelimiter(";")({"a", "b", "c"})
```

Output

```
"a;b;c"
```

Figure 11-9 *A snapshot of the Microsoft documentation on* `Combiner.CombineTextByDelimiter.`

The syntax says two important things:

- The only mandatory argument we need is a delimiter as text.
- The output of this function will be a function and not a text value.

The About section tells us that this function will combine a list of values with the specified delimiter.

Example 1 shows the list input `{"a", "b", "c"}` within the parentheses at the end of the function, like this:

```
Combiner.CombineTextByDelimiter(";")({"a", "b", "c"})
```

This clarifies the reason for using `Combiner.CombineTextByDelimiter`. Because this function can only work with a list, and the `Table.CombineColumn` function also returns a list, they make a perfect match. In short, feed Power Query what it eats! 😄

I don't want you to be mad at me for taking a long detour just to show you a list. Now that you've figured out that the `Table.CombineColumns` function under the hood returns a list (for each row value, as shown in Figure 11-8), you can use any of the list functions on it. 😌

Now Back to Our Regularly Scheduled Program

We are now left with one more transformation to be done. We need to transpose the column into a row, like this:

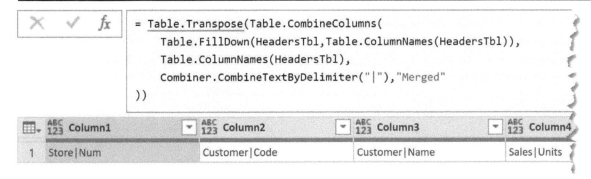

Figure 11-10 *Transposing the table that now contains a single row of headers.*

This is nothing spectacular. We've accomplished the transposition by wrapping the entire code (that returned a table) in the `Table.Transpose` function.

At this stage, we have two tables:

- The single-row table with headers (refer to Figure 11-10) in the MergedHeaders step
- The table in the SplitTables step that contains the rest of the rows (refer to Figure 11-4)

To put these two tables together, we can create a new step called CleanTbl with this ridiculously simple code:

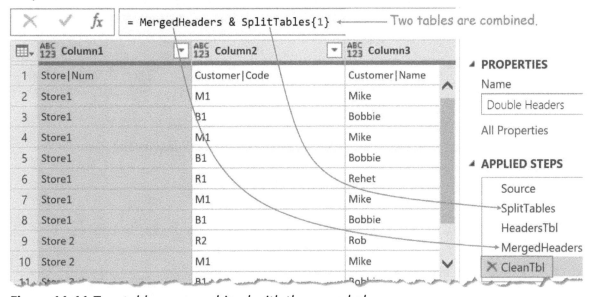

Figure 11-11 *Two tables are combined with the* `&` *symbol.*

A few subtleties to note:

- There is a table on each side of the ampersand (`&`). If either of those two values isn't a table, this doesn't work. The `&` symbol concatenates the same value types (i.e., table with table, list with list, record with record, text with text, etc.).
- The left side (in this case, `MergedHeaders`) refers to the step that returns a table.
- The right side (in this case, `SplitTables`) refers to the step that returns a list of two tables, and `{1}` extracts the second table from that list.

The only thing left to do is to promote the first row as headers. Yes, you can do this by using the UI, but this book is about M, so let's write that last revision to our code:

```
fx   = Table.PromoteHeaders(MergedHeaders & SplitTables{1})
```

#	ABC 123 Store|Num	ABC 123 Customer|Code	ABC 123 Customer|Name
1	Store1	M1 First row promoted	Mike
2	Store1	B1 as Headers	Bobbie
3	Store1	M1	Mike
4	Store1	B1	Bobbie
5	Store1	R1	Rehet

Figure 11-12 *Using* `Table.PromoteHeaders` *to promote the first row to column headers.*

The Real Magic Begins: Building a Custom Function

The example we've just walked through wouldn't have made the cut for this book if we couldn't build it as a plug-and-play solution. After all the mental strain that you have gone through, you should be able to say, "Give me any data that has merged headers for any number of rows, and I'll fix it." 😎

Building that plug-and-play solution calls for building a custom function. Let's peek into the M code (in the Advanced Editor) for our query and talk about the logic for the custom function.

```
1   let
2   Source = Excel.Workbook(File.Contents(FilePath), null, true){[Item=
3   SplitTables = Table.SplitAt ( Source, 2 ),
4   HeadersTbl = Table.Transpose(SplitTable{0}),
5   MergedHeaders = Table.Transpose(Table.CombineColumns(
6       Table.FillDown(HeadersTbl,Table.ColumnNames(HeadersTbl)),
7       Table.ColumnNames(HeadersTbl),
8       Combiner.CombineTextByDelimiter( "|" ),"Merged"
9   )),
10      CleanTbl = Table.PromoteHeaders(MergedHeaders & SplitTables{1})
11  in
12      CleanTbl
```

Figure 11-13 *A peek into the Advanced Editor for the Double Headers query.*

If you look closely, you'll see that we need three inputs from the user for the query to work:

1. The source (i.e., the table undergoing the transformation)
2. How many header rows there are in the table (in this case, two as a hard-coded value)
3. The delimiter choice for combining the headers (in this case, a pipe symbol, |, again hard-coded)

This is exactly what we need as variables in our custom function. Consider this M code for creating a function:

```
1   (InputTable as table, HeaderRowCount as number, optional Delimiter as text) as table =>
2   let
3       Source = InputTable,
4       DelimiterValue = Delimiter ?? "|",
5       SplitTables = Table.SplitAt(Source, HeaderRowCount),
6       HeadersTbl = Table.Transpose(SplitTables{0}),
7       MergedHeaders = Table.Transpose(Table.CombineColumns(
8           Table.FillDown(HeadersTbl,Table.ColumnNames(HeadersTbl)),
9           Table.ColumnNames(HeadersTbl),
10          Combiner.CombineTextByDelimiter(DelimiterValue),"Merged"
11      )),
12      CleanTbl = Table.PromoteHeaders(MergedHeaders & SplitTables{1})
13  in
14      CleanTbl
```

Figure 11-14 *Custom function M code for fixing multiple headers.*

What are we doing here?

We create a new blank query (Home → New Source → Other Sources → Blank Query), name it FixMultipleHeaders, and paste the code above into the Advanced Editor. The code above is a literal copy and paste of the Double Headers query from the Advanced Editor, with a few modifications:

1. The code starts by declaring three variables (`InputTable as table`, `HeaderRowCount as number`, and `optional Delimiter as text`) and returns the output `as table =>`.

2. Line 3 of the code (the Source step) references the `InputTable` variable.

3. Line 4 of the code uses a double question mark, `??` (i.e., the coalesce operator), and replaces the delimiter with the pipe symbol, `|`, if the user inputs nothing (i.e., the field is null). The step `DelimiterValue` is then referenced in line 10.

4. Line 5 of the code references the `HeaderRowCount` variable instead of the hard-coded value.

The code from line 6 onward is the same as the code shown in Figure 11-13.

Using the New Custom Function

Refer to the query Double Headers with Function.

To try out the new custom function, let's start from scratch by creating a new query where the same data from Figure 11-3 is loaded.

ABC 123 Column1	ABC 123 Column2	ABC 123 Column3	ABC 123 Column4	ABC 123 Column5	ABC 123 Column6
1 Store	Customer		null Sales		null
2 Num	Code	Name	Units	MRP	Value
3 Store1	M1	Mike	3	160	
4 Store1	B1	Bobbie	2	210	
5 Store1	M1	Mike	1	100	
6 Store1	B1	Bobbie	3	130	
7 Store1	R1	Rehet	2	220	
8 Store1	M1	Mike	2	200	
9 Store1	B1	Bobbie	3	220	
10 Store 2	R2	Rob	1	70	
11 Store 2	M1	Mike	1	70	
12 Store 2	B1	Bobbie	1	90	
13 Store 2	R1	Rehet	3	110	
14 Store 2	R1	Rehet	2	140	

PROPERTIES
Name
Double Headers with Function
All Properties

APPLIED STEPS
Source

Figure 11-15 *The data has double headers in rows 1 and 2.*

We can call the function in the new step HeadersFixed and enter these values for the arguments:

- `Source` for `InputTable`
- `2` for `HeaderRowCount`
- `"-"` for `Delimiter` (and remember that we marked this input as optional)

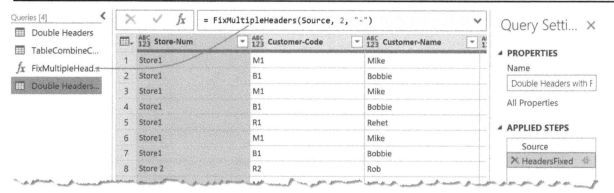

Figure 11-16 *The double headers are fixed.*

I am assuming that this custom function truly makes you happy or, at the very least, make your work more scalable. 👊

Example 2: Removing Junk Rows and Combining Data

If you often get CSV or Excel files as data dumps to work with, you know that it's not uncommon for such files to have a few junk rows at the top before the actual data begins. Consider the following three CSV sales datasets (which are available in the subfolder Remove Junk Rows and Combine Data):

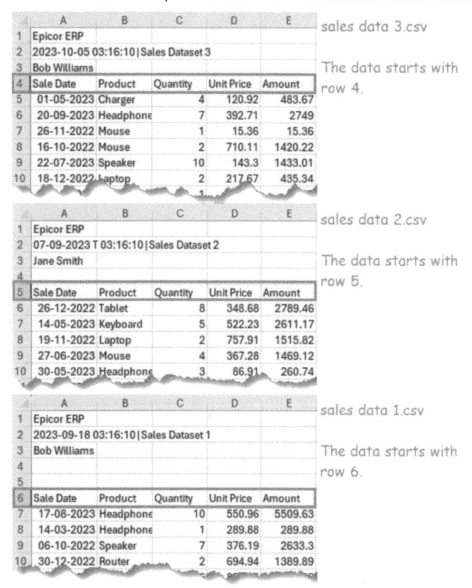

Figure 11-17 *Three CSV files with a few junk rows at the top.*

In this example, we want to combine these three files, but we have to deal with those junk rows. Because each file has a different number of junk rows at the top, we can't simply remove a fixed number of rows from the top of each file. How do we solve this?

The Logic to Solve This Problem

To solve this problem, we've got to take steps like these:

1. In any one data (CSV) file, start skipping the rows from the top until we get to the headers of the data. (Thankfully, all three CSV files have the same headers. 😜)

2. Apply the same logic to all the files and then combine the data.

Identifying the Junk Rows in a Single Dataset

> Refer to the query sales data 1. Find it in the Excel file Remove Junk Rows and Combine Data - Solution, in the Patterns and Recipes folder.

Let's start by loading sales data 1.csv in Power Query.

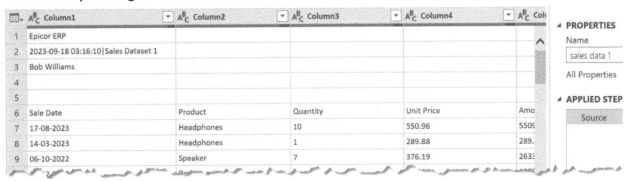

Figure 11-18 *Loading sales data 1.csv in Power Query.*

In this file we need to keep skipping rows (i.e., records) until we reach the headers. To make this more visually comprehensible, we can create a custom column with _ (underscore) as input. We end up with a record for each row.

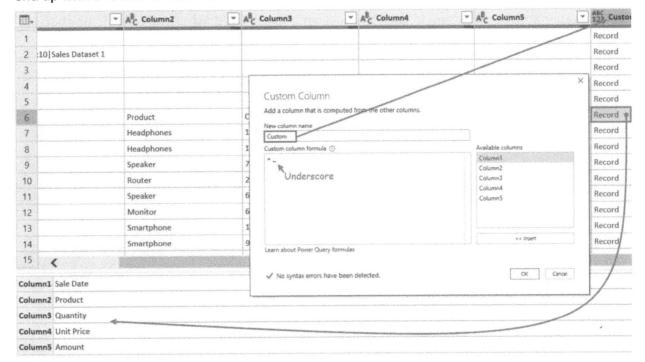

Figure 11-19 *Creating a custom column.*

Next, we need to compare the value of each row (record) with each header: Sale Date, Product, Quantity, Unit Price, and Amount. To work with only the record values, we can transform the record into a list by modifying our custom column formula to look like this:

```
= Record.ToList(_)
```

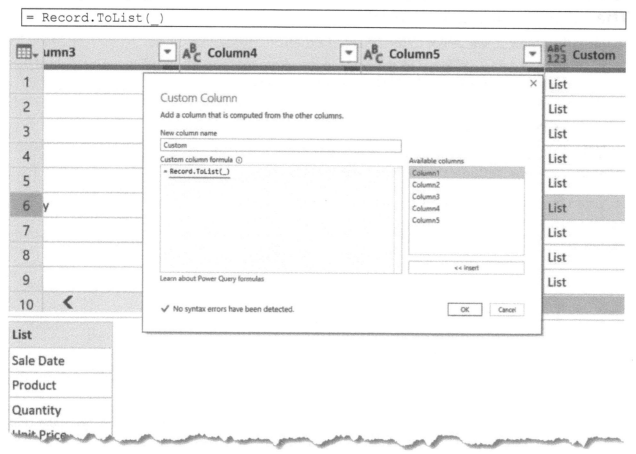

Figure 11-20 *Transforming the custom column records into a list.*

Now we can match the list value in each row against a hard-coded list of columns. To do that, we revise our custom column M code again so it looks like this:

```
=Record.ToList(_) <>
{"Sale Date","Product","Quantity","Unit Price","Amount"}
```

Figure 11-21 *The custom column returns TRUE or FALSE as output when matched with the headers list.*

The code is not difficult. We just compare the list with the column headers (another hard-coded list). But I bet you have some questions, like these:

- Why do we use <> (the not equal sign) between the two lists? Shouldn't the row values be equal to the header list, and shouldn't we use = (equals)?
- Why do we hard-code the column names? What if the column names are not the same in all the CSV files, or what if they change later? Wouldn't hard-coding the column names make the query vulnerable?

Valid questions. Hear me out!

First, the reason we use <> (not equals) as opposed to = (equals) is because the `Table.Skip` function works on the inverse logic—that is, it will stop skipping the rows when it encounters the first `FALSE` value. Here is the function's syntax:

```
= Table.Skip(Table Reference, count or condition)
```

Since we don't have a fixed count of rows, we'll be using a condition to skip the rows. Notice in Figure 11-21 that we get the first `FALSE` value at row 6. That is where the `Table.Skip` function will stop skipping the rows.

Now on to the second set of questions. In this problem, we are considering a rather simple pattern where the column names are the same in all the CSV files. If we were working with files where the column names are not the same, and we wanted to skip the rows until we reached the headers, we could use this slight revision to the custom column formula:

```
= List.MatchesAny(Record.ToList(_), each _ = null or _ = "")
```

In this code, we check whether any of the rows has a blank value. It'll return `TRUE` if a blank or null is found, and otherwise it will return `FALSE`. This image shows what it looks like:

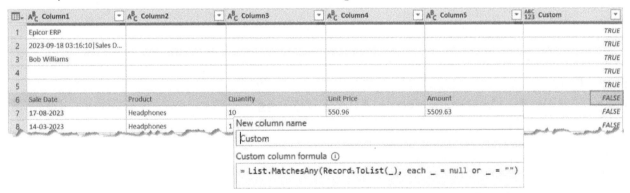

Figure 11-22 *The first `FALSE` appears where the entire row is not blank or null.*

We are making two strong assumptions for this condition to work:

- Each of the top junk rows will have at least one blank or null value.
- The row that contains the headers will not have any blanks or null values.

The point is, you've got to have some pattern to work with. Power Query isn't black magic. 😬

Let's move on from my impaired jokes and get back to writing M code.

Removing the Top Junk Rows

Creating that custom column helped us identify the top junk rows. We don't need it in our solution, though, so we can delete it and use its code in the `Table.Skip` function. To do so, we can delete the Added Custom step and create an entirely new step with the following code:

```
=Table.Skip(
  Source,
  each Record.ToList(_) <>
  {"Sale Date","Product","Quantity","Unit Price","Amount"}
)
```

It results in a table like this:

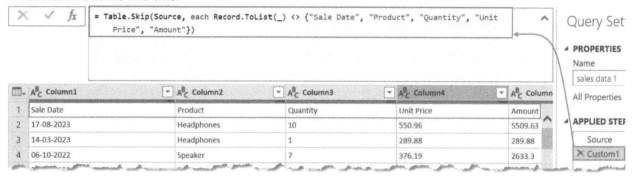

Figure 11-23 *The junk rows are skipped, and headers appear in the first row.*

In the second argument of the `Table.Skip` function, we've used the same code that we used for creating a custom column (refer to Figure 11-21). But there are two more problems:

- The headers are in the first row.
- This kind of transformation needs to be applied to all the CSV files.

To promote the first row as headers, we can revise our M code so it looks like this:

```
=Table.PromoteHeaders(
  Table.Skip(
    Source,
    each Record.ToList(_) <>
    {"Sale Date","Product","Quantity","Unit Price","Amount"}
  )
)
```

But how do we apply this code to all the CSV files? Let's start from the top.

Removing Junk Rows from All CSV Files

As a best practice, we can first create a parameter to save our folder location and then reference it to connect to all CSV files in the folder:

1. Create a new parameter (Home → Manage Parameter → New Parameter).
2. Name the new parameter FolderLocation and enter the folder path in the Current Value box.

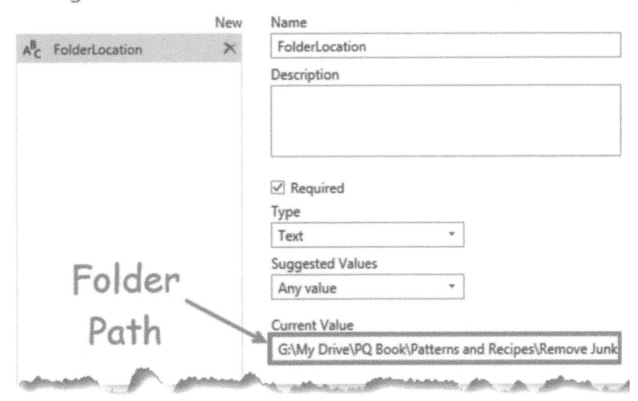

Figure 11-24 *The FolderLocation parameter holds the folder location.*

3. Creating a new blank query (Home → New Source → Other Sources → Blank Query).

4. Use the `Folder.Files` function with the `FolderLocation` parameter to refer to the location that contains all the CSV files.

5. Name the query SalesDataCombined.

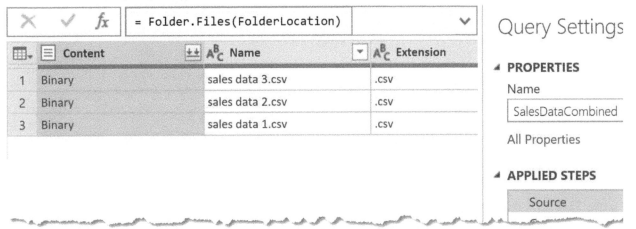

Figure 11-25 *Connecting to the folder location of all the CSV files.*

The Content column indicates that all the CSV files are binary files. (An easy way to think of a binary is as a file of any type.) All those binaries need to be transformed into tables that can be read by Power Query. The function we can use to read the CSV files (i.e., the binaries) is the `Csv.Document` function.

We can create a new step like this:

```
= Table.TransformColumns(Source,
   {"Content", each Csv.Document(_)})
```

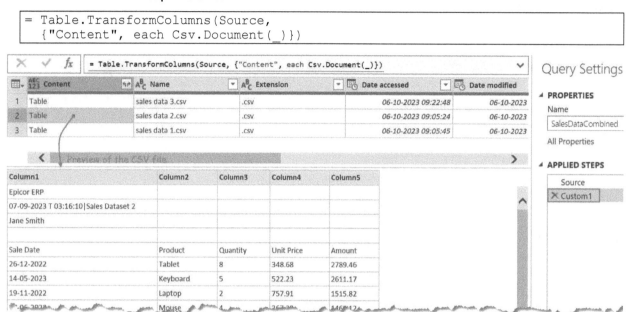

Figure 11-26 *Transforming the binary into a table by using* `Csv.Document`.

We can see the top junk rows in the preview of each table. We've already built the logic to clean a single table, and now it's time to apply the same logic to all the CSV files (i.e., the tables in the Content column).

Here's how we can revise our M code and stack our previous logic in it:

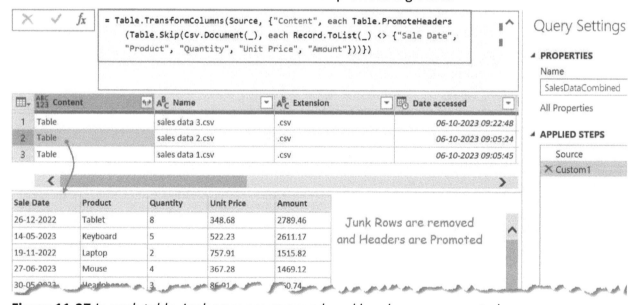

Figure 11-27 *In each table, junk rows are removed, and headers are promoted.*

I know, staring at that M code probably makes you wonder what the hell just happened. Let's spend some time on it. Consider this M code from Figure 11-26, where we transformed each binary into a readable table by using the `Csv.Document` function:

```
= Table.TransformColumns(Source,
   {"Content", each Csv.Document(_)})
```

Note two important things:

- The `Csv.Document` function produces a table as output. However, that table is raw and has junk rows.

- `Table.TransformColumns` works on all the binaries in the Content column, transforming them into raw tables.

Now consider our function from Figure 11-23 that we created to clean up a single table:

```
=Table.PromoteHeaders(
  Table.Skip(
    Source,
    each Record.ToList(_) <>
    {"Sale Date","Product","Quantity","Unit Price","Amount"}
  )
)
```

In this formula, we input a table in the first argument of `Table.Skip` (i.e., Source) and then apply our logic to check each row against valid headers.

So, if we want to nest these two formulas and transform all CSV files, we need to replace the first argument of `Table.Skip`, which only accepts a table (i.e., Source), with `Csv.Document(_)`, which returns a table. I'll say it again: Feed Power Query what it eats! 😋

The code to do it is shown here (refer to Figure 11-27):

```
=Table.TransformColumns(
  Source,
  {"Content",
  each Table.PromoteHeaders(Table.Skip(
  Csv.Document(_),each Record.ToList(_) <>
  {"Sale Date","Product","Quantity","Unit Price","Amount"}))
  })
```

The next obvious step is to combine (i.e., append) all the tables. To do that, we can create a new step, as shown here:

Figure 11-28 *Combining all the transformed tables from the previous step.*

Note that:

- `Custom1` is the table from the previous query step.
- `Custom1[Content]` extracts the transformed tables in the Content column as a list.
- `Table.Combine` combines all the tables in that list.

Don't forget to apply data types before you close and load. 😌

Done!

Example 3: Combining Data with Inconsistent Column Headers

Power Query thrives on patterns for transforming data, but you will not always be able to find patterns, and at times you'll have to rely on user input. In this example, we'll look at one such problem and its solution.

Refer to the three CSV files for January, February, and March sales in the subfolder Combining Data with Inconsistent Headers.

Jan Sales.csv

	A	B	C	D	E
1	SaleDt	Prod	Units	MRP	Amount
2	01-01-2023	Dell Inspiron	5	1000	5000
3	02-01-2023	iPhone 13	3	800	2400
4	03-01-2023	HP Spectre	4	1200	4800
5	04-01-2023	Samsung Galaxy	5	750	3750
6	05-01-2023	Apple MacBook	2	1800	3600
7	06-01-2023		6		5100

Feb Sales.csv

	A	B	C	D	E
1	Date	Product	Units	MRP	Sales
2	01-02-2023	Dell Inspiron	6	1000	6000
3	02-02-2023	iPhone 13	4	810	3240
4	03-02-2023	HP Spectre	5	1205	6025
5	04-02-2023	Samsung Ga	6	760	4560
6	05-02-2023	Apple MacB	3	1810	5430
7	06-02-2023	oogle Pixel		55	4 75

Mar Sales.csv

	A	B	C	D	E
1	Pdt	Dt	Units	Price	Total
2	Dell Inspiron	01-03-2023	7	1010	7070
3	iPhone 13	02-03-2023	5	820	4100
4	HP Spectre	03-03-2023	6	1210	7260
5	Samsung Gal	04-03-2023	5	770	3850
6	Apple MacBo	05-03-2023	4	1820	7280
7	oogle	03-2025		60	160

Figure 11-29 *These CSV files do not have the same headers.*

If you look closely, you'll see two anomalies:

- The CSV files have similar but not identical headers.
- The order of the columns is not the same across all the files.

It's not shown here, so we don't know for sure, but the CSV file for April might have slightly different column headers than the rest of the files.

Our task is to append data from all three CSV files, and the result should look like this:

Date	Product	Units	MRP	Amount
01-01-23	Dell Inspiron	5	1000	5000
02-01-23	iPhone 13	3	800	2400
03-01-23	HP Spectre	4	1200	4800
04-01-23	Samsung Galaxy S25	5	750	3750
05-01-23	Apple MacBook Pro	2	1800	3600
06-01-23	Google Pixel 8	6	850	5100
07-01-23	Lenovo ThinkPad	5	950	4750
08-01-23	Surface Pro	4	1100	4400

Jan + Feb + Mar data combined

Figure 11-30 *Here is how the output should look like.*

The Logic to Solve This Problem

Before we start throwing our M punches, let's draw a rough outline of what a good solution would look like:

- Since we have no pattern for column headers for the existing and forthcoming files, we need a bit of user intervention to provide input for what the correct column names should be. This means creating a query with two columns:
    - Column 1 should contain the current column names from all the CSV files.
    - Column 2 should allow the user to rename each column.
- This table then becomes the source for renaming all the CSV files.
- Once the renaming is done, we can combine the data.

Important note: As soon as a new file is added to the folder, the user will have to refresh the query for renaming the columns, add or edit the column names, if necessary, and then refresh the query for renaming the columns and combining data from all the CSV files.

With the logic laid out, let's start!

Query 1: Creating a Query for User Input

Refer to the query HeaderList. Find it in the Excel file Combining Data with Inconsistent Headers - Solution, in the Patterns and Recipes folder.

Let's begin with a new query, named HeaderList, and connect to the folder with CSV files by using the function `Folder.Files`.

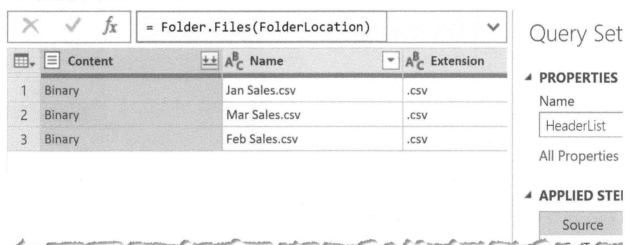

Figure 11-31 *Connecting to the folder that contains CSV files.*

Just as in the previous example, we create the parameter `FolderLocation`, which serves as a single point of change if the folder location changes. We reference it in the `Folder.Files` function.

Next, we need to convert the binaries/CSV files (in the Content column) into readable tables. As a new step, we can use the `Table.TransformColumns` function like this:

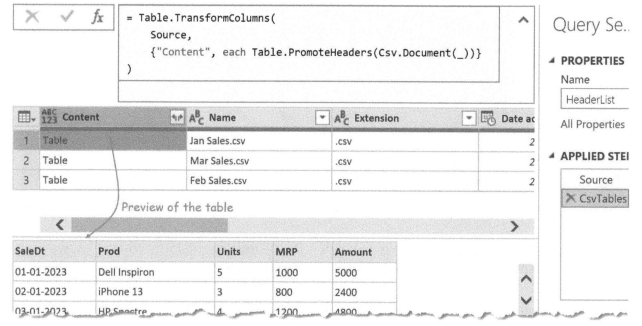

Figure 11-32 *Transforming the binaries into tables.*

The formula is straightforward if we read it from the inside out:

1. `Csv.Document` converts the binary into a table.
2. `Table.PromoteHeaders` marks the first row as headers.
3. These two steps are repeated for each table in the Content column.

We can now combine the three tables and extract the column names as a list. Here is a new step for that:

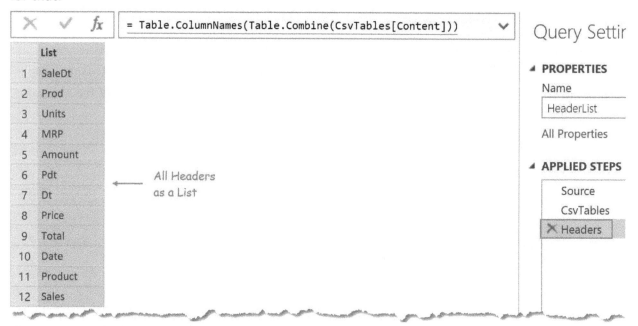

Figure 11-33 *The headers from all CSV files are extracted as a list.*

By now you should recognize this pattern of extracting column names 😄:

1. The `Table.Combine` function combines all the tables in the Content column.

2. The `Table.ColumnNames` function extracts the column names as a list.

Let's load this query in Excel and start feeding in input for the correct column names.

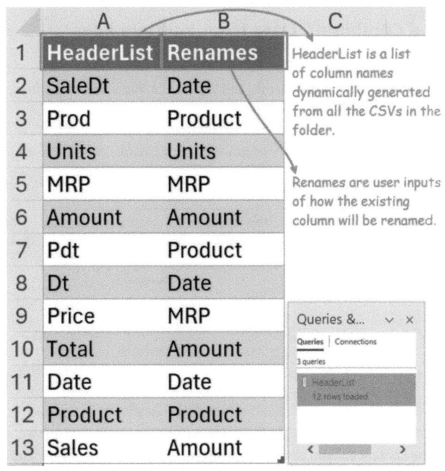

	A	B
1	HeaderList	Renames
2	SaleDt	Date
3	Prod	Product
4	Units	Units
5	MRP	MRP
6	Amount	Amount
7	Pdt	Product
8	Dt	Date
9	Price	MRP
10	Total	Amount
11	Date	Date
12	Product	Product
13	Sales	Amount

HeaderList is a list of column names dynamically generated from all the CSVs in the folder.

Renames are user inputs of how the existing column will be renamed.

Queries &...

Queries | Connections

3 queries

HeaderList
12 rows loaded

Figure 11-34 *The table with existing column names and renamed columns entered by the user.*

Now this table can be the source for renaming all the columns to make their names consistent and then seamlessly combining the data.

We can load this table, which now has two columns, from Excel into Power Query (Data → From Table/Range). We can then name the query RenamedHeaders.

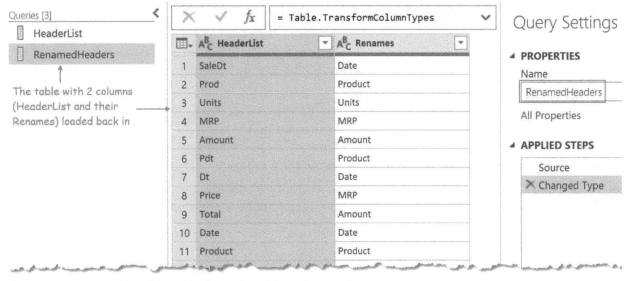

The table with 2 columns (HeaderList and their Renames) loaded back in

Figure 11-35 *Loading the table from Excel into Power Query.*

There is still some minor work to be done with this query, but we'll come back to it in a bit, armed with more context. For now, let's work on a second query, which will use the first query to rename columns from all CSV files.

Renaming Headers and Combining Data from Multiple Files

Refer to the query Combine&Rename.

Let's create a new blank query, name it Combine&Rename, and repeat the initial two steps from the HeaderList query:

1. The Source step uses `Folder.Files` to populate the CSV files from the folder.

2. In the CsvTables step, `Table.TransformColumns` converts each CSV file into a table and promotes the first row as headers.

With the initial two steps done, our query looks like this:

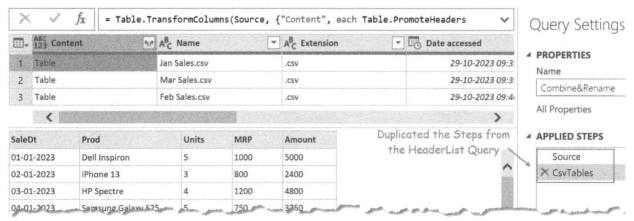

Figure 11-36 *Creating a new query and duplicating the first two steps from the HeaderList query.*

At this stage, the three tables in the Content column contain inconsistent headers. Before we expand them and combine their data, we need to rename their columns to make them consistent.

The renaming in this case should work like this:

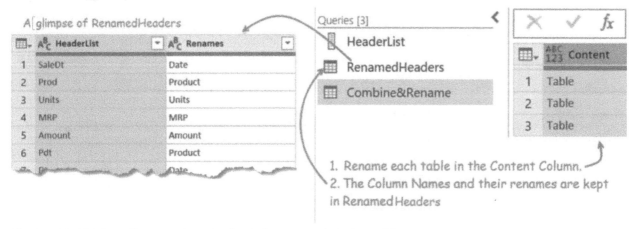

Figure 11-37 *Visually mapping the logic for renaming the tables.*

Let's take a quick detour to look at how renaming works. As a trial exercise, we can rename the Name and Extension columns to FileName and FileType, respectively. Here is what the M code looks like:

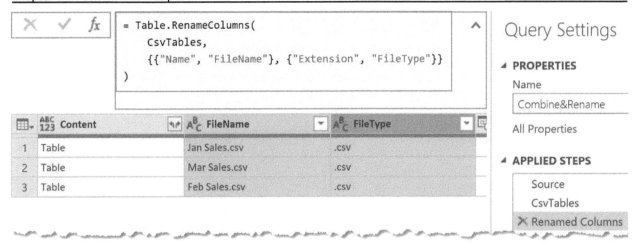

Figure 11-38 *Creating a renamed step to see the UI-generated M code.*

This M code uses the function `Table.RenameColumns` (no surprise!). The first input is the table name (that is, the previous step—in this case, CsvTables) where the columns will be renamed. The renaming uses nested lists, where each nested list is a pair of text values for the original column and the renamed column (i.e., `{"Name", "FileName"}`).

We already have the column names and their renames in the RenamedHeaders query (refer to Figure 11-35), but that is a table at this point, and we need a nested list for the `Table.RenameColumns` function to work (refer to Figure 11-38). We need to feed Power Query what it eats! 😄

Before we carry out the renaming, we need to first transform the RenamedHeaders query (the table) into a nested list such that each row becomes a list. Let's create a new step with the following code:

Figure 11-39 *Transforming the RenamedHeaders table to a nested list.*

The `Table.ToRows` function transforms each record into a list and returns a nested list.

> **Tip:** The `Table.ToColumns` function does the opposite and transforms each column of a table into a list and returns a nested list. (For a review, see Figure 5-9 in Chapter 5.)

Now that we have all the necessary ingredients, we can return to our working query Combine&Rename and rename all the tables. To maintain hygiene, we can also delete the pseudo Renamed Columns step that we created.

Consider this M code for renaming the tables in the Content column:

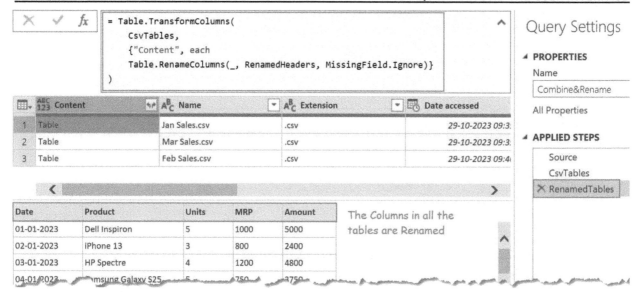

Figure 11-40 *Renaming columns in all the tables.*

This is how it works:

1. Just like before, we loop through all the tables in the Content column.
2. For each table, we use the `Table.RenameColumns` function, where the first input is the table (denoted by the _), the second input is the nested list (i.e., `RenamedHeaders`), and the third optional input is `MissingField.Ignore` to ignore errors in the event that there are any columns missing from the tables but present in the renaming list (`RenamedHeaders`).

Finally, we can now combine data from the three tables in the new step:

Figure 11-41 *Combining the renamed tables from the previous step.*

The `Table.Combine` function references the Content column as a list and combines the renamed tables. Because the headers in all the tables are consistent, the data gets combined seamlessly.

A Slight Quirk

When a new CSV file brings in a few more inconsistent columns, the HeaderList query captures the column names and loads them into Excel, but the corresponding Renames column values do not move as new rows are added to the table. The user has to manually ensure that each renamed value corresponds to the correct column name. How do you make sure this happens automatically, without any manual intervention?

> Refer to the queries HeaderList 2, RenamedHeaders 2, and Combine&Rename 2.

This is a problem that we can mostly solve by using the UI, and you can find the solution in the same Excel file that contains the current query. It involves the three queries shown here:

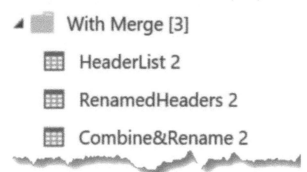

Figure 11-42 *Revised queries to tackle the reordering problem for new column names.*

Here's how it works:

1. The HeaderList 2 query captures all the column names and loads that data into Excel.
2. The user adds rename values against the column names, and this query is loaded back into Power Query as RenamedHeaders 2.
3. We convert the query HeaderList 2 (i.e., a list) into a table and apply a left outer merge between this table and RenamedHeaders 2 and expand the Renames column.
4. Now HeaderList 2 is a two-column table and shows the renamed values on the right side when the data is loaded in Excel. If any new column names are added, they will appear as null values, and the user gets to fill in those null values.
5. Finally, we need Renamed Headers 2 to be a nested list, and we can add a step for this in the Combine&Rename 2 query, right before the renamed tables.

It all works smoothly. 😎

Example 4: Capturing and Reporting Errors

Refer to the query Products in the Excel file Reporting Errors.

In Chapter 9, when we were talking about errors, I left you hanging in an example using the `try` keyword where the number and the error message appeared in the same column (refer to Figure 9-17). I promised to eventually provide elaborate examples of capturing and reporting errors not just from one column but dynamically from all the columns of a table. We're now up to that point!

As you can see here, the Source step contains a table with a few error cells:

	ABC 123 Product_ID	ABC 123 Product_Name	ABC 123 Category	ABC 123 Brand	ABC 123 Price_USD	ABC 123 Sto
1	P001	Error	Furniture	OfficePro	249.99	
2	P002	Smartphone X12	Electronics	TechGiant	799.99	
3	P003	Cotton T-Shirt	Clothing	ComfyWear	Error	
4	P004	Stainless Steel Pot	Kitchenware	ChefChoice	59.99	
5	P005	Wireless Mouse	Error	TechGiant	29.99	
6	P006	Yoga Mat	Sports & Fitness	ZenFit	34.99	
7	P007	LED Desk Lamp	Lighting	BrightHome	39.99	
8	P008	Leather Wallet	Accessories	LuxeLeather	49.99	

Figure 11-43 *Error values in the table.*

We'd like to capture all errors as a table that shows the reason and message for each error and then load this data into either Excel or Power BI. Ideally, the output should look like this:

1²₃ Row	A⁰C Column	ABC 123 Reason	ABC 123 Message
1	1 Product_Name	DataFormat.Error	Invalid cell value '#N/A'.
2	3 Price_USD	DataFormat.Error	Invalid cell value '#N/A'.
3	5 Category	DataFormat.Error	Invalid cell value '#N/A'.

Figure 11-44 *The expected output, with the error reason and message displayed.*

This is a ridiculously simple problem that can mostly be tackled using the user interface. Here's how:

1. Add an index column (Add Column → Index Column → From 1).

2. Rename the index column Row in the formula bar:

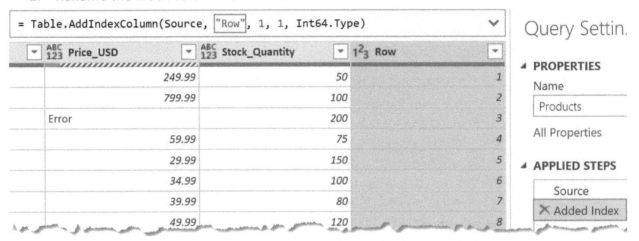

Figure 11-45 *Adding an index column and renaming it Row in the formula bar.*

3. Select the Row column, right-click, and select Unpivot Other Columns. The unpivoted table looks like this:

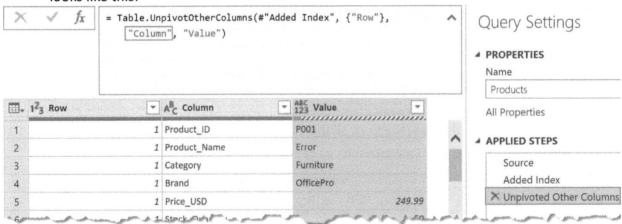

Figure 11-46 *The table is unpivoted, and the Attribute column is renamed Column.*

I sense that you realize where we are going with this. 😄

4. Keep only the error values in the Value column (Value column → Home → Keep Rows → Keep Errors).

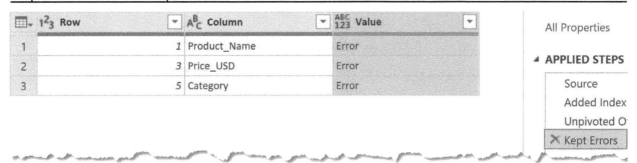

Figure 11-47 *Keeping the errors in the Value column.*

5. To capture the error reason and message, add a new custom column with the `try` keyword, like this:

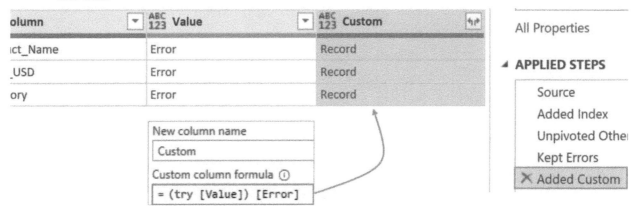

Figure 11-48 *Using `try` in the custom column.*

Recall from Chapter 9 how the `try` keyword works (refer to Figure 9-12). If an error is evaluated, `try` returns a record with two fields: HasError and Error. We can reference the Error field after the `try` like this:

```
=(try[Value])[Error]
```

This gives us access to the five error fields shown in Figure 9-13.

All that is left to do is to expand the Custom column with the Reason and Message fields, and the output is served:

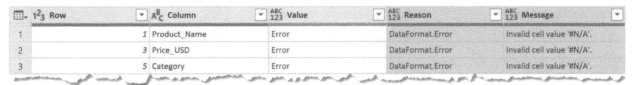

Figure 11-49 *The table now shows the error reason and message.*

Now you can delete the Value column and load this data into Excel or Power BI and do any sort of fancy reporting you want on this data. 😄

> **Note:** Consider these two things before we finish the chapter:
> - We could have expanded additional columns from our record in Figure 11-48.
> - We also could have used the `try` and `catch` keywords while creating the custom column in Figure 11-48. In that case, the custom column code would have looked like this:
>
> ```
> = try [Value] catch (e) => e
> ```

Exercise

Here is just one challenging exercise to test your overall understanding. Ready?

Note: Open the Excel file Exercise - Unsolved in the Patterns and Recipes folder and then use the Power Query Editor to work through this exercise.

Exercise 1: Unpivot Multiple Column Groups

Say hello to a problem that we only partially solved in Chapter 3 (refer to Figure 3-22).

Male Customers			Female Customers		
Date	Product	Units	Date	Product	Units
17-Apr-23	A	82	17-Apr-23	Z	76
18-Apr-23	B	11	18-Apr-23	G	80
19-Apr-23	C	82	19-Apr-23	H	71
20-Apr-23	B	57	20-Apr-23	I	84
21-Apr-23	A	12	21-Apr-23	G	75
22-Apr-23	A	78	22-Apr-23	K	89

←———— Pivoted Data

Date	Product	Units	Customer Type
17-04-2023	A	82	Male
18-04-2023	B	11	Male
19-04-2023	C	82	Male
20-04-2023	B	57	Male
21-04-2023	A	12	Male
22-04-2023	A	78	Male
17-04-2023	Z	76	Female
18-04-2023	G	80	Female
19-04-2023	H	71	Female
20-04-2023	I	84	Female
21-04-2023	G	75	Female
22-04-2023	K	89	Female

←———— Expected Output - Unpivoted Data

Figure 11-50 *The data and the expected output.*

Here are a few assumptions about the pivoted data in this example:

- The number of main headers (e.g., Male, Female, Kids) can change.
- Each main header has the same three subheaders: Date, Product, and Units.
- There can be only two header rows: one for main headers and one for subheaders.

For this exercise, create a more dynamic solution than the one discussed in Chapter 3.

Note: When you're done with this exercise, you can compare your answer against the one I provide in the Solutions chapter at the end of this book or refer to the Excel file Exercise - Solved or do both. 😄

Chapter 12: Miscellaneous Tips and Tricks

This book wouldn't be complete without a smattering of tips and tricks at the end. I'm using this chapter to share some of my favorite Power Query tips and tricks I have learned over the years.

> **Note:** For this chapter, we'll be using the file Tips and Tricks.xlsx (which you'll find in the Tips and Tricks folder). As you work through this chapter, you'll be able to walk through the examples by using the queries provided in this file.

Power Query Keywords

In the M language, there are a few interesting keywords that you can use within queries to make them more efficient. Let's look at them, one by one.

The #shared Keyword

Refer to the query Shared.

In the midst of a coding spree 40,000 feet above sea level, you feel the need to browse the documentation for M functions, but your flight doesn't offer Wi-Fi. What do you do?

Use the `#shared` keyword. Here's how. In the formula bar, just type `=#shared` (all lowercase) and press Enter. The result is a record showing all the functions:

f_x	= #shared

Shared	Record
Value.ResourceExpression	Function
Resource.Access	Function
Kusto.Contents	Function
Kusto.Databases	Function
AzureDataExplorer.Contents	Function
AzureDataExplorer.Databases	Function
CommonDataService.Database	Function
PowerPlatform.Dataflows	Function
DataLake.Contents	Function
DataLake.Files	Function
List.NonNullCount	Function

Figure 12-1 *#shared results in a record containing all the Power Query functions.*

Furthermore, you can transform this record into a table by using the `Record.ToTable` function to conveniently work with the table in the UI.

```
X    ✓    fx    | = Record.ToTable(#shared)
```

⊞▾ Aᴮ꜀ Name ▾	ᴬᴮᶜ₁₂₃ Value ▾
1 Shared	Table
2 Value.ResourceExpression	Function
3 Resource.Access	Function
4 Kusto.Contents	Function
5 Kusto.Databases	Function
6 AzureDataExplorer.Contents	Function
7 AzureDataExplorer.Databases	Function
8 CommonDataService.Database	Function

Figure 12-2 *Transforming records into a table.*

Once you have a table that contains all the functions, you can do pretty much anything that you would otherwise do with any other table in Power Query. To start, you can click on any function in the Value column to see detailed documentation about that function. 😎

The #sections Keyword

Refer to the query Sections.

#sections is an interesting keyword, particularly when you want to dynamically reference other queries. Consider a scenario where you want to reference (i.e., work with) all the queries that start with the word "Test." How would you do that?

In the query Sections, notice that you can use the =#sections keyword (all lowercase) in the formula bar like this:

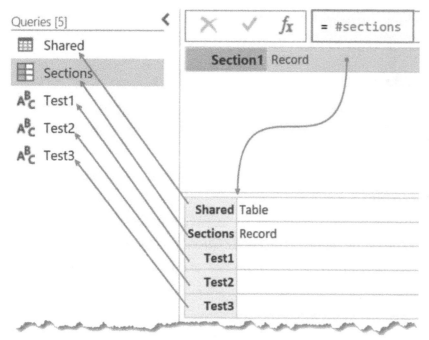

Figure 12-3 *The #sections keyword results in a record of all the queries in the Power Query window.*

You can preview all the queries in the Section1 field of the record. So, to extract all the queries in the table, you would:

1. Extract the column from the record, like this:

```
=#sections[Section1]
```

2. Wrap that in the `Record.ToTable` function to convert it into a table for ease of use:

```
=Record.ToTable(#sections[Section1])
```

The result appears like this:

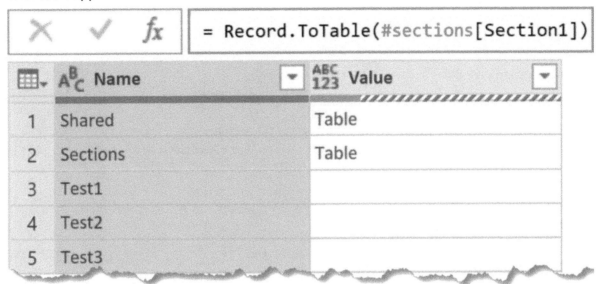

Figure 12-4 *Transforming* `#sections` *into a table.*

You can see a slight error in the Value column here because self-referencing the Sections query means a circular reference is created. From this point onward, you can filter the table to keep all the queries that begin with "Test." 😎

The is Keyword

> Refer to the query isKeyword.

The `is` keyword is a very handy comparer keyword, but it only works for value types (lists, tables, data types, etc.) and generates `TRUE` or `FALSE` as output. Here is how it works:

```
1  let
2      CheckTable = #table(null, {{null}}) is table,   // will return true
3      CheckList = {1,2,3} is list,                     // will return true
4      CheckText = "Some Text" is number                // will return false
5  in
6      CheckText
```

Figure 12-5 *The* `is` *keyword returns* `TRUE` *if the value types are matching and otherwise returns* `FALSE`.

Note that:

- You can only compare value types with the `is` keyword. Writing something like `= 4 is 4` will result in an error because the number 4 is not a value type.
- You can use the `is` keyword anywhere in your queries (steps, columns, custom functions, etc.).

The Dot Dot (..) Keyword

Refer to the query DotDot.

Dot dot (. .) is a list expansion keyword. You can create a list with start and end values with two dots in between. Here are a few examples:

```
1   let
2       // returns a list of numbers from 1 to 10
3       OneToTen = {1..10},
4
5       // Returns Uppercase Letters from A to G
6       AtoG = {"A".."G"},
7
8       // Returns Weekdays from Sunday to Saturday
9       SunToSat = List.Transform({1..7}, Date.DayOfWeekName),
10
11      // Returns Month Names from January to Decemeber
12      MonthNames = List.Transform({1..12}, each Date.MonthName(#date(2024,_,1)))
13  in
14      MonthNames
```

Figure 12-6 *Using two dots to create lists.*

You can use these lists in many ways to enhance your queries.

The Coalesce Operator (??)

Refer to the query Coalesce.

Quite often you'll find yourself writing if statements to do things like check whether a certain value is null and then replace it with another value. You can reduce the amount of code you use to do this by using the coalesce operator (i.e., ??).

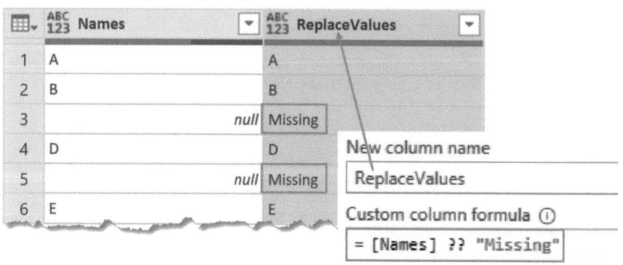

Figure 12-7 *Using ?? to replace null values with the text value* "Missing".

Note that:

- The coalesce operator can only be used to replace null values.
- The syntax is pretty straightforward:

```
= ValueToCheck ?? ReplacementValue
```

- You can use any type of replacement value (number, text, table, list, record, etc.), so the following formula will also produce legitimate output (even though it doesn't make any sense 😄):

```
= [Names] ?? {1,2,3}
```

- Under the hood, the coalesce operator (`??`) uses the `if` function, so I don't believe it to be any faster or slower than the `if` function. It's just shorter!

Miscellaneous Power Query Tricks

Here are a few nifty Power Query tricks that are extremely useful for writing crisper M code.

Using Autocomplete in Power Query

Autocomplete in Power Query is the most terrible thing to happen to the M language, and there's been no good solution to this point. In case you've not witnessed its atrocity, let me show you.

In this example, I am writing a `Text.Lower` formula in the Custom Column box. Halfway through the formula, I press the Tab key to autocomplete the formula. Here's what I get:

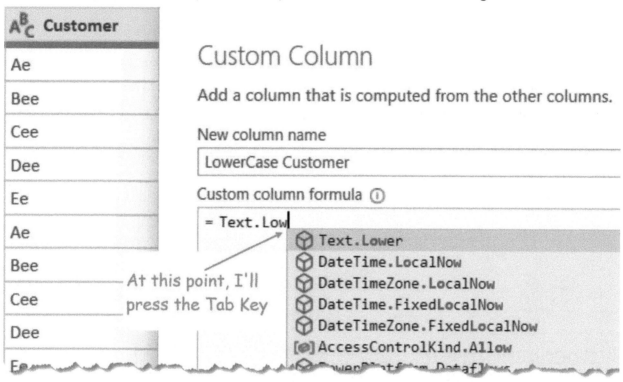

Figure 12-8 *Pressing the Tab key to autocomplete the* `Text.Lower` *function.*

But as I press the Tab key, Power Query goes bonkers and adds `Text` before the function, so now I have `TextText.Lower`, and obviously this drives me nuts.

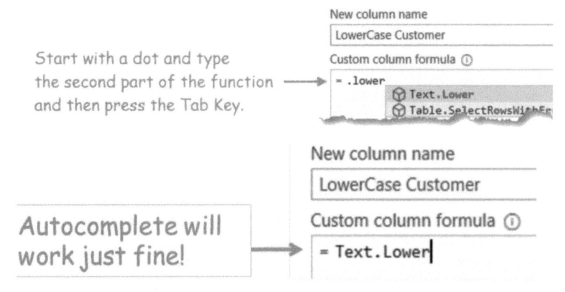

A^B_C Customer
Ae
Bee
Cee
Dee
Ee
Ae
Bee
Cee

Custom Column

Add a column that is computed from the ot

New column name

LowerCase Customer

Custom column formula ⓘ

= TextText.Lower|

↑

Text written twice

Figure 12-9 *Power Query autocompletes the function by adding* Text *at the start.*

The trick is to start with a dot instead:

Start with a dot and type
the second part of the function
and then press the Tab Key.

New column name

LowerCase Customer

Custom column formula ⓘ

= .lower
   ⓦ Text.Lower
   ⓦ Table.SelectRowsWithEr

New column name

LowerCase Customer

Custom column formula ⓘ

= Text.Lower|

Autocomplete will
work just fine!

Figure 12-10 *Autocomplete works when you start with the dot instead.*

This trick can be used in the Custom Column box, the formula bar, and even the Advanced Editor: Just start with the dot. As a bonus, this technique won't crop your existing function if you're wrapping one function in another. 😊

Using the true Parameter in the Excel.Workbook Function

Refer to the query true parameter.

You'll often find the Promoted Headers step added to a query when you're connecting to an Excel file. It looks something like this:

Figure 12-11 *The Promoted Headers step is automatically added when connecting to an Excel file.*

You can remove the Promoted Headers step by using the optional `useHeaders` argument in the `Excel.Worbook` function. Here is how it's done:

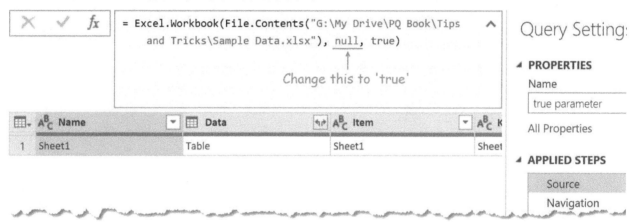

Figure 12-12 *Replacing the null value with* `true` *in the* `Excel.Workbook` *function in the Source step.*

With the `true` argument in the `Excel.Workbook` function, the first row of each worksheet in the Excel file is considered a header row, and you can now get rid of the Promoted Headers step.

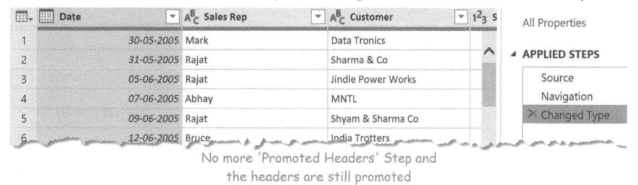

No more 'Promoted Headers' Step and
the headers are still promoted

Figure 12-13 *Headers are promoted even without the Promoted Headers step.*

Nifty, right? 😑

> **Gotcha!** 🙁 The file path to Sample Data.xlsx in the Source step might be broken in your computer. The Sample Data file is provided in the Tips and Tricks folder. Be sure to fix the file path in the Source step if you want the query shown here to work.

Using Projections

Refer to the query Projections.

Let's say we are working on a query, and we'd like to keep the Date and Sales columns and remove the rest of the columns:

Figure 12-14 *Keeping only the Date and Sales columns and removing the rest.*

The most obvious solution would be to select the two columns Date and Sales in Power Query, right-click, and select Remove Other Columns.

Another nifty way of getting the job done is to use projections. Here is the syntax:

```
= TableReference [[Column1], [Column2]]
```

Note that:

- We start by referring to a table.
- Next, in the square brackets, we reference the columns separated by a comma. Each column reference is also in square brackets. The output is a table.

Here it is in action on our query:

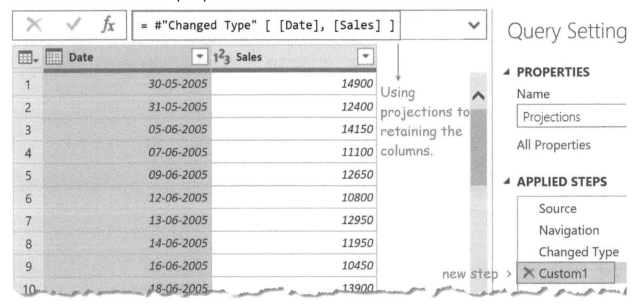

Figure 12-15 *Using projections to retain the Date and Sales columns.*

> **Note:** I use this technique only to simplify my code. I have not seen any performance upgrade or degradation in using this technique compared to using the `Table.SelectColumns` function.

The meta Keyword

Refer to the query Test.

Let's dig up an old grave from Chapter 2, where we discussed how to extract an intermediate step from a query. I noted at the end of Example 2 that once the query is transformed as a record, it becomes useless and cannot be loaded into Excel. (If that doesn't ring a bell, I'll let you go back and jog your memory a bit.)

Say that we are trying to extract an intermediate step from the Test query:

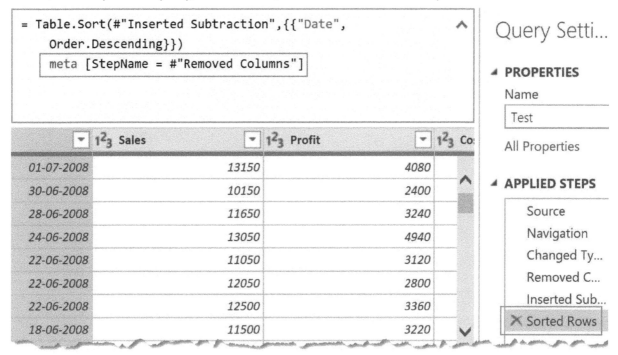

Figure 12-16 *The Test query has multiple steps.*

This time, instead of turning the entire query into a record, we're going to use the `meta` keyword, which will keep the query intact and usable.

On the last step of the query, Sorted Rows, we can add the `meta` keyword in the formula like this:

```
= Table.Sort(#"Inserted Subtraction",{{"Date",
    Order.Descending}})
    meta [StepName = #"Removed Columns"]
```

Figure 12-17 *Adding the* `meta` *keyword in the last step.*

Note that:

- The `meta` keyword allows us to add metadata to any value (or step) in Power Query.
- These metadata values can be specified in a record, as shown above.
- In this case, we used StepName as the field name and referenced the Removed Columns step.

- There is no impact on the output, but the last step (Sorted Rows) now stores the output of the Removed Columns step as metadata.

Next, we create a new query (Home → New Source → Other Sources → Blank Query), name it Meta Keyword, and reference our Test query in the Source step, like this:

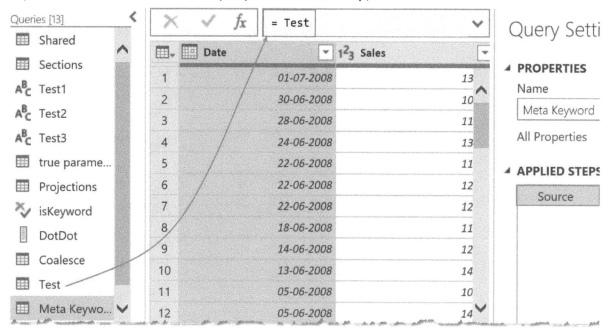

Figure 12-18 *Referencing the Test query.*

At this point, we still get the last step of the query (i.e., Sorted Rows) and not the intermediate step that we wanted (i.e., Removed Columns). We need to extract the metadata by using the `Value.Metadata` function, like this:

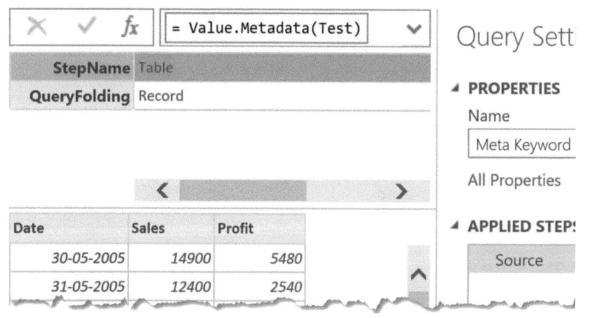

Figure 12-19 `Value.Metadata` *returns a record with the StepName field.*

Now that we can see our StepName field, we can simply extract the table from the intermediate step (Removed Columns) by referencing the field name, like this:

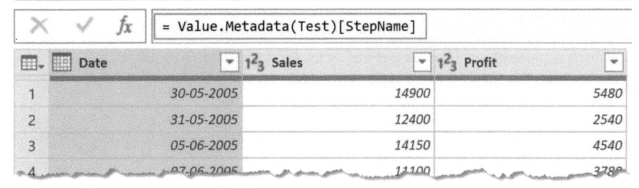

Figure 12-20 *Extracting an intermediate step in a new query.*

Solutions

The best way to view these solutions is to look at the Excel file for each chapter.

Chapter 1: Working with Lists

Here are the solutions for the exercises in Chapter 1.

> **Note:** Refer to the Excel file List Exercises - Solved in the Lists folder.

Exercise 1

```
let
    // the .. expands the list between
    // the start and end values.
    Solution1 = {"a".."j"},

    // you can also create the list manually
    Solution2 =
    {"a", "b", "c", "d", "e", "f", "g", "h", "i", "j"}
in
    Solution2
```

Exercise 2

```
let
    Source = Table.FromRows(Json.Document(Binary.Decompress(Binary.
FromText("ZZDNDsIgEIRfhXD2sP1Tr7VGE6Me1OihelgrCY0tGJYefHuhxWj0Qs-
gyM/sNZclXSA8jhOUjfiwKd0YQZcAvo5IXEk0jnm62d7cW2bkDiMes0F4WRzDIvhKWWt/
YovGWKJ2EmB22gqQbzdEiOxit6oq8IgP4UQSCJAvW/CrRh222h3W/Mw2OXJGs79ijPbF9kwXOATB-
N4LfHTJPVyr0r6hqLyvYcMAnCIxqS+LUPptlfx5OsrWA5ka5qtKJPSN5fNjNdJT5F4sTPLy8=",
BinaryEncoding.Base64), Compression.Deflate)), let _t = ((type nullable text)
meta [Serialized.Text = true]) in type table [#"Sales Rep" = _t, Customer =
_t, Amount = _t]),

    #"Changed Type" =
    Table.TransformColumnTypes(Source,
    {{"Sales Rep", type text},
     {"Customer", type text},
     {"Amount", Int64.Type}}),

    // #"Changed Type"[Amount] will result in list.
    // List.Sum will sum its values.
    ExtractAndSumAmount = List.Sum(#"Changed Type"[Amount])
in
    ExtractAndSumAmount
```

Exercise 3

```
let
    Source = Table.FromRows(Json.Document(Binary.Decompress(Binary.From-
Text("fVHLTsMwEPwVK+ceNi/KtQ0CCUEPbVUOIYdtsOSIxEZe59C/r70NIgmQi+XZHc/
ujMsyekb6slK6aBWdisKfMcQ5zFC1KqNCoW3lxdcO/taheO8BkjtRmEBLYoClVlAYjXoy5kM8t-
kEtztY871cpPNljJ0n50gM6FEdrdFNTYOTA8/4sTx4ONtJ8bIpRoG3OCsPE193xhXfNWHYC-
madJNZ/IDi/YfRsc7N58ZukQwSJhGuXWkDPa9zX1rUPt2AWsWWmhGVROaEnhaFu4z2EOZ7m/
qcZJsSEydYNOsmB6++9/W0Fia/ta/uSXpOM0GVXVFQ==", BinaryEncoding.Base64),
Compression.Deflate)), let _t = ((type nullable text) meta [Serialized.Text =
true]) in type table [#"Sales Rep" = _t, Customer = _t, Amount = _t, #"Cus-
tomer~" = _t, #"Amount~" = _t]),

    ColNamesList = Table.ColumnNames(Source),

    #"Converted to Table" =
    Table.FromList(ColNamesList,Splitter.SplitByNothing(),
    null, null, ExtraValues.Ignore),

    #"Filtered Rows" =
    Table.SelectRows(#"Converted to Table", each
    Text.EndsWith([Column1], "~")),

    RemoveColsList = #"Filtered Rows"[Column1],

    RemovedColumns =
    Table.RemoveColumns(Source, RemoveColsList)
in
    RemovedColumns
```

Exercise 4

```
let
    Source = Table.FromRows(Json.Document(Binary.Decompress(Binary.
FromText("ZZDNDsIgEIRfhXD2sP1Tr7VGE6Me1OihelgrCY0tGJYefHuhxWj0Qs-
gyM/sNZclXSA8jhOUjfiwKd0YQZcAvo5IXEk0jnm62d7cW2bkDiMes0F4WRzDIvhKWWt/
YovGWKJ2EmB22gqQbzdEiOxit6oq8IgP4UQSCJAvW/CrRh222h3W/Mw20XJGs79ijPbF9kwXOATB-
N4LfHTJPVyr0r6hqLyvYcMAnCIxqS+LUPptlfx5OsrWA5ka5qtKJPSN5fNjNdJT5F4sTPLy8=",
BinaryEncoding.Base64), Compression.Deflate)), let _t = ((type nullable text)
meta [Serialized.Text = true]) in type table [#"Sales Rep1" = _t, Customer1 =
_t, Amount1 = _t]),

    ColNamesList = Table.ColumnNames(Source),

    #"Converted to Table" =
    Table.FromList(ColNamesList,
    Splitter.SplitByNothing(), null, null,
    ExtraValues.Error),

    #"Inserted Text Before Delimiter" =
    Table.AddColumn(#"Converted to Table",
    "Text Before Delimiter",
    each Text.BeforeDelimiter([Column1], "1"), type text),

    RenameList =
    Table.ToRows(#"Inserted Text Before Delimiter"),

    RenamedTable = Table.RenameColumns(Source, RenameList)
in
    RenamedTable
```

Chapter 2: Working with Records

Here are the solutions for the exercises in Chapter 2.

Note: Refer to the Excel file Records Exercises - Solved in the Records folder.

Exercise 1

```
Let
    Source =
    [Name = "Chandeep",
    Cities Lived =
      {"Dubai", "Mumbai", "Bangalore", "Gurgaon", "Pune"}]
in
    Source
```

Exercise 2

```
let
    Source = Table.FromRows(Json.Document(Binary.Decompress(Binary.
FromText("i45WMjQwVNJRcszJTE4F0m6ZeYl5QFasDkjGCCjilJ8EJH0Ti7JTSzLz0qEyx-
kAx54zEopxMkC7PEKiwCZDjkliWmQKkPYKggqZAjmsZSJ1/QWpRYklmfl6xUmwsAA==",
BinaryEncoding.Base64), Compression.Deflate)), let _t = ((type nullable text)
meta [Serialized.Text = true]) in type table [#"Employee ID" = _t, Name = _t,
Department = _t]),

    #"Changed Type" =
    Table.TransformColumnTypes(Source,
    {{"Employee ID", Int64.Type},
    {"Name", type text},
    {"Department", type text}}),

    Row3 = #"Changed Type"{2}
in
    Row3
```

Exercise 3

```
let
    Source = Table.FromRows(Json.Document(Binary.Decompress(Binary.FromTex-
t("dZExCsMwDEWvUjzHIH3ZqTO2uUD3kCnZC6W9f63SwHdNB4EMj/cleVkCBBZFo2kYwu1x31/
b83SpvdXSLGEdDggRhaBr7eElDFlrmmufHWpMKZr8xCWPKwzl1nTE6cjQ2Jrm7+BAJujcb+fvi-
UWlT/ORDAxNfdpnpESQSm/yCxifSbU3eRyUIfz5FT/T+gY=", BinaryEncoding.Base64),
Compression.Deflate)), let _t = ((type nullable text) meta [Serialized.Text
= true]) in type table [Date = _t, Product = _t, Quantity = _t, #"Selling
Price" = _t]),

    #"Changed Type" =
    Table.TransformColumnTypes(Source,
    {{"Date", type date},
    {"Product", type text},
    {"Quantity", Int64.Type},
    {"Selling Price", Int64.Type}}),

    #"Added Custom" =
    Table.AddColumn(#"Changed Type", "Records",
    each [
    Year = Date.Year([Date]),
    Month = Date.MonthName([Date]),
    Sales = [Quantity] * [Selling Price],
    Commission = Sales * 0.1]),
```

```
      #"Expanded Records" =
      Table.ExpandRecordColumn(#"Added Custom",
      "Records",
      {"Year", "Month", "Sales", "Commission"},
      {"Year", "Month", "Sales", "Commission"})
in
      #"Expanded Records"
```

Chapter 4: Navigation

Here are the solutions for the exercises in Chapter 4.

Note: Refer to the Excel file Navigation Exercises - Solved in the Navigation folder.

Exercise 1

```
let
    Source = {"A".."J"},

    Custom1 = Source{2}
in
    Custom1
```

Exercise 2

```
let
    Source = Table.FromRows(Json.Document(Binary.Decompress(Binary.
FromText("i45WclTSUTI0ABJBqSlKsTrRSk4gASMg4ZSTmJwNFnIGCZmiCLmAhAyRtLmCBIz-
BakpTwSJuMF1gJbEA", BinaryEncoding.Base64), Compression.Deflate)), let _t =
((type nullable text) meta [Serialized.Text = true]) in type table [Prod =
_t, Units = _t, Color = _t]),

    #"Changed Type" =
    Table.TransformColumnTypes(
    Source,{{"Prod", type text},
    {"Units", Int64.Type},
    {"Color", type text}})

    Custom1 = #"Changed Type"{0}
in
    Custom1
```

Exercise 3

```
let
    Source = Table.FromRows(Json.Document(Binary.Decompress(Binary.
FromText("i45W8krMU9JRMjTQM1KK1YlWcktNAnEN9YzBXN/EIhDXRM8UzHUsAHPNoFzfxEoQ1x-
LK9SoFGWVkCTIqFgA=", BinaryEncoding.Base64), Compression.Deflate)), let _t =
((type nullable text) meta [Serialized.Text = true]) in type table [Month =
_t, #"Visitors 000" = _t]),

    #"Changed Type" =
    Table.TransformColumnTypes(Source,
    {{"Month", type text},
    {"Visitors 000", type number}})

    Custom1 =
    #"Changed Type" {[Month = "Feb"]} [Visitors 000]
in
    Custom1
```

Chapter 5: Manipulating Between Lists, Records, and Tables

Here are the solutions for the exercises in Chapter 5.

Note: Refer to the Excel file Manipulation Exercises - Solved in the Manipulating Between Lists Records and Tables folder.

Exercise 1

```
let
    List1 = {1,2,3},
    List2 = {4,5,6},
    List3 = {7,8,9},
    // Initiate the record in square brackets, each value
    // will be pair of column name and the list reference
    Record = [
        Rec1 = List1,
        Rec2 = List2,
        Rec3 = List3
    ]
in
    Record
```

Exercise 2

```
let
    Record1 = [Name = "Bob", Age = 20],
    Record2 = [Name = "Mary", Age = 21],
    Record3 = [Name = "Tanya", Age = 19],
    // Table.FromRecords will accept a list of records
    Table = Table.FromRecords({Record1, Record2, Record3})
in
    Table
```

Chapter 6: if then else

Here is the solution for the exercise in Chapter 6.

Note: Refer to the Excel file if then else Exercises - Solved in the if then else folder.

Exercise 1

```
let
    Source =
    Excel.CurrentWorkbook(){[Name = "Sales"]}[Content],

    #"Changed Type" =
    Table.TransformColumnTypes(Source,
    {{"Date", type date}, {"Sales Rep", type text},
    {"Region", type text}, {"Sales", Int64.Type},
    {"Profit", Int64.Type}}),

    #"OR Condition" =
    Table.AddColumn(#"Changed Type", "Commission",
    each if List.Contains(
            {[Sales] > 14500, [Profit] > 5000}, true)
            then [Sales] * 0.1 else 0)
in
    #"OR Condition"
```

Chapter 7: Iteration

Here are the solutions for the exercises in Chapter 7.

Note: Refer to the Excel file Looping Exercises - Solved in the Iteration folder.

Exercise 1

```
let
    Source = {"a".."f"},
    #"Using Each" = List.Transform(
    Source,
    each Text.Upper(_)
),
    #"Using Function" = List.Transform(
    Source,
    Text.Upper
)
in
    #"Using Function"
```

Exercise 2

```
let
    Source = {2,4,6,8,10},
    #"Using Function" =
    List.Transform(Source,(x)=> x + 10)
in
    #"Using Function"
```

Exercise 3

```
let
    Source = {1..5},
    #"Using Function" =
        List.Transform(Source,(x)=> List.Product({1..x}))
in
    #"Using Function"
```

Chapter 8: Custom Functions

Here are the solutions for the exercises in Chapter 8.

Note: Refer to the Excel file Custom Functions Exercises - Solved in the Custom Functions folder.

Exercise 1

Here is the query for creating the FY custom function:

```
// FY
(Dates as date,
optional #"Year End Month Num" as number) =>
let
    YearEndingMonth =
        if #"Year End Month Num" = null
        then 12
        else #"Year End Month Num",
    Year =
        Date.Year(Date.AddMonths(Dates, - YearEndingMonth))
in
    Year
```

Here is the query for using the FY custom function:

```
let
    Source =
    Excel.CurrentWorkbook(){[Name="Dates"]}[Content],

    #"Changed Type" =
    Table.TransformColumnTypes(Source,
    {{"Dates", type date}}),

    #"Added Custom" =
    Table.AddColumn(#"Changed Type",
    "Fiscal Year", each FY([Dates], 3))
in
    #"Added Custom"
```

Exercise 2

Here is the query for creating the custom function for removing null columns:

```
// fxRemoveNullCols
(inputTable as table,
optional FirstRows as number) as table =>
let
    TopRowsTable =
    if FirstRows = "" or FirstRows = null
    then inputTable
    else Table.FirstN(inputTable, FirstRows),

    ColList =
        Table.SelectRows(
            Table.Profile(TopRowsTable)
            [[Column], [NullCount], [Count]],
            each [Count] = [NullCount])[Column]
in
    Table.RemoveColumns(inputTable, ColList)
```

Here is the query for using the fxRemoveNullCols function:

```
let
    Source =
    Excel.CurrentWorkbook(){[Name = "Data"]}[Content],

    #"Changed Type" =
    Table.TransformColumnTypes(Source,
    {{"Letter", type text}, {"Column1", type text},
    {"Value", Int64.Type}, {"Blank", type text}}),
    Custom1 = fxRemoveNullCols(#"Changed Type", 3)
in
    Custom1
```

Chapter 9: Errors

Here are the solutions for the exercises in Chapter 9.

Note: Refer to the Excel file Errors Exercises - Solved in the Errors folder.

Exercise 1

```
let
    Source =
    Excel.CurrentWorkbook(){[Name="Table1"]}[Content],

    tryotherwise =
    Table.AddColumn(Source, "Custom",
    each try [Units] * [Price] otherwise null)
in
    tryotherwise
```

Exercise 2

```
let
    Source =
    Excel.CurrentWorkbook(){[Name="Table1"]}[Content],

    trycatch =
    Table.AddColumn(Source, "Error or Sales",
    each try [Units] * [#"Price$"] catch(e)=> e[Message])
in
    trycatch
```

Chapter 11: Patterns and Recipes

Here is the solution for the exercise in Chapter 11.

Note: Refer to the Excel file Exercise - Solved in the Patterns and Recipes folder.

Exercise 1

```
let
    Source =
    Excel.CurrentWorkbook(){[Name="Data"]}[Content],

    FirstRecordAsList = Record.ToList(Source{0}),

    RemovedNulls = List.RemoveNulls(FirstRecordAsList),

    SecRecordAsHeaderList =
    List.Distinct(Record.ToList(Source{1})),

    Skip2RowsFromSource = Table.Skip(Source,2),

    AllColsAsList =
    List.Transform(
        Table.ToColumns(Skip2RowsFromSource),
        List.RemoveNulls),

    ListSplitPairsOf3 = List.Split(AllColsAsList,3),

    NestedListToTables =
    List.Transform(ListSplitPairsOf3,
    each Table.FromColumns(_, SecRecordAsHeaderList)),

    ConvertedToTable =
    Table.FromList(
        NestedListToTables,
```

```
        Splitter.SplitByNothing()),

    AddedIndex =
    Table.AddIndexColumn(
        ConvertedToTable, "Customer", 0, 1, Int64.Type),

    AddedCustomer =
    Table.TransformColumns(
        AddedIndex,
        let CustValue = RemovedNulls
        in {"Customer", each CustValue{_}}),

    ExpandedColumn =
    Table.ExpandTableColumn(
        AddedCustomer, "Column1",
        SecRecordAsHeaderList),

    #"Changed Type" =
    Table.TransformColumnTypes(
        ExpandedColumn,
        {{"Date", type date}, {"Product", type text},
        {"Units", Int64.Type}, {"Customer", type text}})
in
    #"Changed Type"
```

Index

Symbols

=> (goes to) operator, 130
& (ampersand) operator, 59–62
?? (coalesce) operator, 137, 212–213
.. (dot dot) keyword, 212
_ (underscore), 43, 89. See also each
    _ (underscore)

A

adding. See inserting; summing
Advanced Editor, 1–2
    M language in, 4–5, 9
ampersand (&) operator, 59–62
and keyword, 81–82, 85–86
appending tables, 59–62
applied steps, IF statements in, 82–83
arrays. See lists
autocomplete, 213–214

B

blank rows, checking for, 57–58
blank values. See null values

C

catch keyword, 156
coalesce (??) operator, 137, 212–213
columns
    combining data with inconsistent
        headers, 198–205
    comparing in nested tables,
        162–169
    creating by expanding records,
        39–42, 49
    data types, setting, 11
    deleting, 10
    expanding, 19–26
    extracting
        list of, 58–59
        and summing as lists, 35
        as table, 56
    inserting, 92–94, 115–120
    removing, 36, 59
    removing errors, 31–34
    renaming, 36, 202–204
    summing, 42–44
    transforming into lists, 75
    unpivoting, 26–30, 208
Combiner.CombineTextByDelimiter
    function, 185–186

combining
    data
        after removing junk rows,
            190–197
        with inconsistent headers,
            198–205
    double headers, 181–190
    tables, 100–101
commas in M language, 6–7
comments in Power Query, 12
comparing columns in nested tables,
    162–169
completed months, listing, 125–128
complex tables, creating, 52–53
concatenating
    with nested tables, 159–161
    text in lists, 91
consecutive counting with nested
    tables, 169–173
converting. See also transforming
    lists to nested lists, 32
    queries to records, 45–46
cross-joins, creating, 53–55
Csv.Document function, 195–197,
    200
current parameters, 104
Custom Column box, M language in,
    5–6
custom functions
    definition of, 130
    double headers problem, 188–190
    fiscal years, 146
    FQ (fiscal quarters), 134–138
    PMT (loan payments), 131–134
    removing null columns, 146
    syntax, 130–131
    TRIM (removing spaces), 138–145

D

data types of columns, setting, 11
Date.From function, 29, 123
Date.QuarterofYear function, 135
dates
    completed months between,
        125–128
    generating list of, 123–125
DateTime.LocalNow function, 123
deleting. See removing
dot dot (..) keyword, 212
double headers problem, 181–190
do...while loops. See List.Generate
    function
dynamic columns, expanding, 19–26
dynamic lists, creating, 16, 22–23

E

each keyword, 89
each _ (underscore), 88–96, 129, 166
error messages, creating, 154
errors
    capturing and reporting, 205–207
    query termination, 149–151
    removing from columns, 31–34
    row-level, 147, 148
    step-level, 147, 148–149
    try . . . catch syntax, 156–157, 158
    try keyword, 151–156
    try . . . otherwise syntax, 147–151,
        158
evaluation order, 13–14
even numbers, generating, 120–122
examples
    appending tables, 59–62
    calculating fiscal quarters, 134–138
    capturing and reporting errors,
        205–207
    combining data with inconsistent
        headers, 198–205
    comparing columns in nested
        tables, 162–169
    concatenating text in lists, 91
    consecutive counting with nested
        tables, 169–173
    custom TRIM function, 138–145
    double headers problem, 181–190
    expanding dynamic columns,
        19–26
    extracting intermediate steps,
        44–47
    generating even numbers, 120–122
    generating list of dates, 123–125
    IF statements with and keyword,
        81–82
    inconsistent headers in multiple
        files, 2–3
    inserting columns, 92–94
    inserting multiple columns with
        List.Accumulate function,
        115–120
    junk rows in multiple files, 3
    List.Accumulate function explana-
        tion, 102–104
    listing completed months, 125–128
    nested tables concatenation,
        159–161
    removing errors from columns,
        31–34
    removing junk rows and combining
        data, 190–197
    replacing multiple values with List.
        Accumulate function, 110–115
    row-level errors, 148

Level up your skills with our structured courses!

Scan me

{M}

M Language Power Query
Push Beyond Power Query's User Interface & Solve Tricky Data Cleaning Problems.

⟨DAX⟩

DAX & Data Modeling
A step by step guide to solving real time business problems in Power BI.

P🖱Q

Power Query Course
Learn to automate your mundane Data-Cleaning tasks using Power Query.

PBI
Beginner

Power BI Beginner
A Beginners course to help you learn the ABC's of Power BI from scratch.

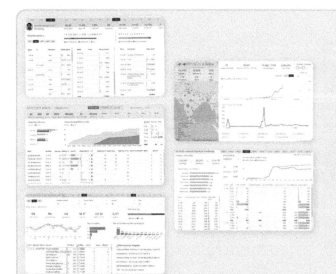

Let us build your Excel / Power BI reports on time, accurate and stunning.

Drop us an email :
chandeep@goodlyinsights.com

POWER QUERY BEYOND THE USER INTERFACE
Solving Advanced Data Cleaning Problems using M

by
Chandeep Chhabra

Holy Macro! Books
PO Box 541731
Merritt Island, FL 32953

Power Query Beyond the User Interface
Solving Advanced Data Cleaning Problems using M

First Publication: April 2025

Author: Chandeep Chhabra

Copy Editor: Kitty Wilson

Tech Editors: Geert Delmulle

Indexer: Cheryl Lenser

Compositor: Bronkella Publishing

Cover Design: Chris Dorning

Published by: Holy Macro! Books, PO Box 541731, Merritt Island FL 32954

Distributed by Independent Publishers Group, Chicago, IL

ISBN 978-1-61547-081-5 (print) 978-1-61547-167-6 (digital)

Library of Congress Control Number: 2024951813

Version: 20250108